AF471096

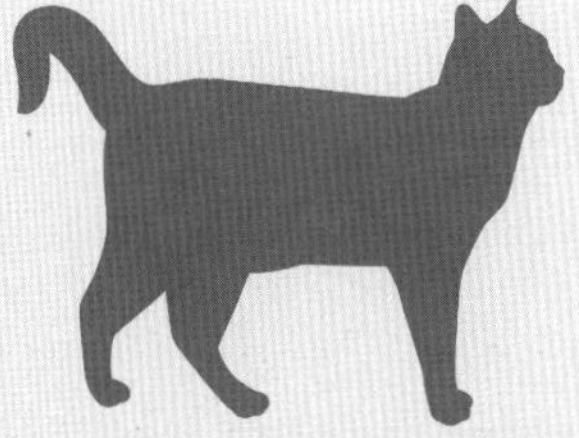

for Karin and all of the creatures......

# Cat Walk

## Jackie Morris

with love
Jackie Morris

GRAFFEG

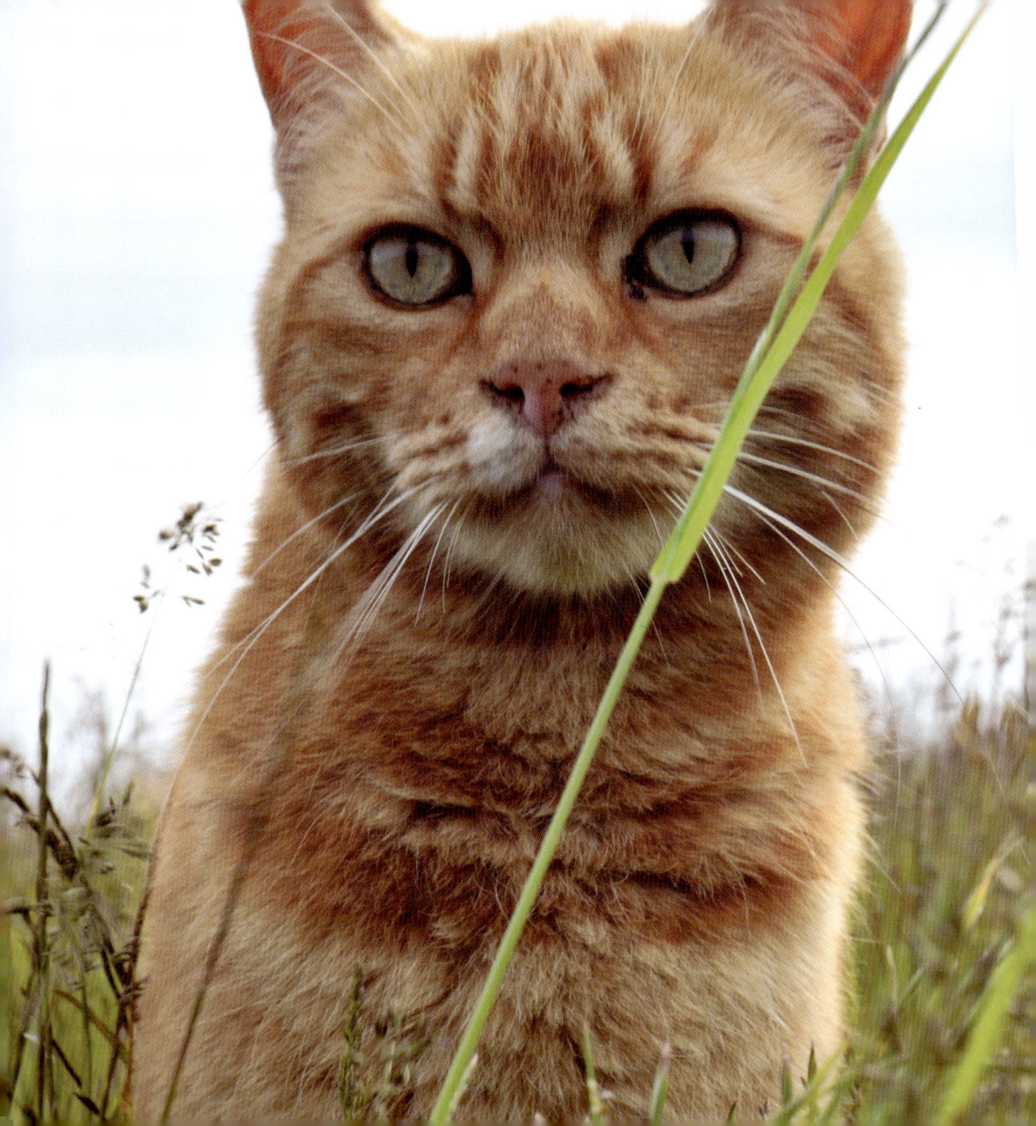

# Contents


5 Jackie Morris

7 Tom Cox cat walks

11 Cat Walk

12 Meet the cats

28 Walking in the Easter sunshine

50 Summer secrets

84 Autumn creeps into the landscape

102 An island of winter snow

128 A warm place to curl

142 The fresh green of early spring

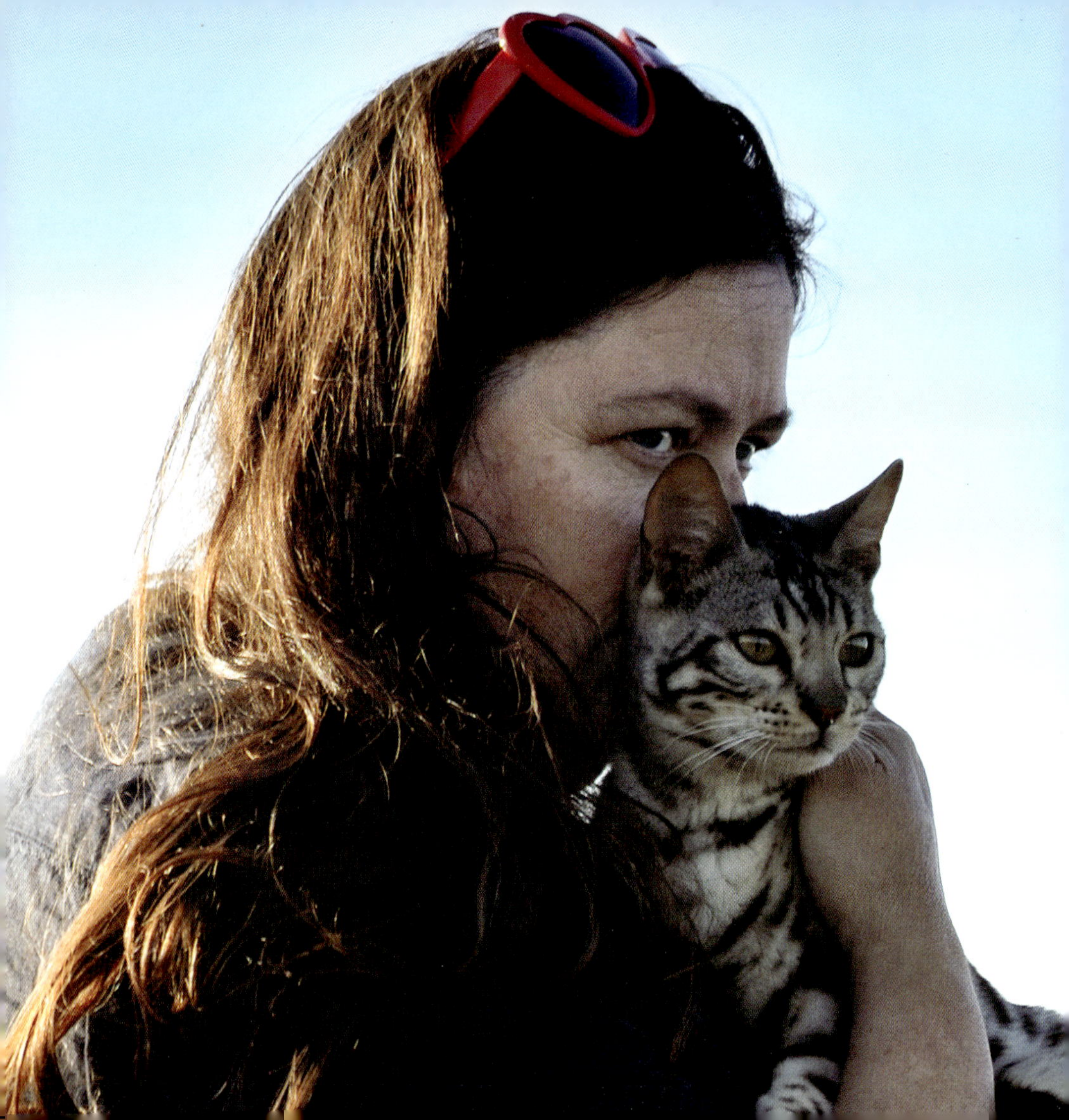

# Jackie Morris

Jackie Morris is the author of some books, the illustrator of more, and now and again takes photographs.

When someone once commented that 'your camera takes very good pictures', she responded, 'yes, and I have a pencil that draws quite well and some brushes that are quite good at painting'.

Jackie has lived in the same small house beside the sea on the St Davids Peninsula since 1992, when she visited from Bath for a weekend and fell in love with the wild beauty of the coastline.

Jackie loves cats, dogs and wild things.

Author of *The Snow Leopard*, *I am Cat*, *East of the Sun, West of the Moon*, *Tell Me a Dragon* and many more.

www.jackiemorris.co.uk/blog
www.facebook.com/ElmotheGinger

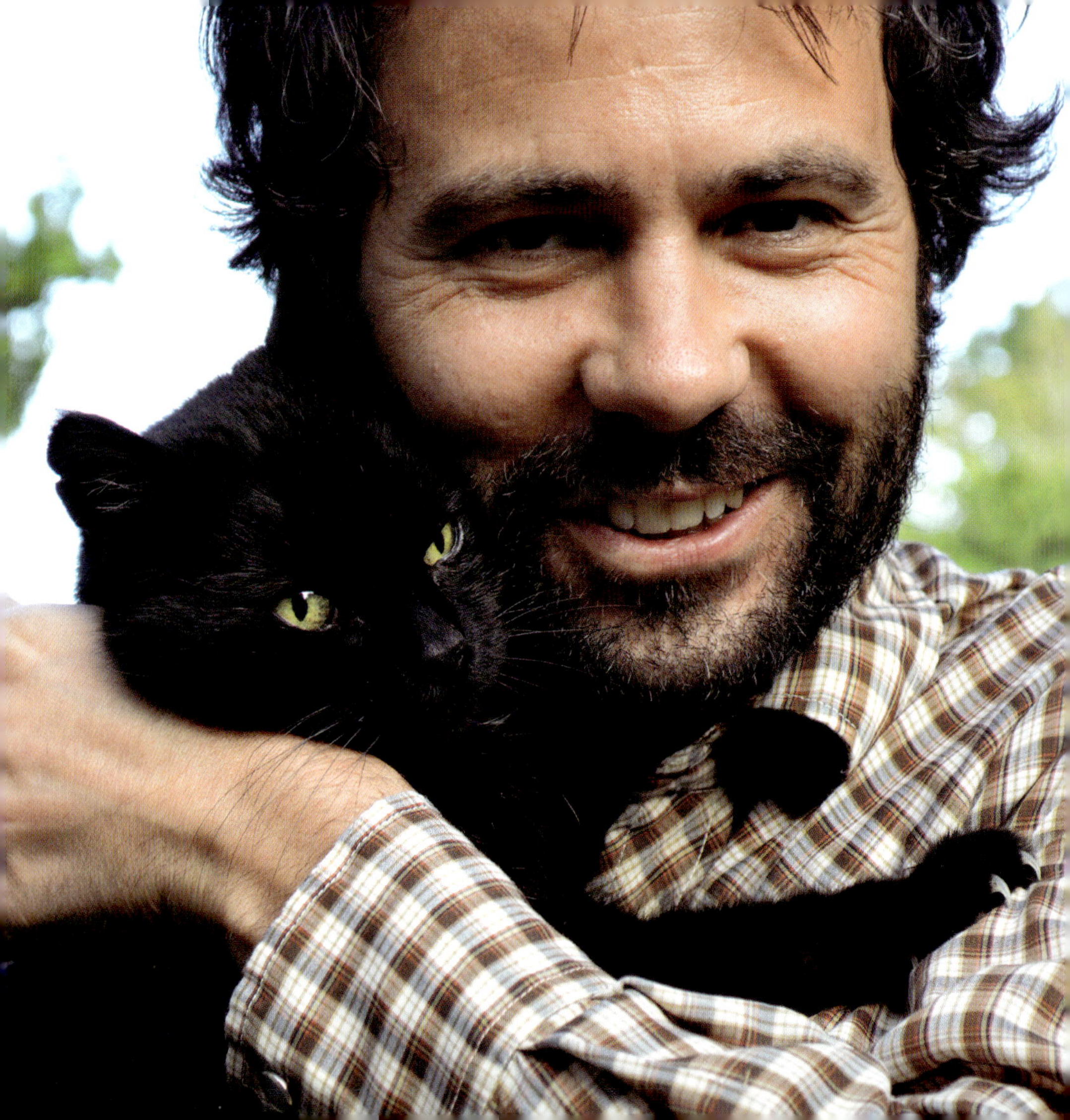

# Tom Cox cat walks

"Of all God's creatures, there is only one that cannot be made slave of the leash," wrote Mark Twain. "That one is the cat." Presumably Twain didn't meet a lot of black rhinos or badgers in his lifetime, but you can see what he's getting at. You occasionally see a cat being walked on a lead, but you can usually tell that, even if it's pretending, it's not quite comfortable about it, and knows that other cats are laughing at it behind its back. As for the idea of taking a cat for a walk without a lead, well, that's absurd, isn't it? With a cat's stubborn, independent nature, it could never happen. That's what we're told, anyway.

In my late teens and early twenties, I would regularly go for a walk with a cat. His name was Monty: a white and ginger chap with the slight aura of a seventeenth-century nobleman about him. I didn't encourage Monty to walk with me. I simply set off one day from our back gate, into the Forestry Commission land behind my parents' house in north Nottinghamshire, and he trotted behind me. Over the next few years, we would walk anywhere between one and three miles together. If a dog came down the footpath towards us in the distance, he'd run and hide in some foliage, and I'd whistle him when the coast was clear.

Because of this experience, when I first met Jackie Morris, in summer 2009, there seemed nothing unusual about the idea of setting off from her house in Pembrokeshire, up a green lane towards lichen-speckled cliffs, pursued by four cheerful cats. "Oh, there's Kiffer, kissing a cow," I thought, as Jackie's cat Kiffer kissed a cow, as if I saw cats on country walks over Britain, kissing cows. The dainty Pixie did get a bit tired towards the end, and travelled some of the way back on my shoulders, like a purring ginger scarf, but I felt like I was getting a glimpse into a perfect parallel existence for humans and cats: something that might happen everywhere if we lived in an unindustrialized world without cars and hard man dogs bred to maul.

Cat walking is not for everyone but do it in the right place and you'll see another one of the many ways in which these small furlords – these enigmatic artistic companions we're told only

love us for our food but clearly don't – are misunderstood. I've
not lived in places where it's been possible to walk my cats over
the last decade and a half but I recently moved to rural Devon
and, setting off into the gardens behind my house, I saw that
my own cats Shipley and Roscoe were following.

As they now venture further and further with me, shooting up
trees with kittenish energy and leaping out on each other from
bushes, I see the same happiness and mystery in their eyes that
I saw in those of Jackie's cats: a glow that's the antithesis to the
slightly dull glaze you often see in the eyes of an indoor cat or
a showcat with an unbecoming length of cord attached to his or
her neck. "You think you've got the measure of me," says the
glow. "You will never get the measure of me. I might look kind of
cuddly but I know stuff you couldn't even dream of."

**Tom Cox**
Author of *Under The Paw*, *Talk To The Tail* and *The Good,
The Bad And The Furry*.

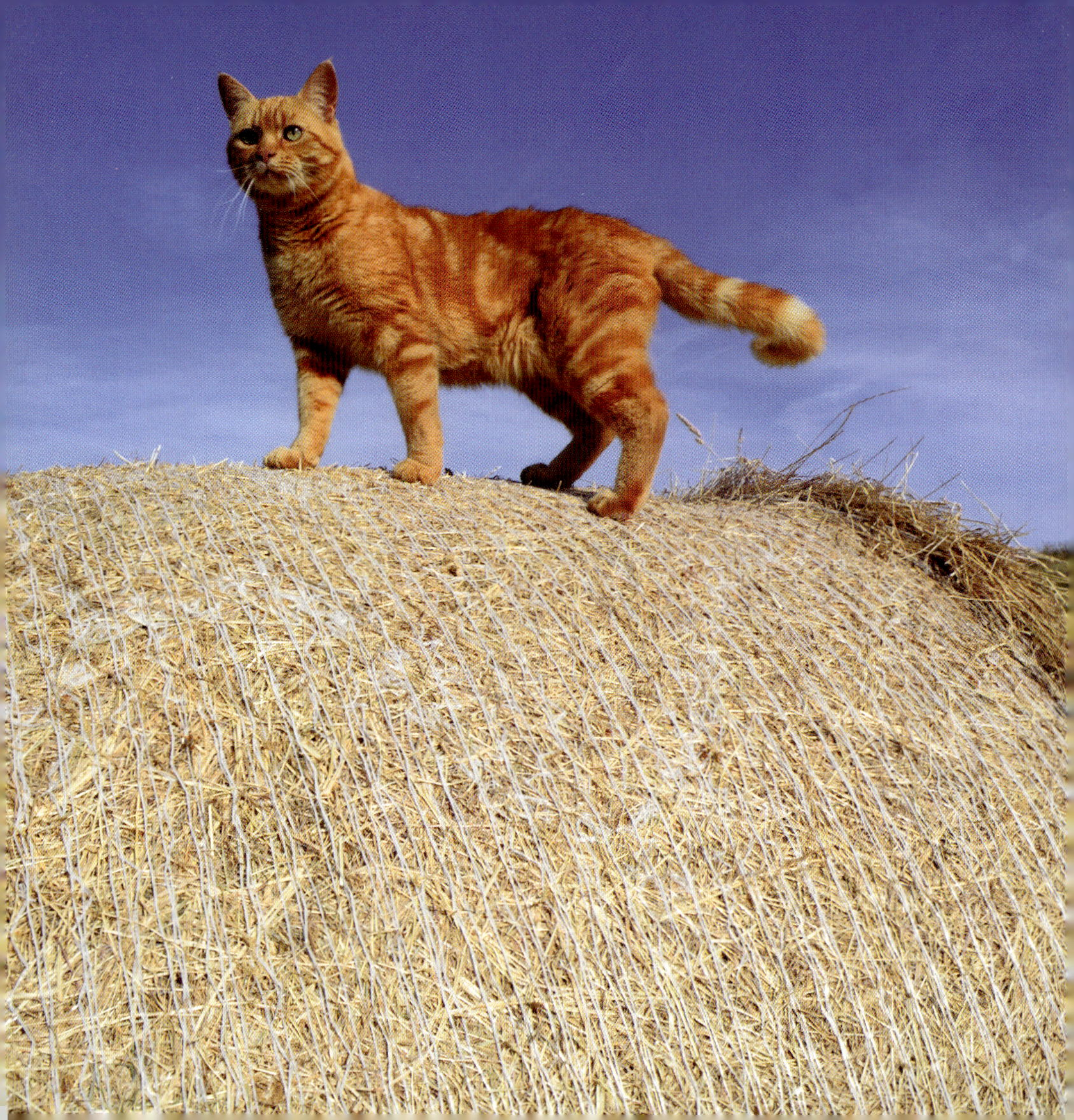

# Cat Walk

Cat Walk has grown over years, out of time, along many footpaths walked with cats, from thousands of photographs. It is set in a small part of Pembrokeshire, Wales, an area of land that is only as big as it is comfortable for a cat to walk.

While working on the book many people at festivals and book signings would ask me what I was working on: always a picture book, now and again a short novel, and this. Trying to describe it was like trying to herd cats. I would say, "well, it's a book about cats, but it's not really about cats.

It's about living in a place long enough to be accustomed to it and yet find something different, fascinating in a fall of light, the appearance of a rainbow, the wind and its ways, the seasons. It's about walking the same paths, a kind of travel book that goes nowhere, only in a circle, out from home and then back.

It's about the wild wheel of the year from summer's heat to winter's wild cold and snow. It's about the characters of small cats, set in a very special place. It is a celebration of cats and that place, and a celebration of love. It is what it is."

# Meet the cats

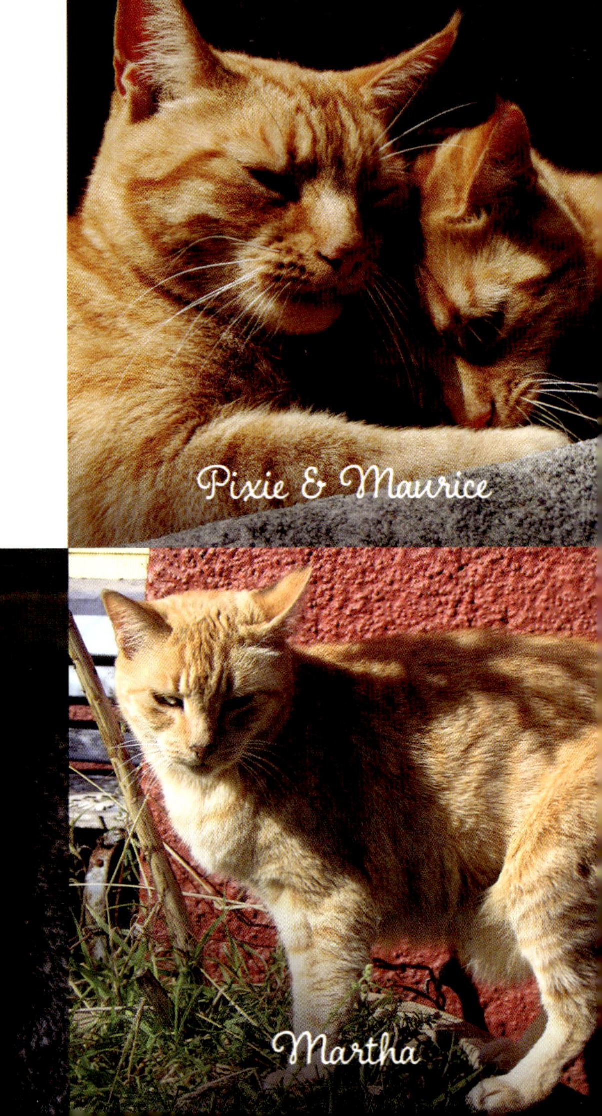

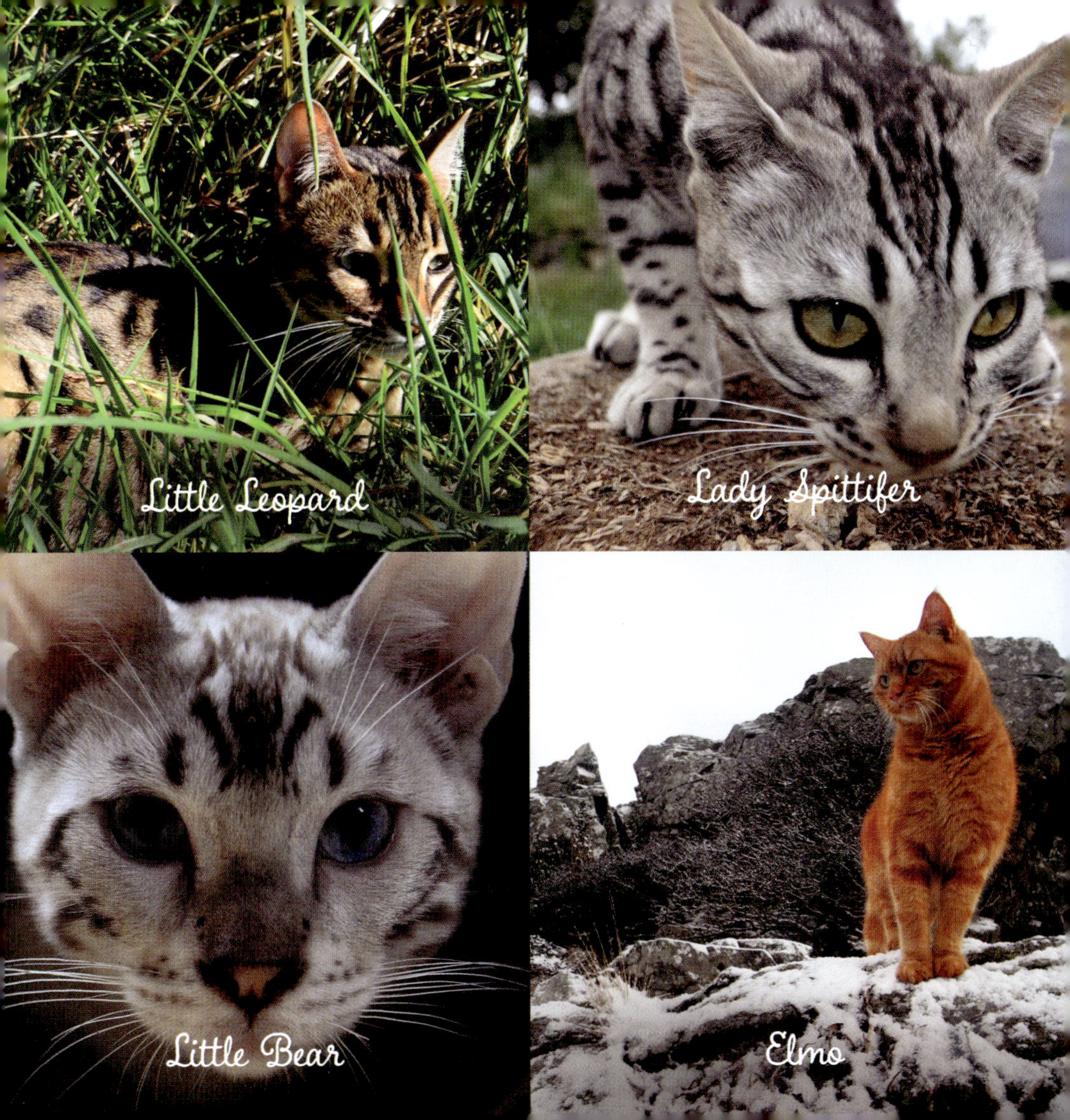

Little Leopard
Lady Spittifer
Little Bear
Elmo

# Pixie & Maurice

Pixie: Small and ginger, sweetest natured, the best walker. Pixie would walk for miles and sit with me on the cliff tops watching the seals, watching birds fly beneath us or simply resting, eyes tight shut, thinking cat thoughts.

As a kitten she would ride on your arm as a hawk rides on a falconer's glove. Later, as a cat, when she tired we would pick her up and she would drape around your neck like the warmest scarf, or ride in your arms, light as a baby.

Gentle Pixie. She loved dogs, especially Bella.

Maurice: Littermate of Pixie, soul cat. He would leap from the ground to my arms if I called him. Dark ginger, he and Pixie would curl in warm places wrapped in each other's dreaming.

Pixie and Maurice came from a farm at St Elvis near Solva, a place of beautiful cats, mostly ginger. The farmer's wife, Helen, has red hair like the cats, beautiful. All the cats of St Elvis have small tufts like lynx ears.

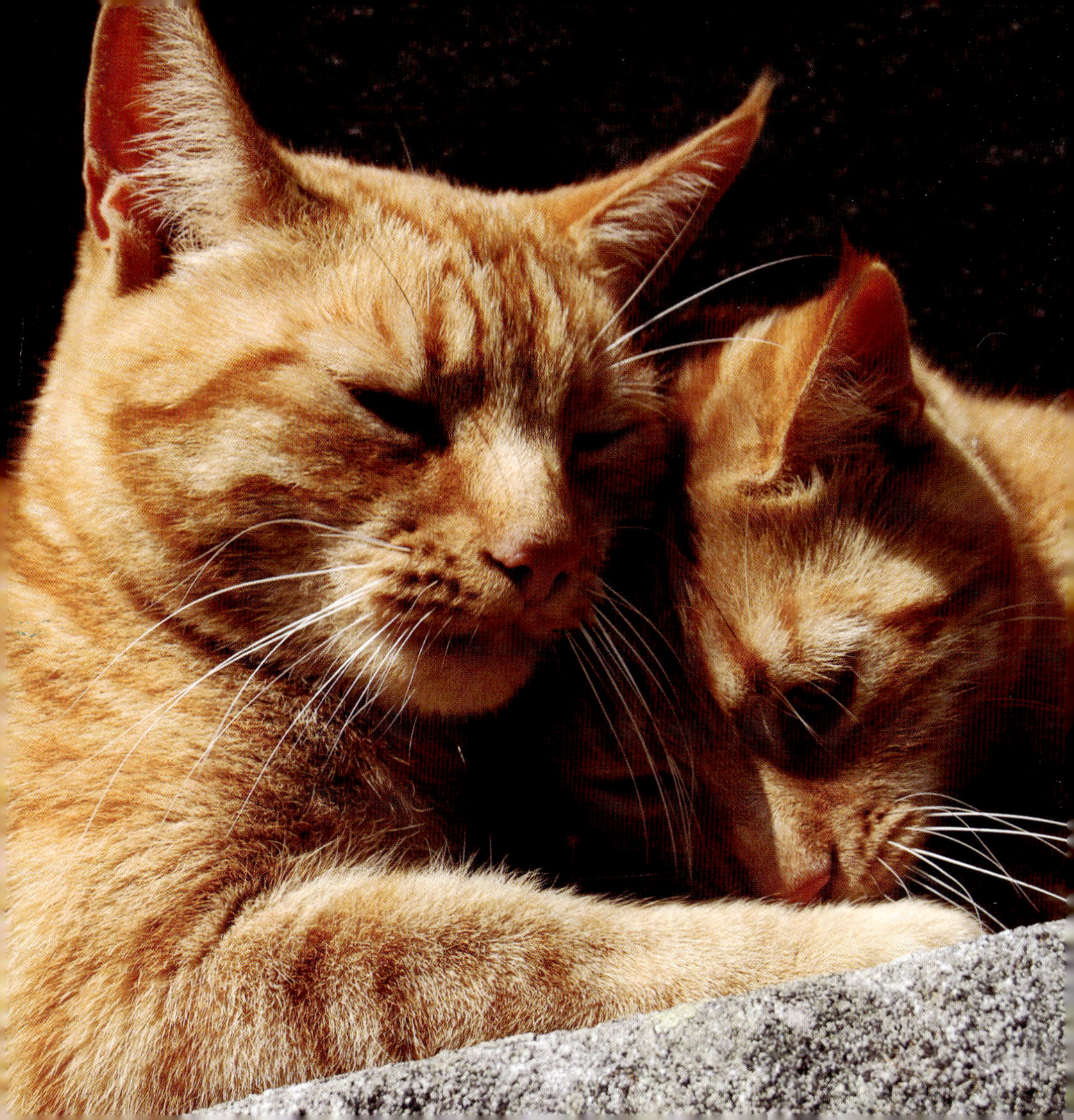

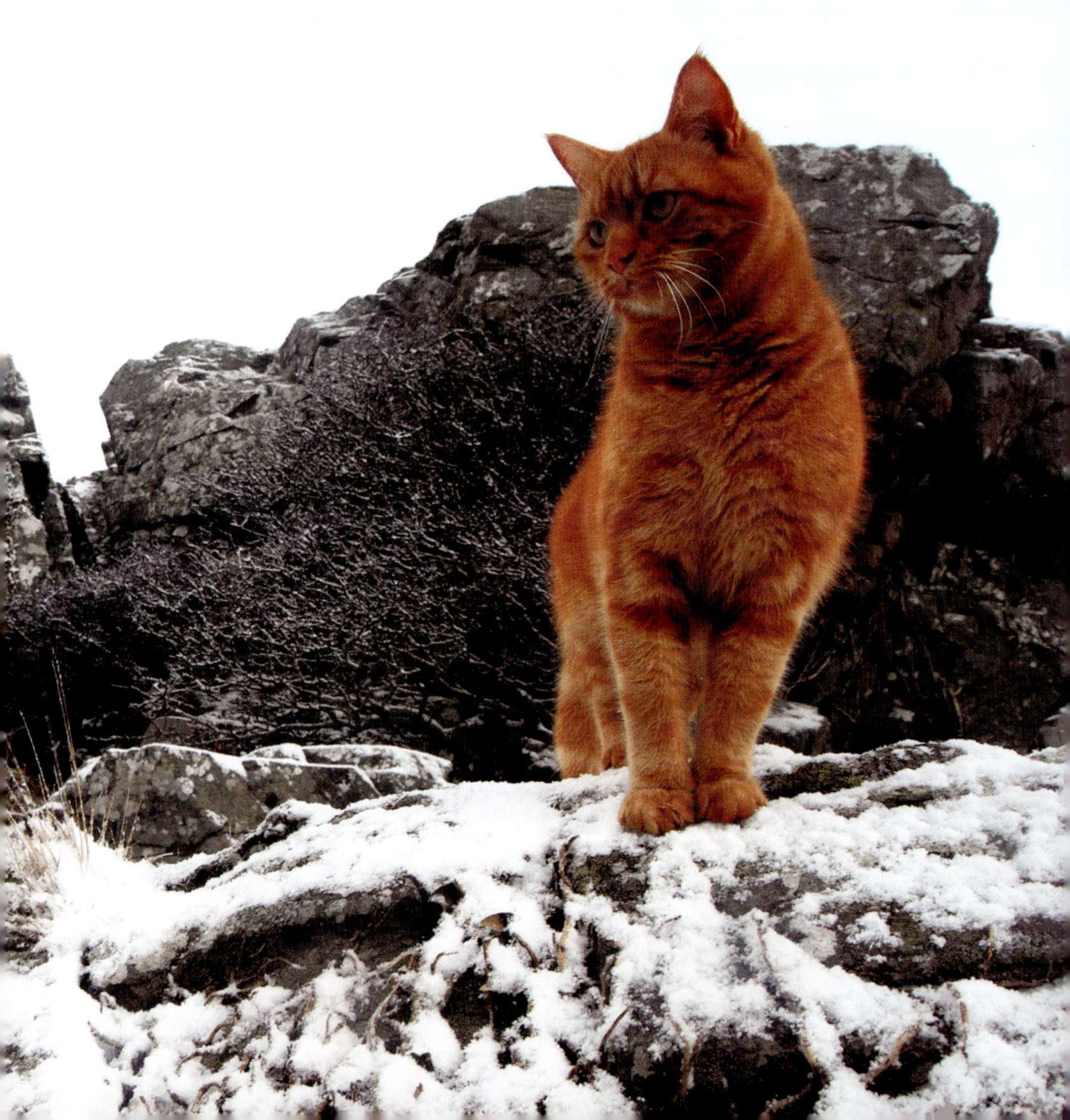

# Elmo

Elmo: Younger brother to Pixie and Maurice.

Elmo would walk beside his brother with tails entwined. And being young and foolish he would often times go hunting during walks, distracted by the rattle of a bush as a snake slithered by or the squeak of a small thing, or the bright flash of a beetle's back.

He spent odd nights of his youth alone up the hillside when calling and calling failed to bring him back in line, and always would be found close to where we had lost him, at first light, waiting, eyes and heart full of the adventure and of tales of the night and wild, watchful gods.

# Martha

Martha and her brother Arthur came to live with me when my first cat disappeared. I had raised him from a scrap of a kitten when his mother was killed on a farm. They, Arthur and Martha, were my first two gingers. I had wanted a ginger cat ever since seeing the picture books of Orlando in the library, though I never read the stories as I couldn't read. But I did fall in love with the shape of a ginger cat. They arrived in a cardboard box, six weeks old, small bundles of fluff, and right from the first would bound and bounce up the hill through the tall grass, following where ever we went. Exhausted at the top we would carry them back.

Arthur left to live with my neighbour for a while. Glyn lived alone and loved to walk with the cat as his companion. Arthur died too young, run over by a careless delivery driver.

Martha was, for a long time, the matriarch of the Cat Pride. She loved the children and would watch over them while they slept.

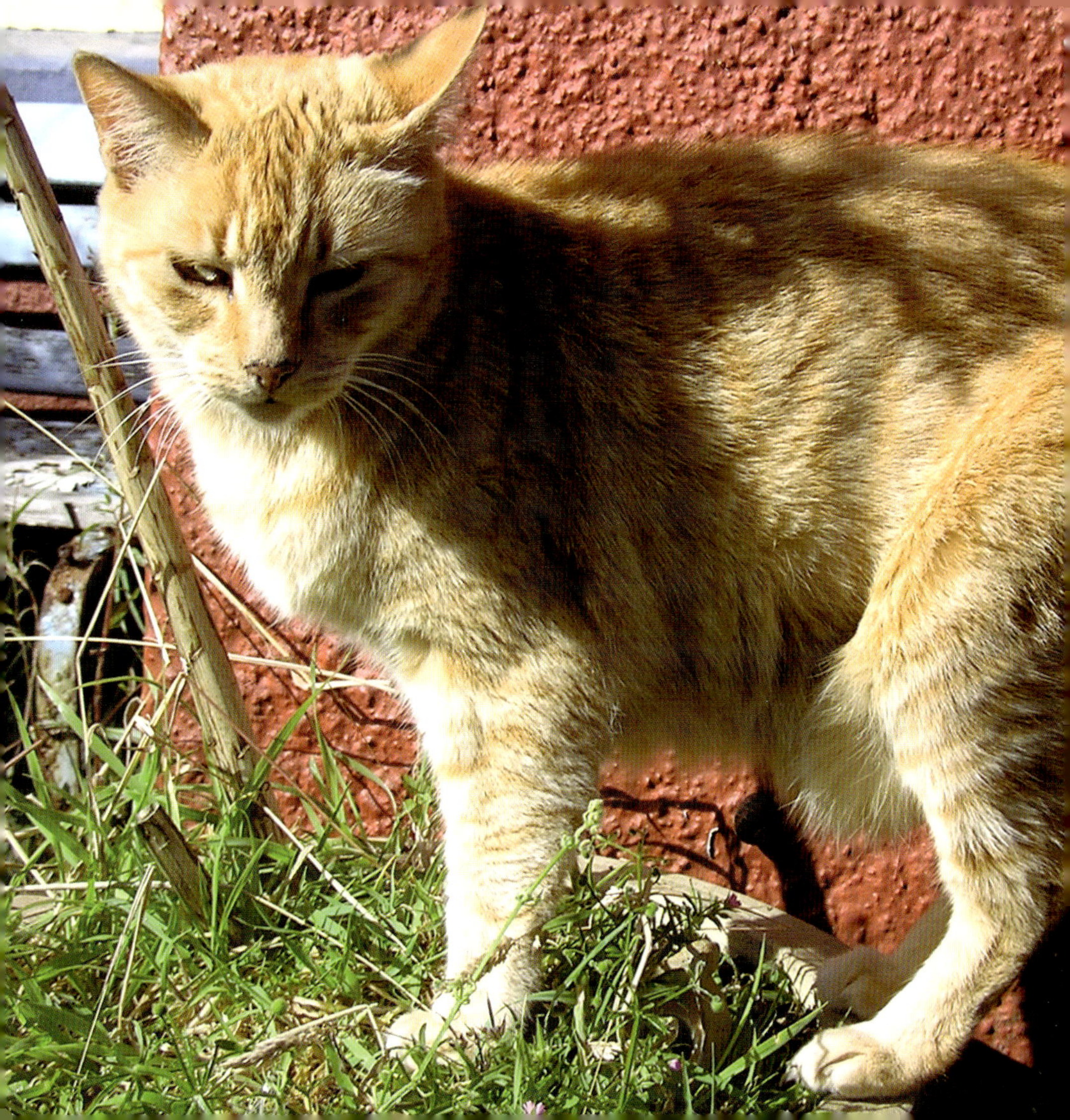

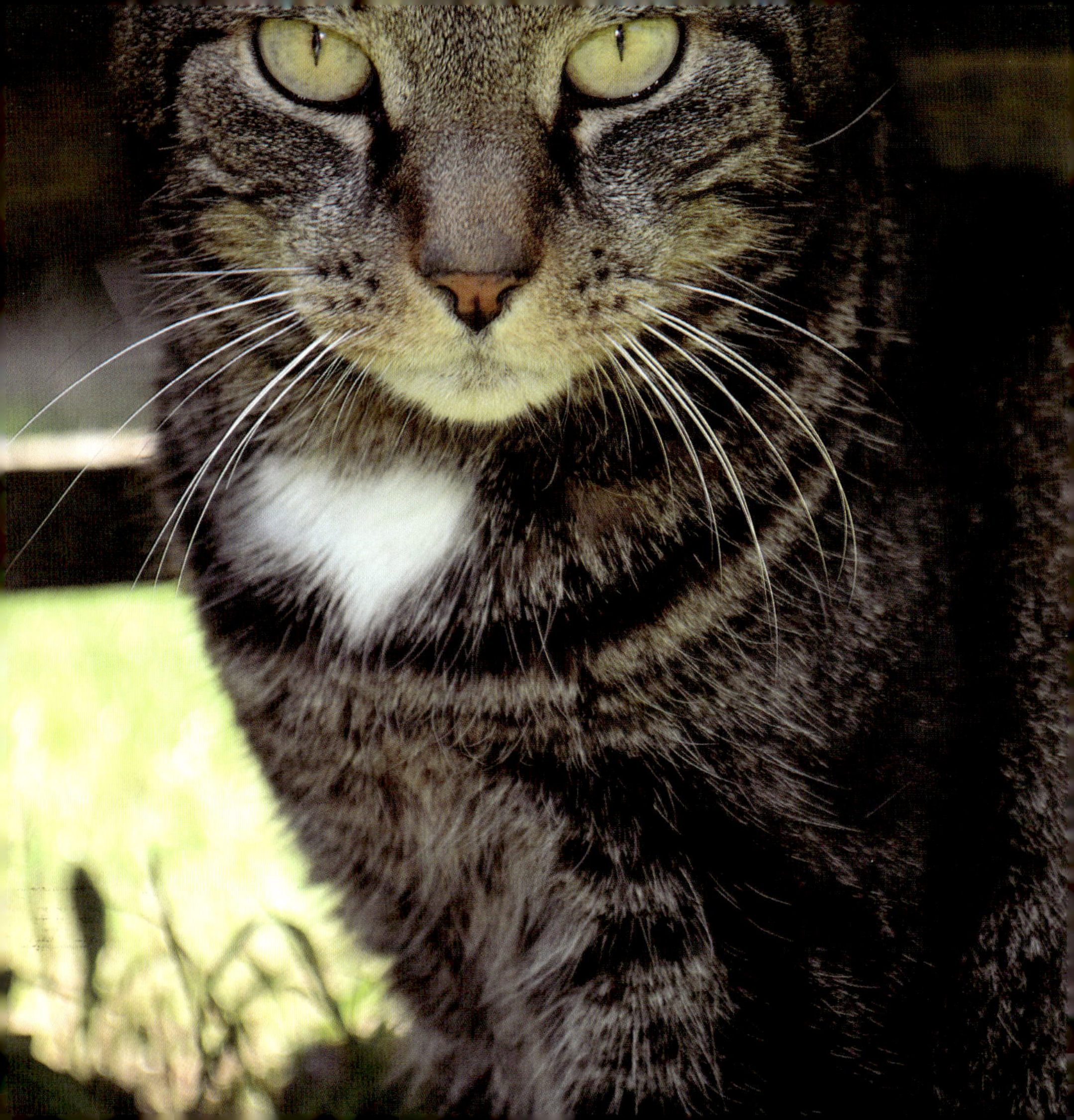

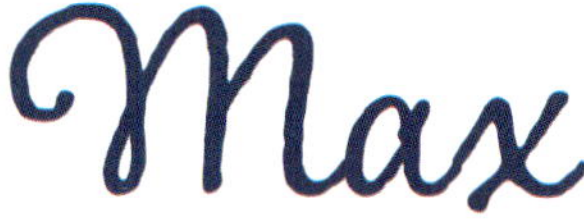

# Max

Oldest of the Cat Pride now, handsome camera-shy tabby, farm cat, Max seldom comes on walks.

Now, by day, he sleeps in the woodshed in summer. In winter he finds warm secret places inside the house, tucked away. While the other cats will curl together in fur piles of cat dreams Max sleeps alone. Now and again, in winter he will allow Elmo to curl beside him, bright flame fur against his midnight dark tabby coat.

Standoffish as a cat can be, if you are lucky Max will come and sit beside you or curl on your lap, and then you know that you should sit still, rest. For to be sat on by Max is an honour not to be dismissed lightly.

Max does not like kittens.

# Lady Spittifer of Silverstorm

Lady S, so called because she is a pedigree posh cat, a Bengal from Silverstorm Bengals in Snowdonia. She came to live with the Pride with her brother, Lord Genji, the shining one (named after the main character in a thousand year old Japanese novel) about 9 months after Pixie died.

The two kittens of great destruction were like two sides of the same coin, always together. They slept in subtle nests, hidden in the garden, camouflaged in dappled light in long grass. If I called to them two bright heads would pop up from unexpected places.

Always ready for a walk, they loved the high hills. Sadly Lord Genji lived true to his name. Considered too beautiful to live long on this earth he was called back to the wild gods before even a year old. So Spit became used to living alone.

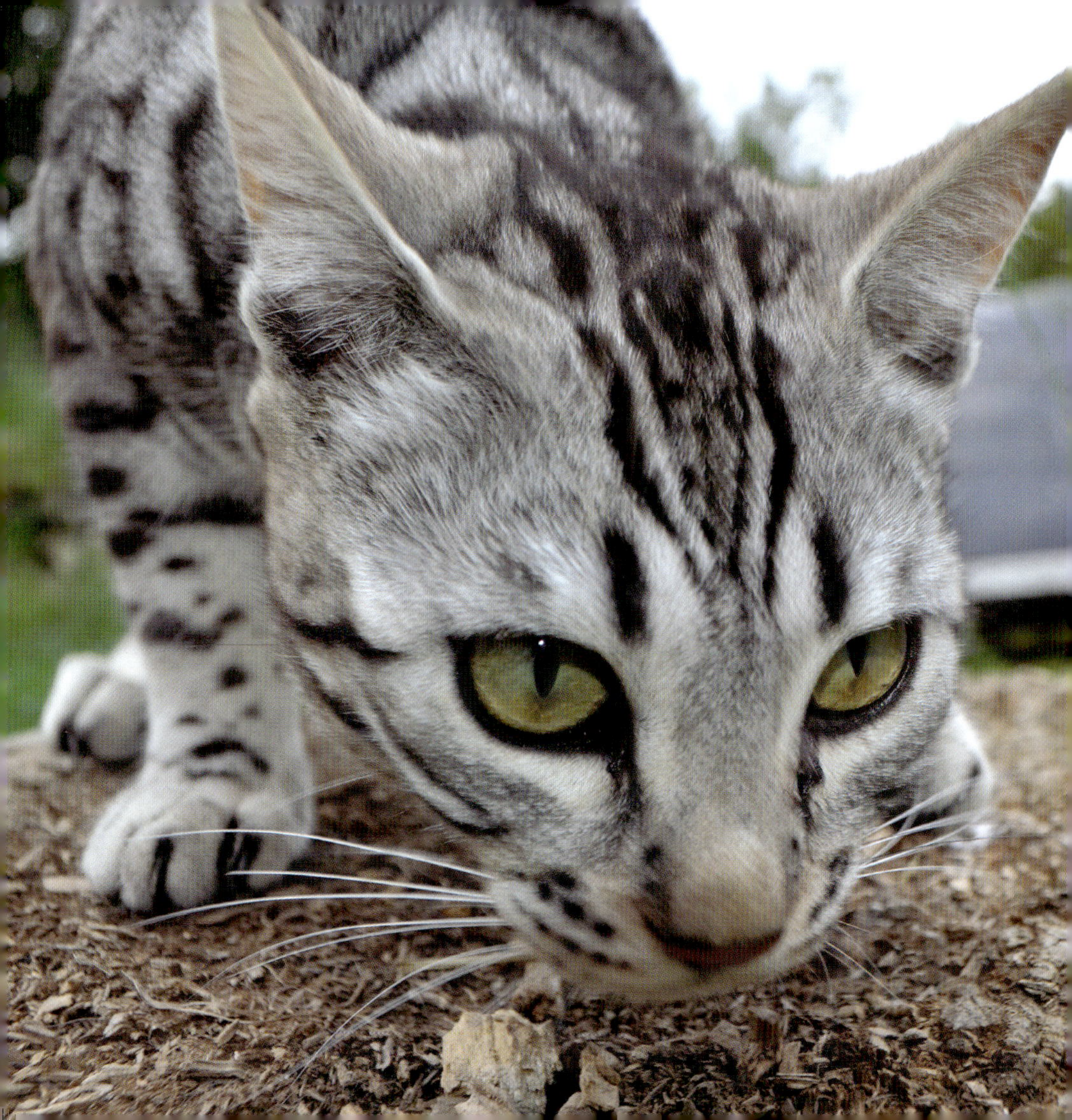

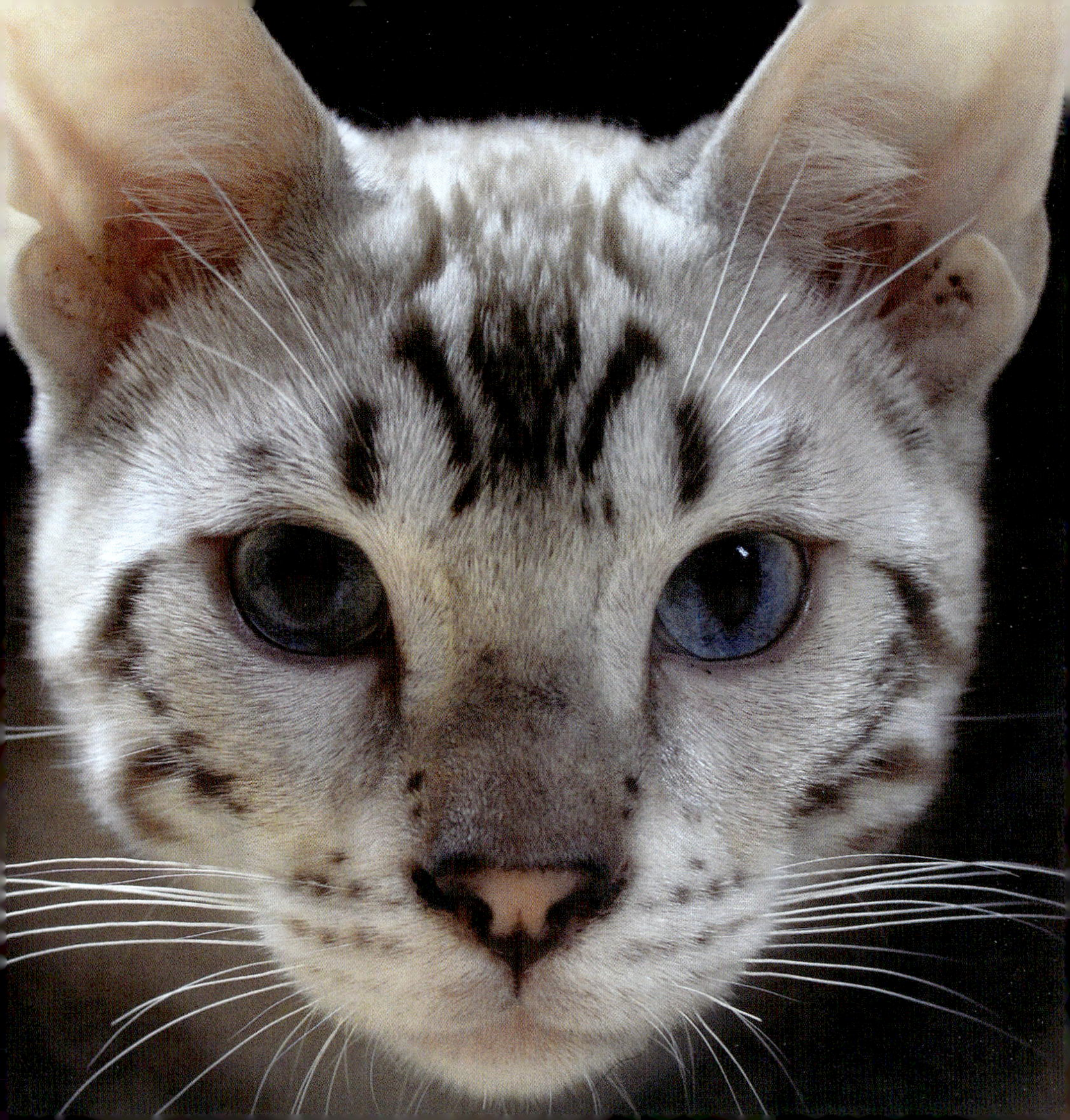

# Little Bear and Little Leopard

Then came Little Bear and Little Leopard. And the Bear and the Leopard love to walk. Little Bear is always ready to 'help' with anything that is being done, from reading to writing to walking and sleeping, even washing up. Bengal cats love water. With a coat that sparkles like sunshine on snow and harebell-blue eyes he looks like an angel. One of his other names, for cats have many, is Lucifer.

# Little Leopard

Little Leopard is sprinkled with gold dust, spotted like a
cheetah, has eyes like green amber and in nature reminds me
of Pixie. Tiny cat, ready for any adventure. I often think he is out
exploring and then find him stretched luxurious as only a cat
can be in a pool of sunshine on my bed, waiting.

Mischief cat, he moves through the long grass in the fields,
stalking trouble.

He hunts swift bees buzzing in the rosemary flowers of the herb
garden.

He hides beneath the bed then reaches out a clawed paw to
catch a foot as you walk past.

He watches while I write, the movement of the pen too tempting
for his cat nature to resist.

He looks like a creature come to life from the wall painting of an
Egyptian pharaoh.

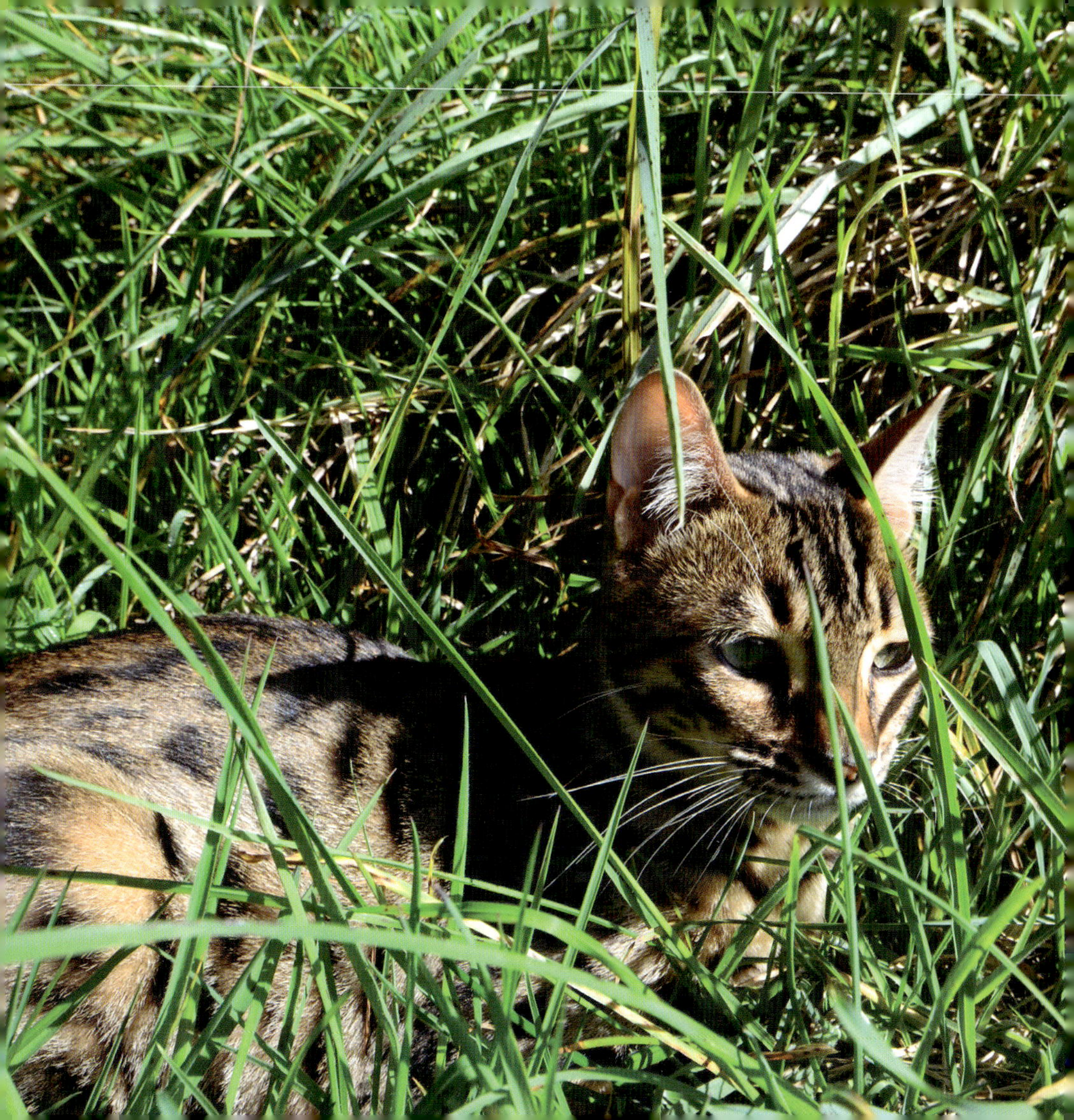

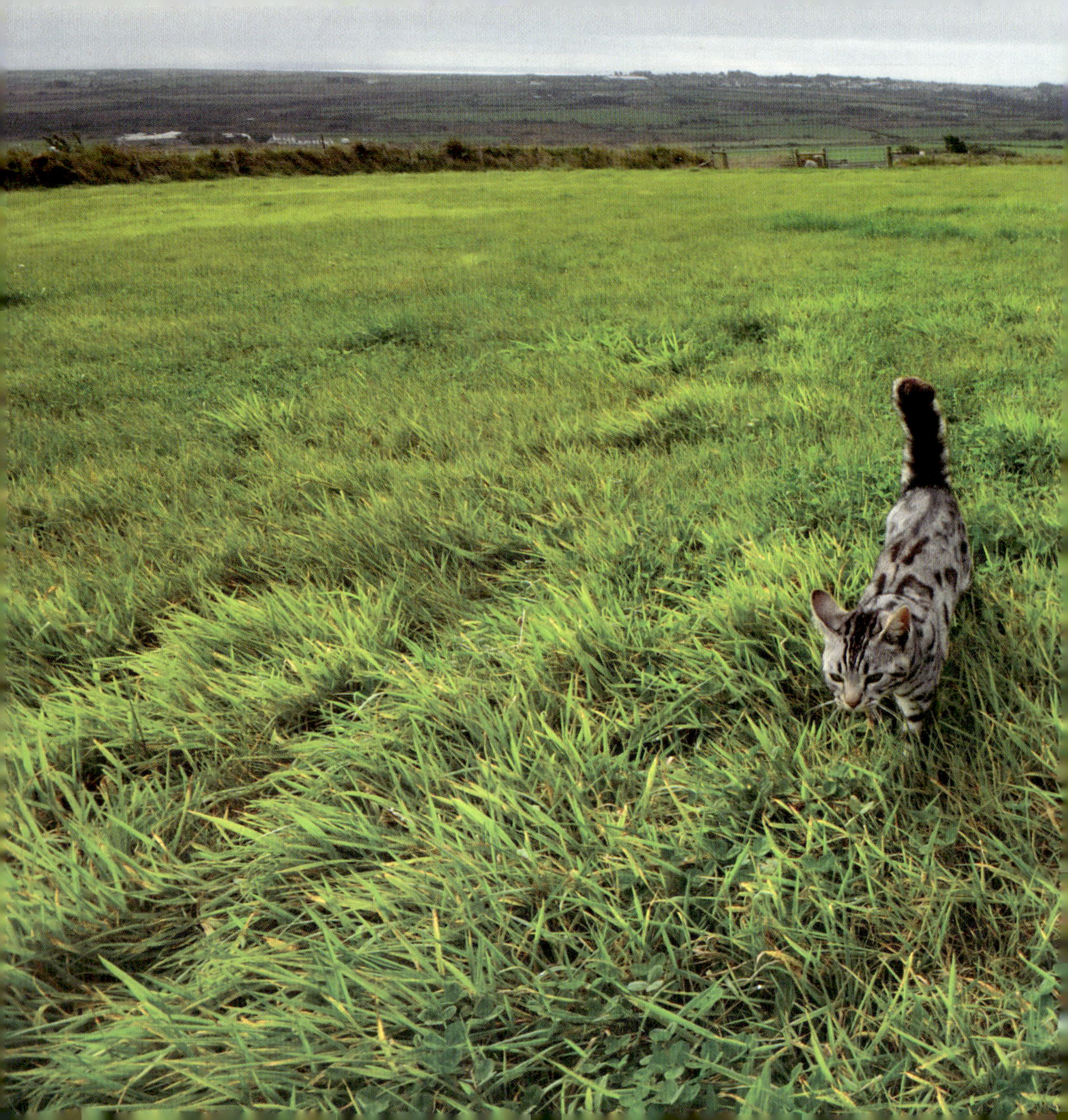

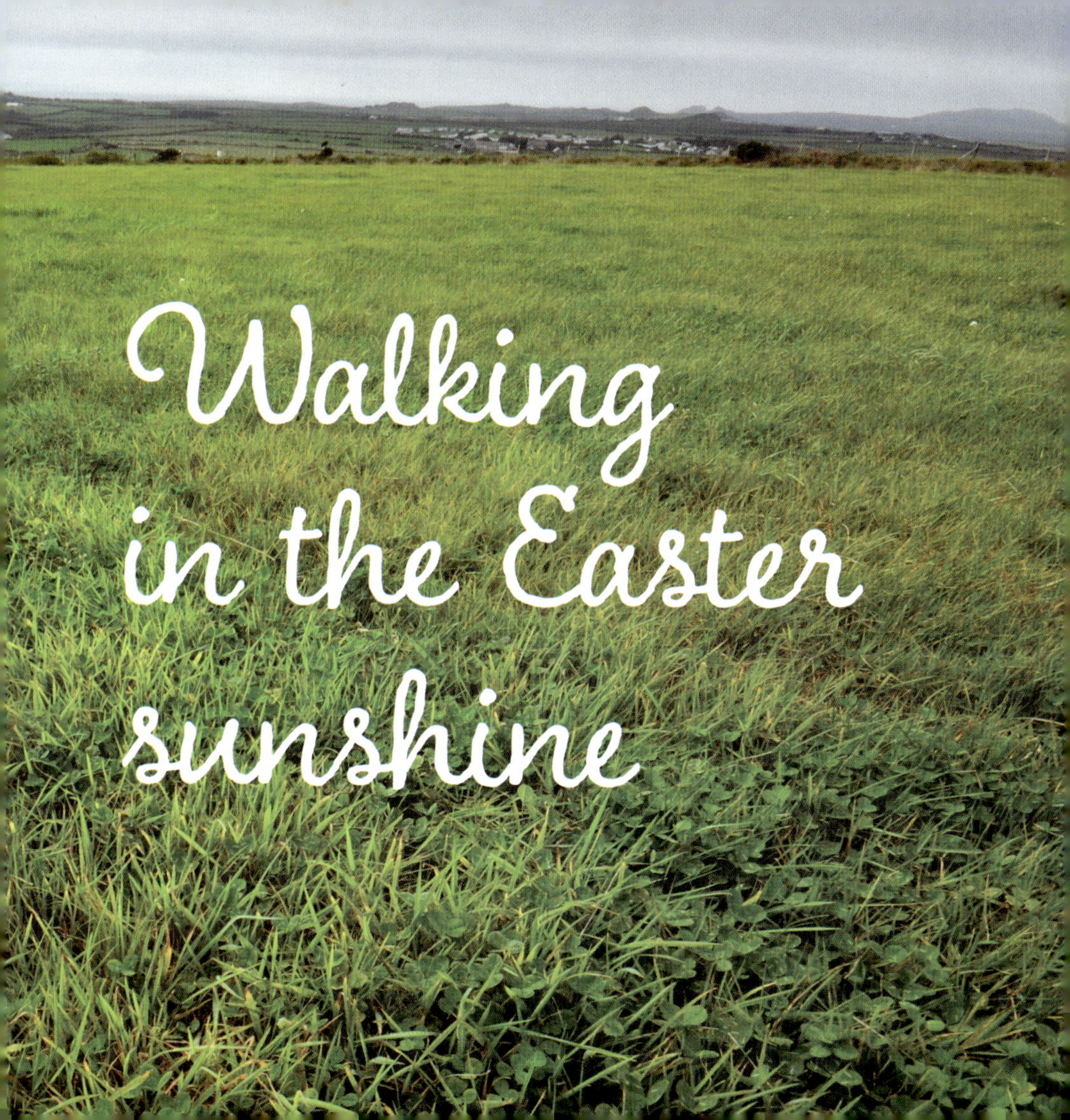

Walking
in the Easter
sunshine

Walking the lane in Easter sunshine. Small eggs, gold and silver lie hidden along the path, tangled in dry and twisted gorse branches.

Dried and fallen needles of gorse rest in the spaces between stones in the old wall. Here there is shelter from cold salt winds.

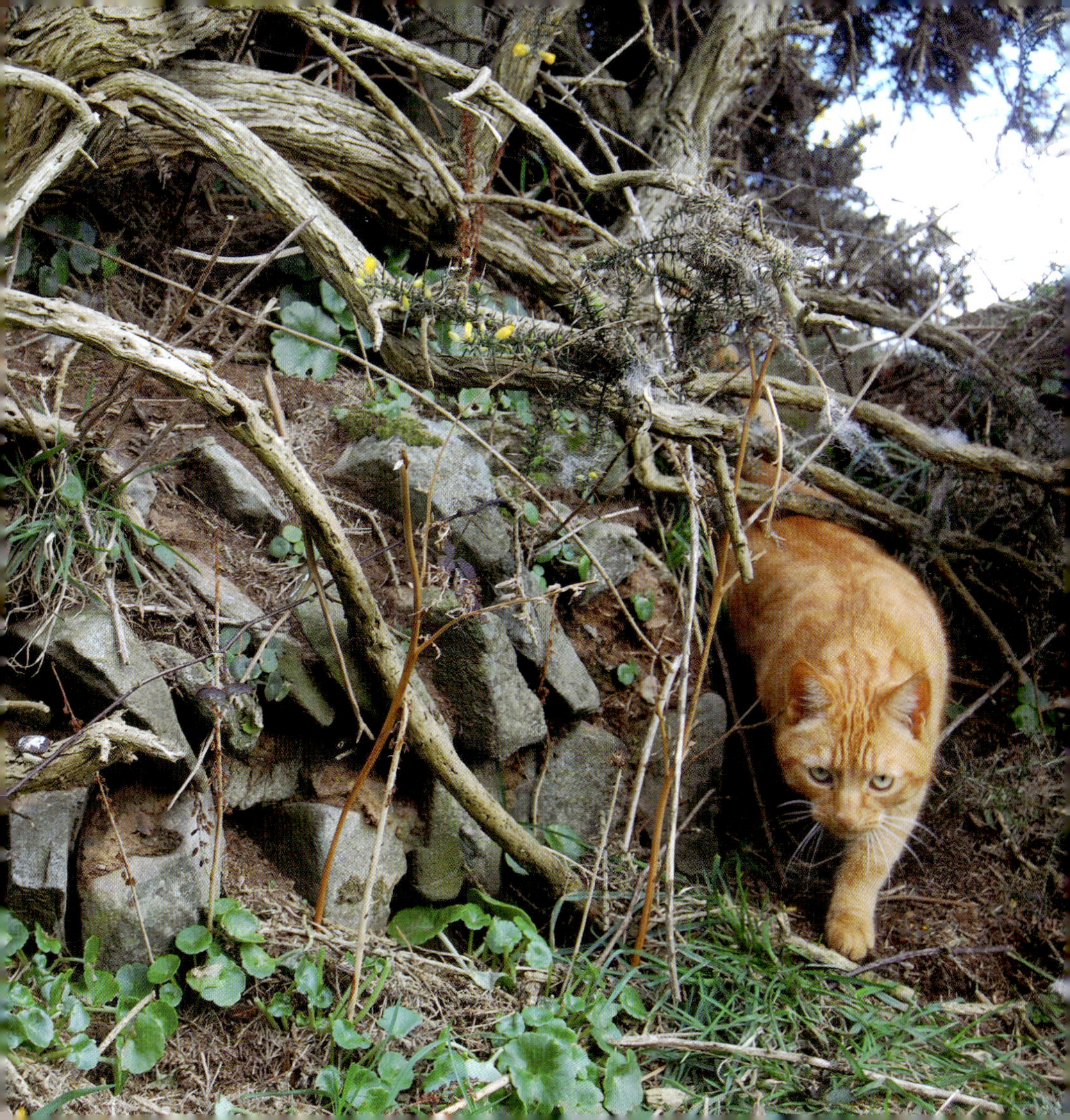

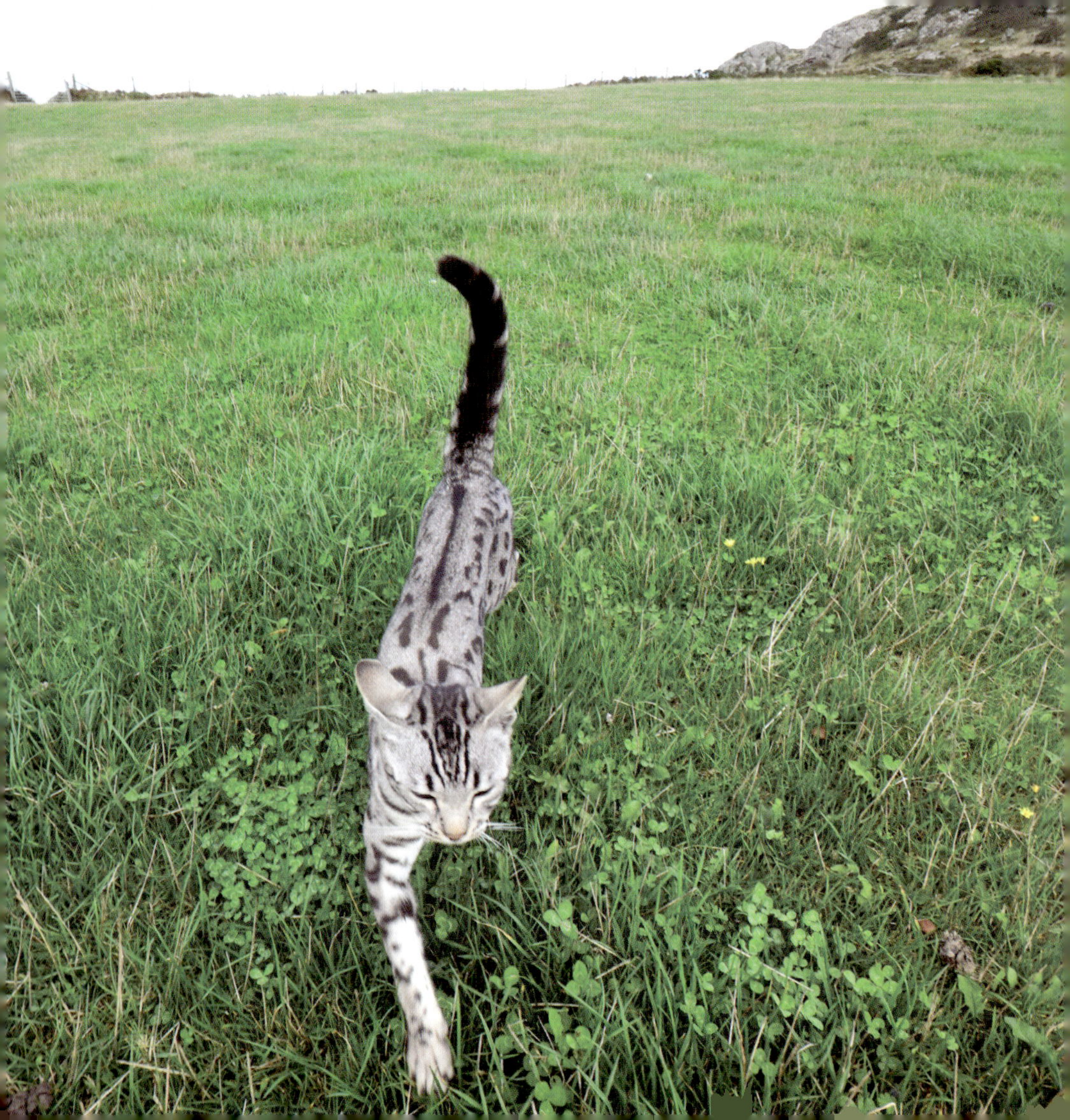

Stepping out into the fresh spring grass as days begin to move into a balance of light and dark. Sometimes it feels that winter still clings to the land. We wait, for the swallows, for wheatears to dance on the stone walls, for the cuckoo to say that spring is here and summer soon and winter gone.

Outside for the first time in his small life Leopard
wanted to be everywhere, see everything. In a
rare moment of stillness, whiskers alert for the
message of movement, he looked so beautiful in
the spring growth of the wild garden.

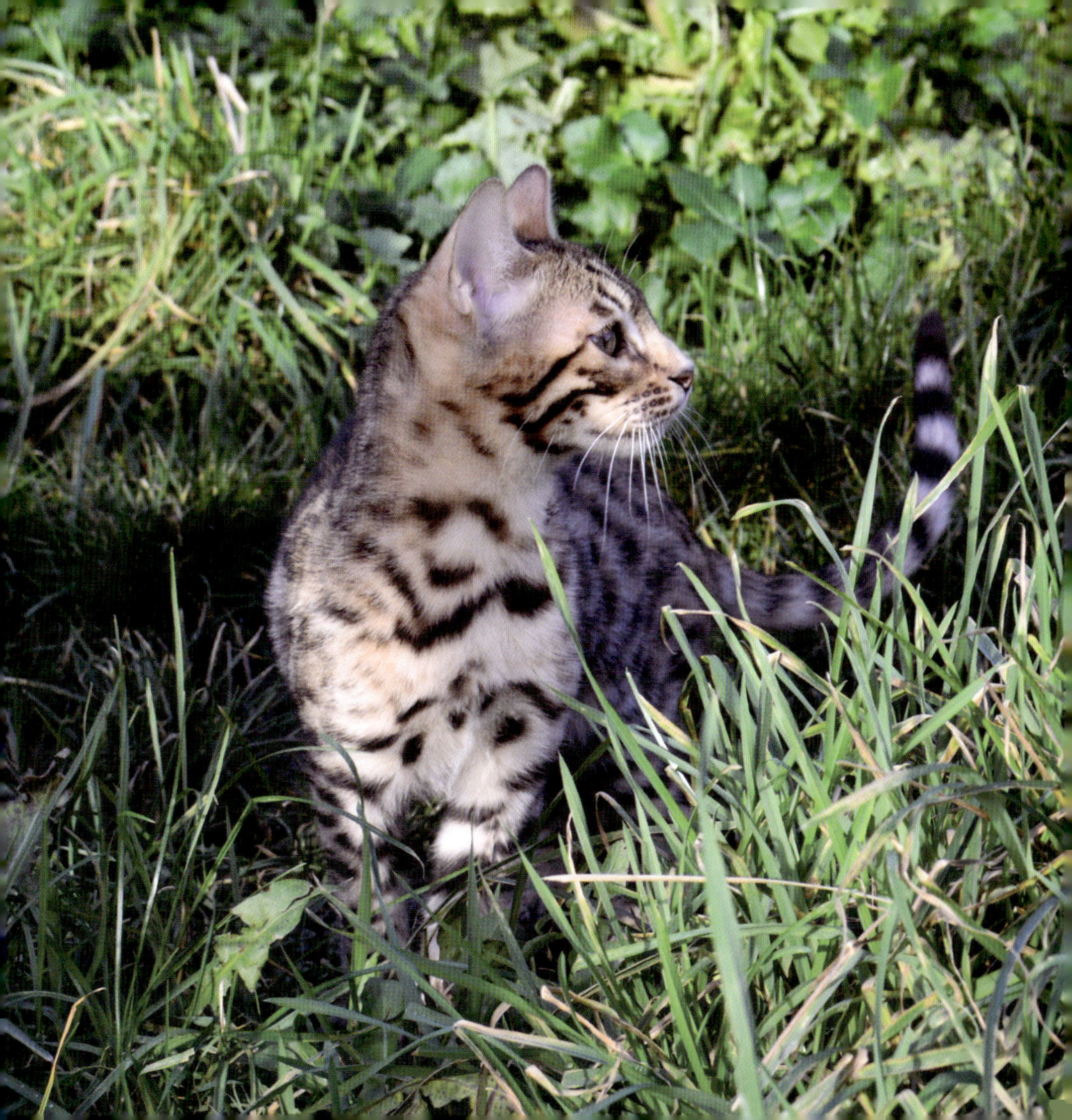

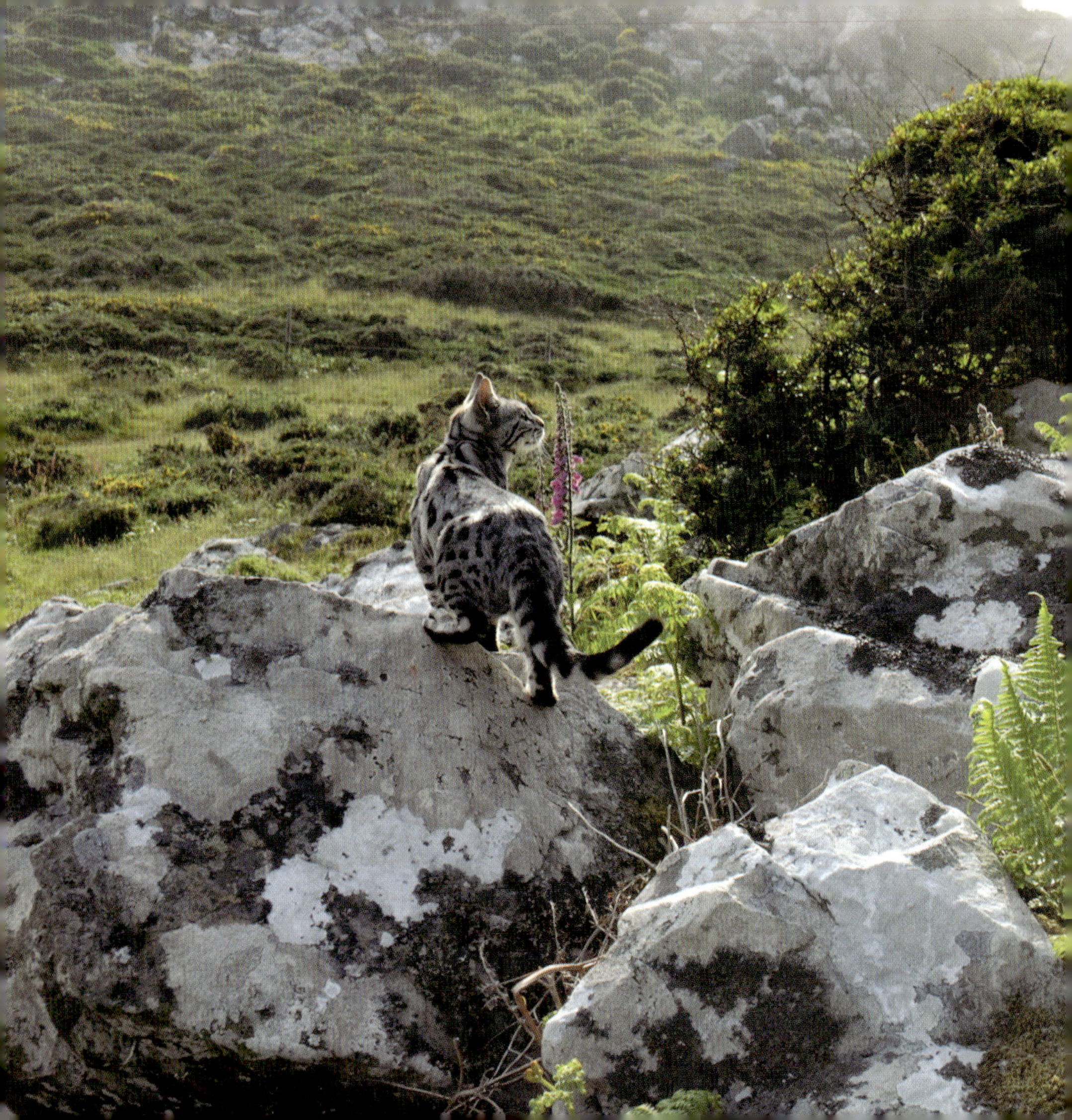

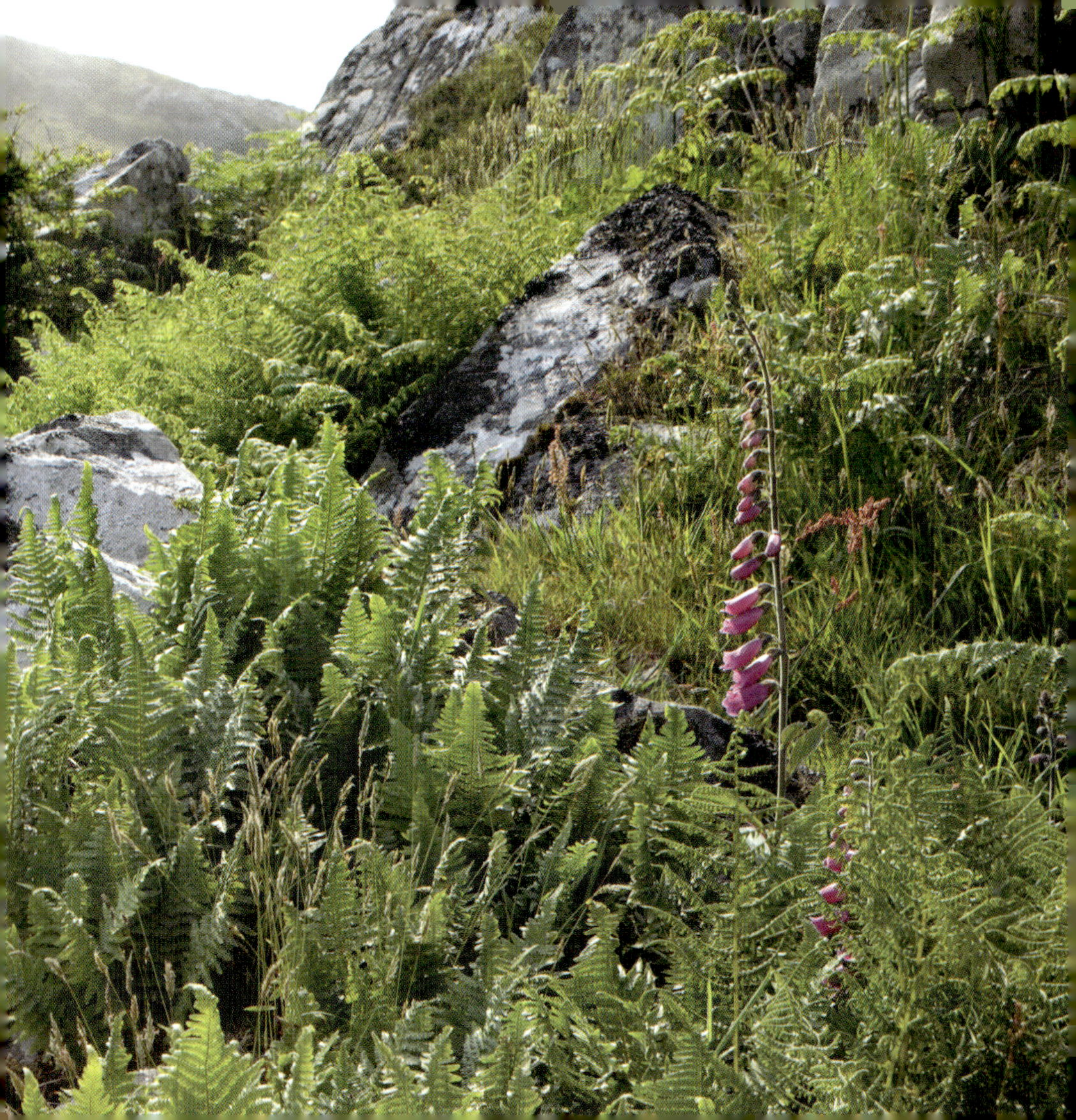

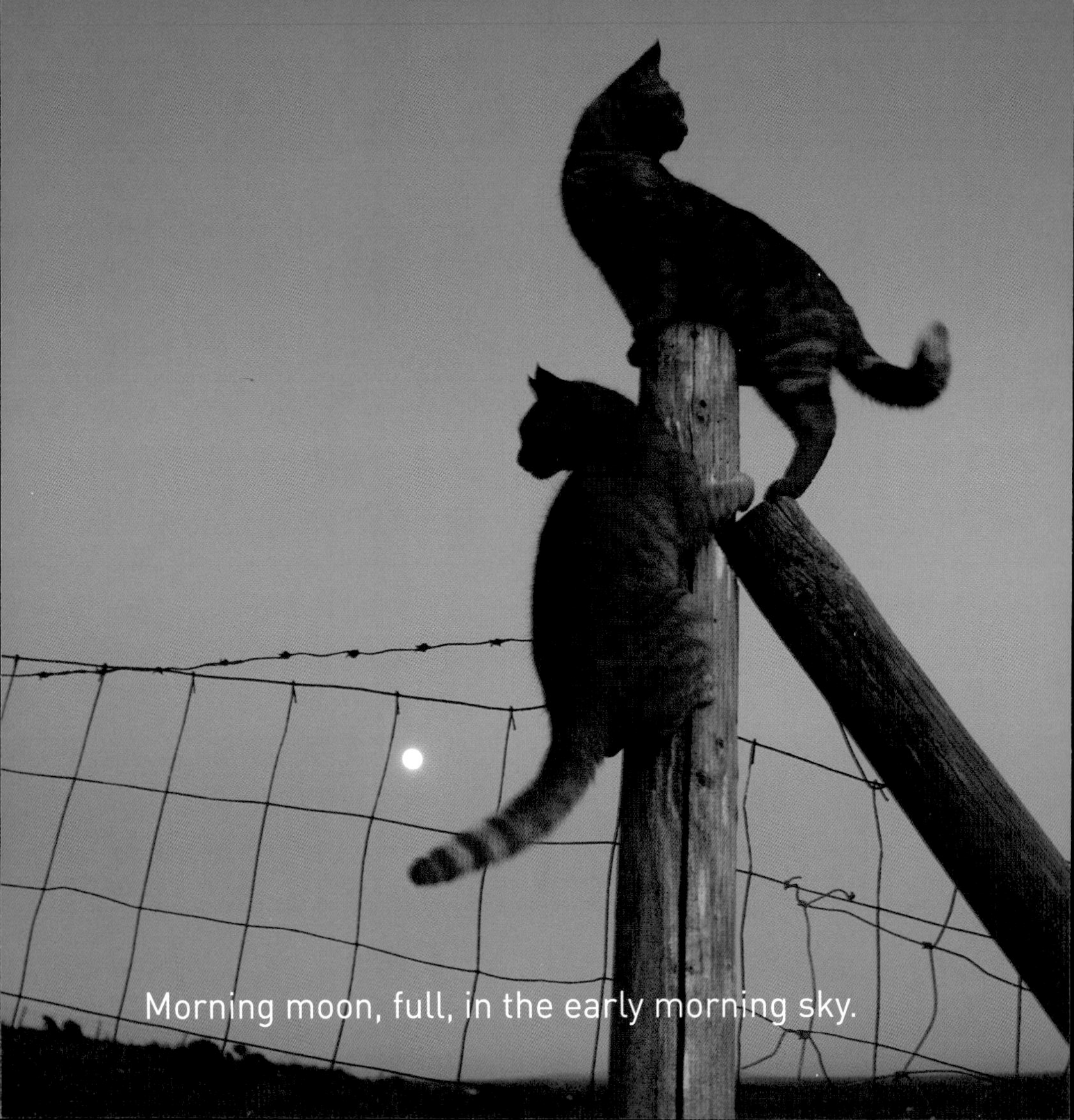
Morning moon, full, in the early morning sky.

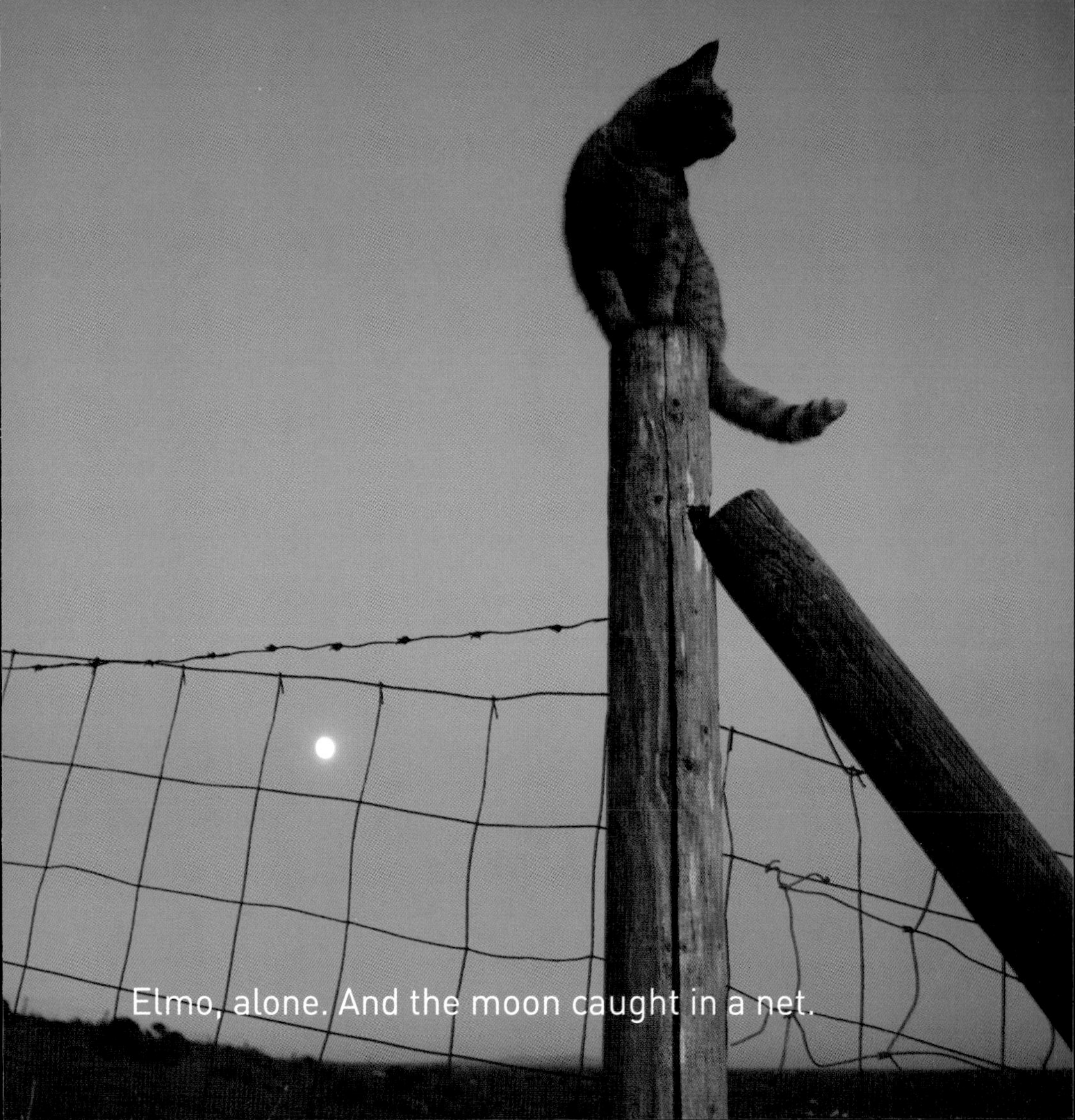
Elmo, alone. And the moon caught in a net.

Lady S seemed to be crafted from the very rock
and lichen on which she sat and yet she moves
with the grace and fluidity of water. Bright eyed,
silver dappled, a miniature leopard cat.

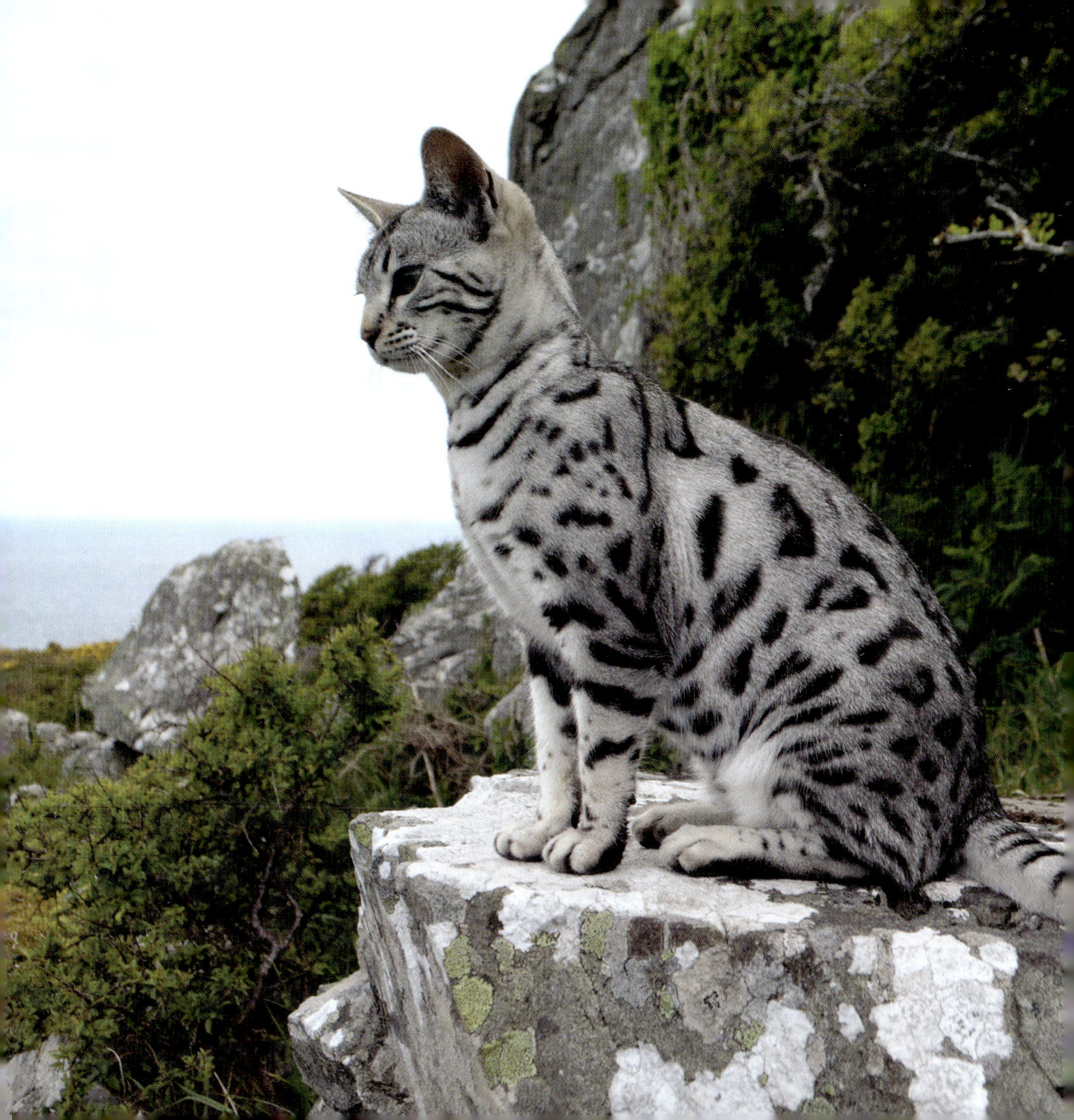

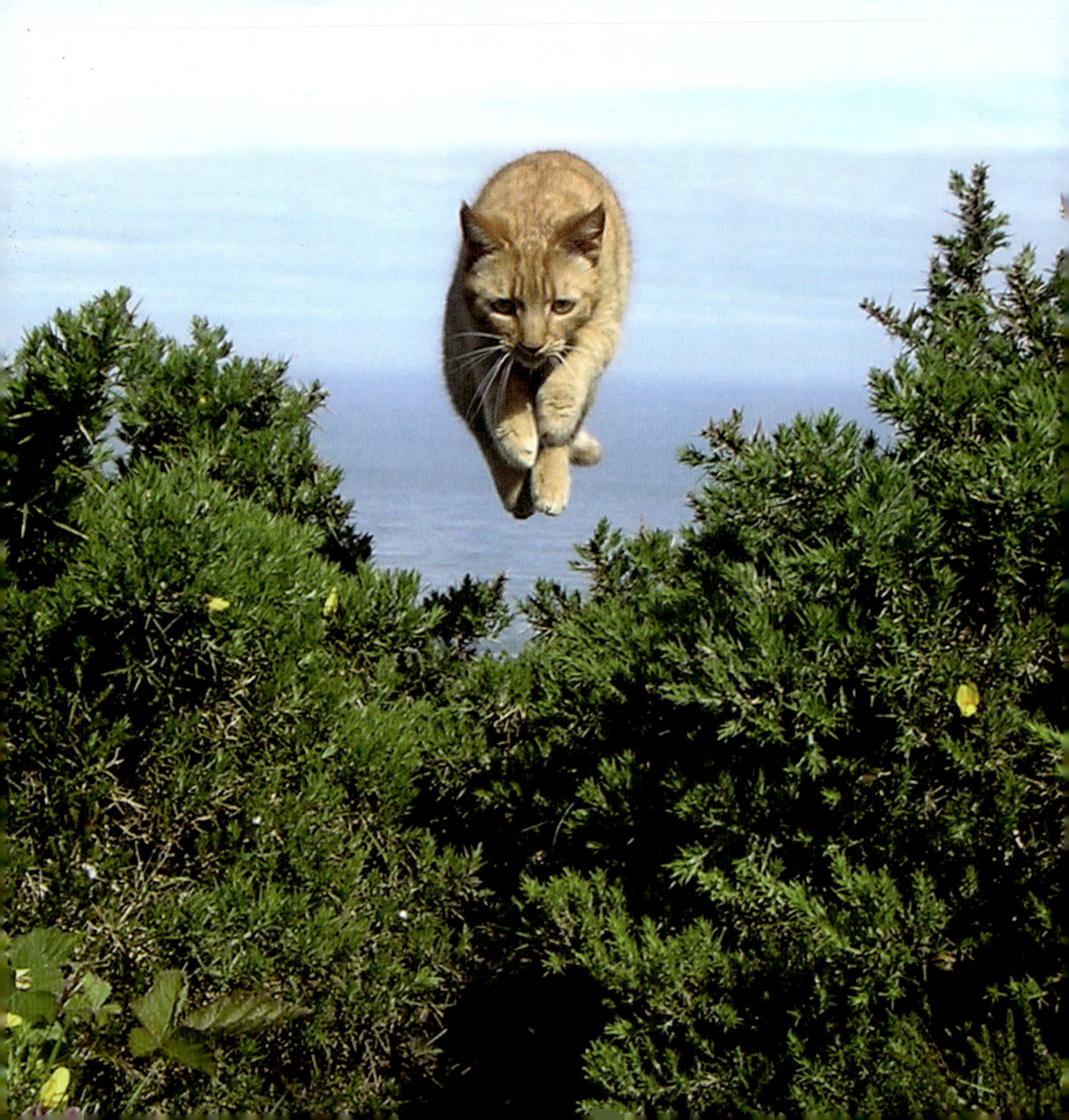

The path was narrow. The width of a badger. In places the gorse reached across, making dark green tunnels. Sometimes the cats would push their way through or slide sinuous beneath where the gorse scratched with leaves sharp as claws. Sometimes they would leap.

Pixie cat, smallest of small, walked along narrow paths between earth and sky, beside the great sea. Around her the grasses were golden, softened by seeds. Above her ravens danced on the wind. Beside her, memories.

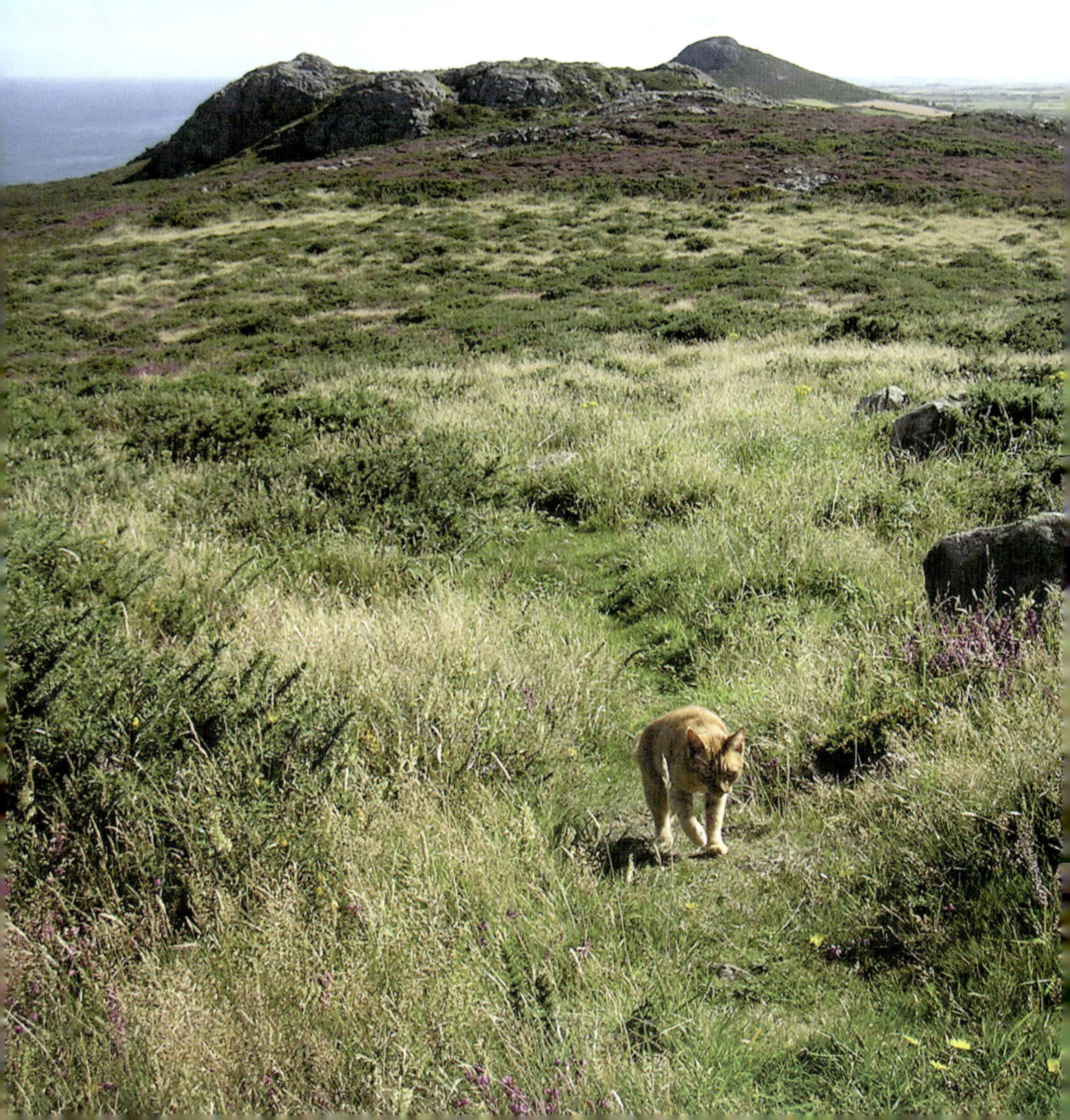

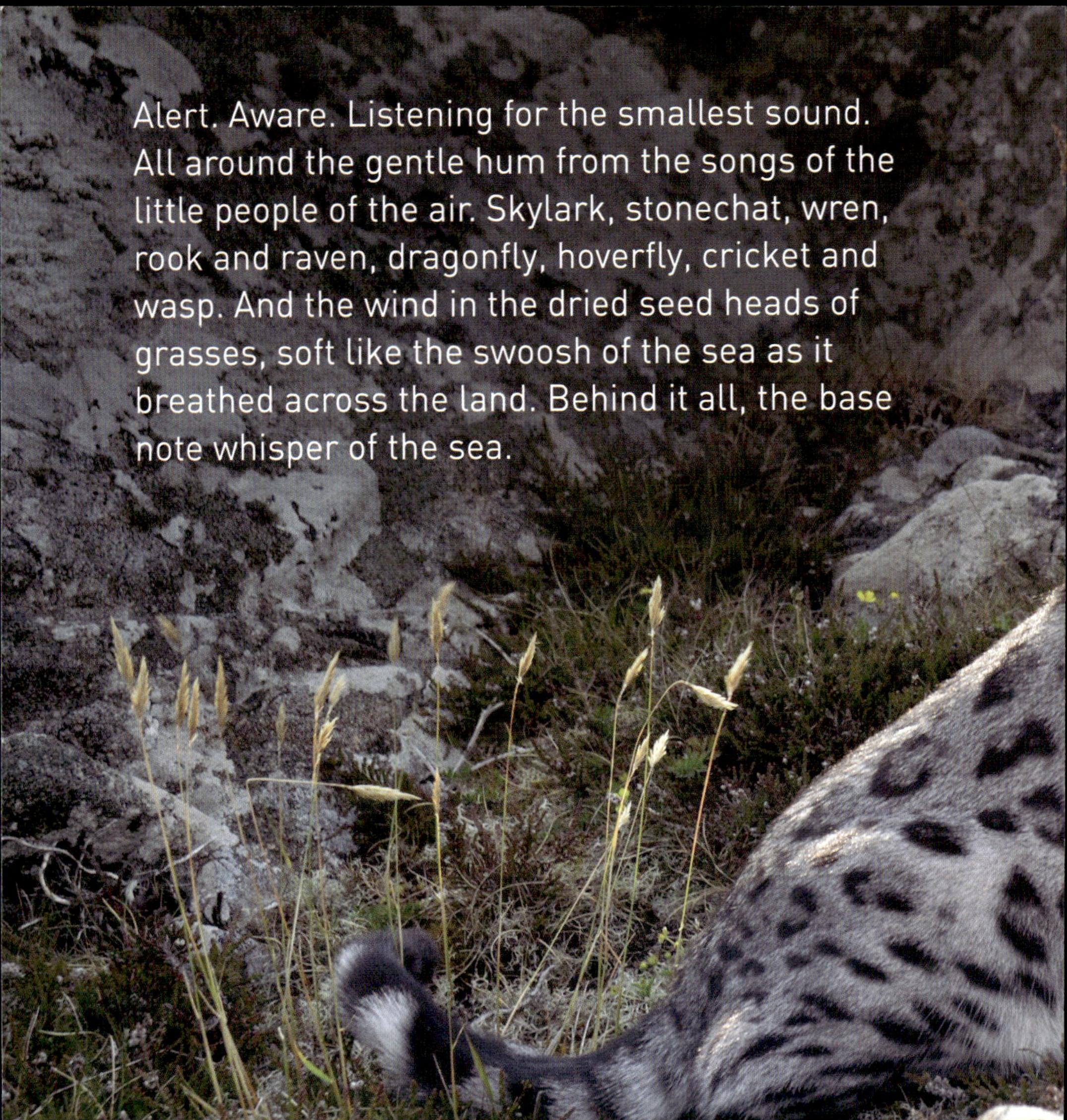
Alert. Aware. Listening for the smallest sound.
All around the gentle hum from the songs of the
little people of the air. Skylark, stonechat, wren,
rook and raven, dragonfly, hoverfly, cricket and
wasp. And the wind in the dried seed heads of
grasses, soft like the swoosh of the sea as it
breathed across the land. Behind it all, the base
note whisper of the sea.

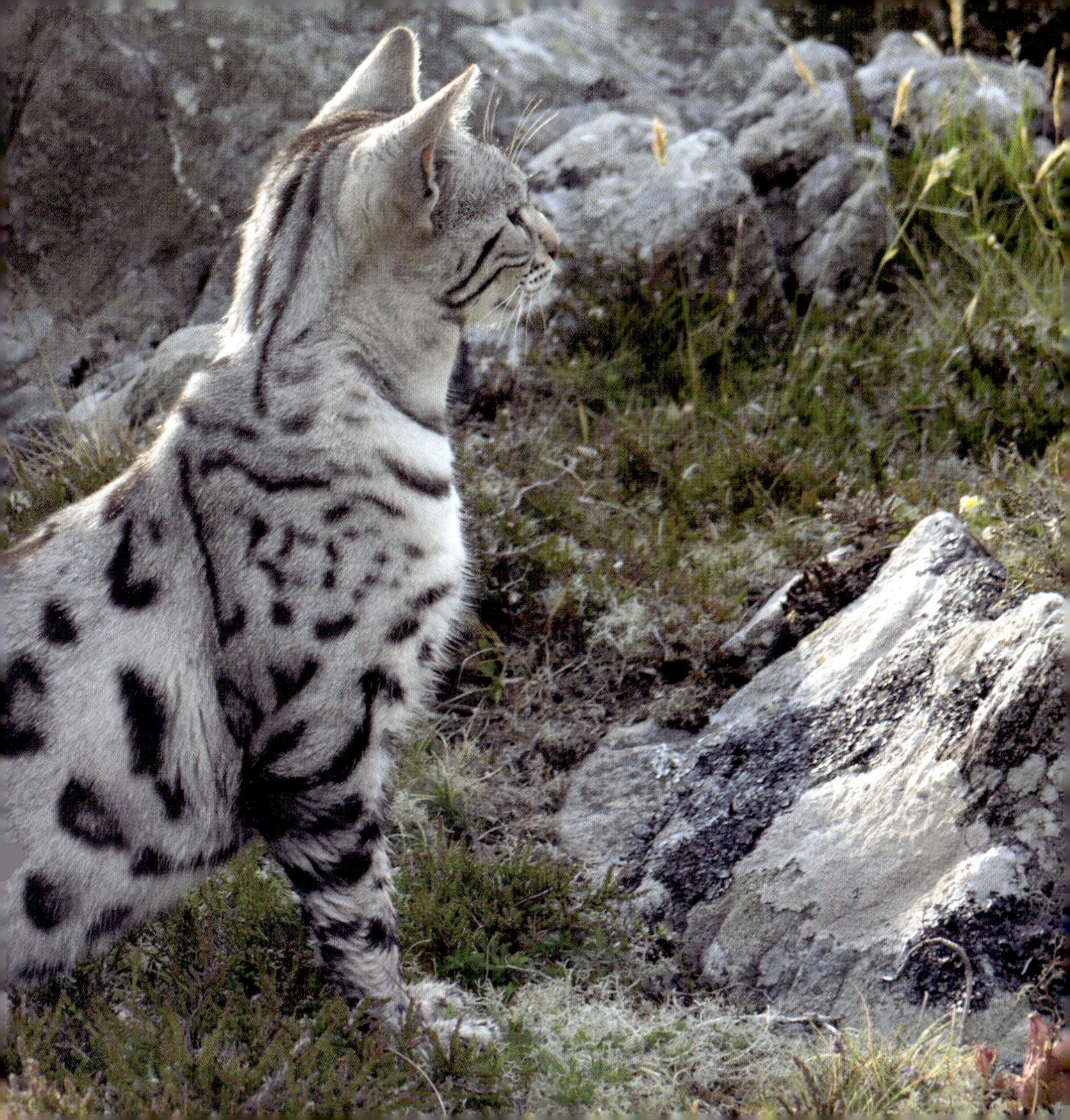

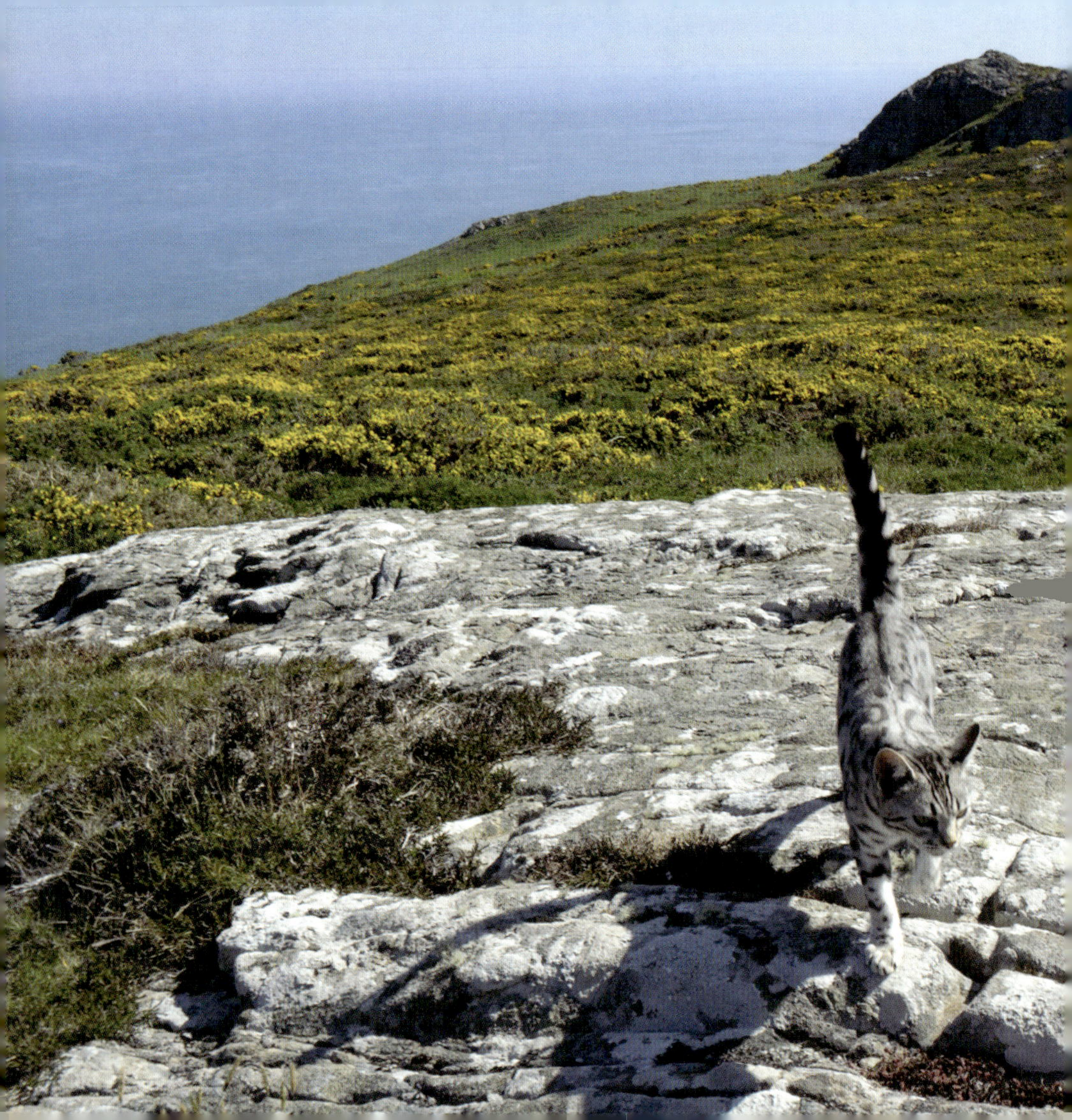

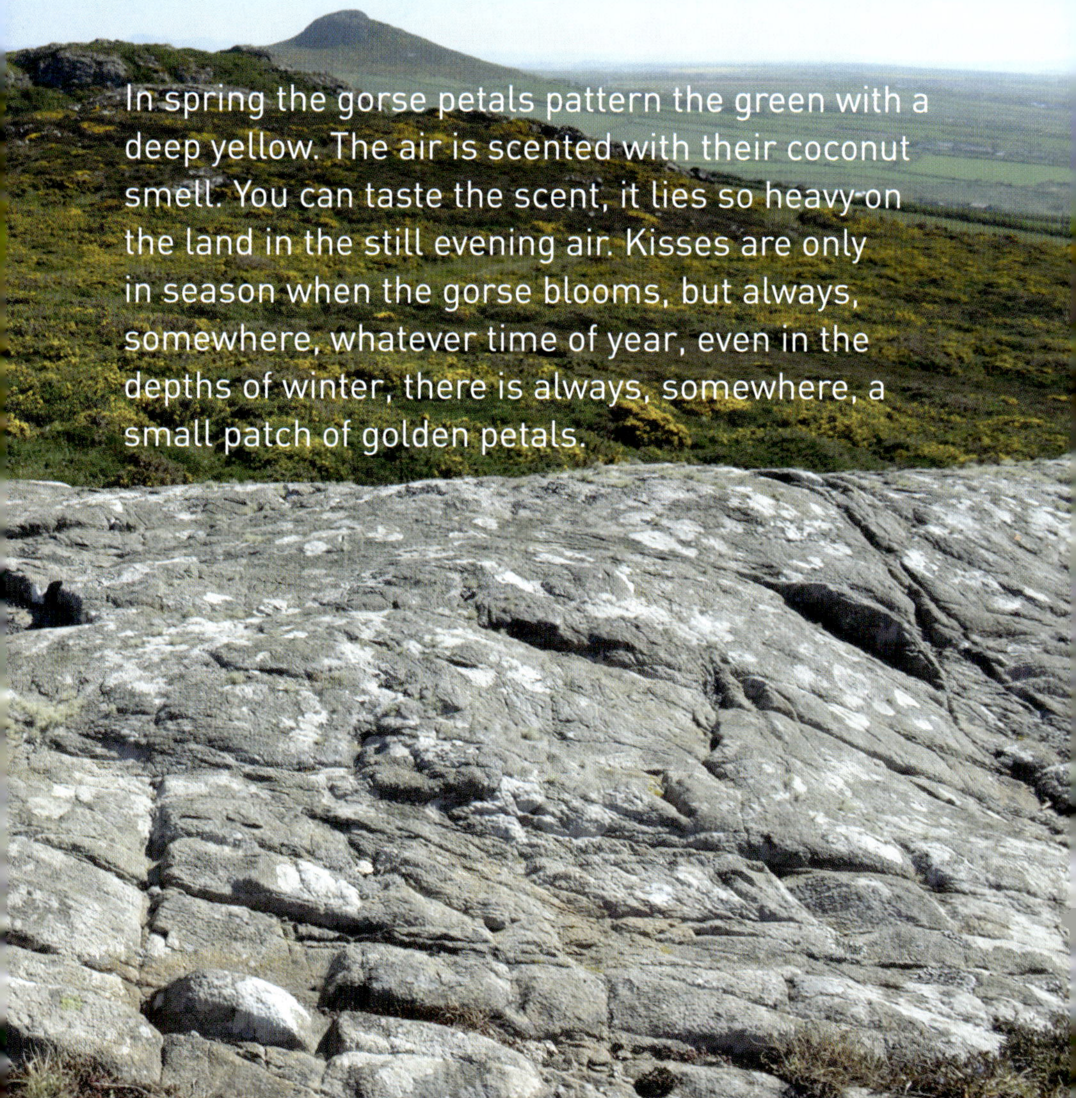

In spring the gorse petals pattern the green with a
deep yellow. The air is scented with their coconut
smell. You can taste the scent, it lies so heavy on
the land in the still evening air. Kisses are only
in season when the gorse blooms, but always,
somewhere, whatever time of year, even in the
depths of winter, there is always, somewhere, a
small patch of golden petals.

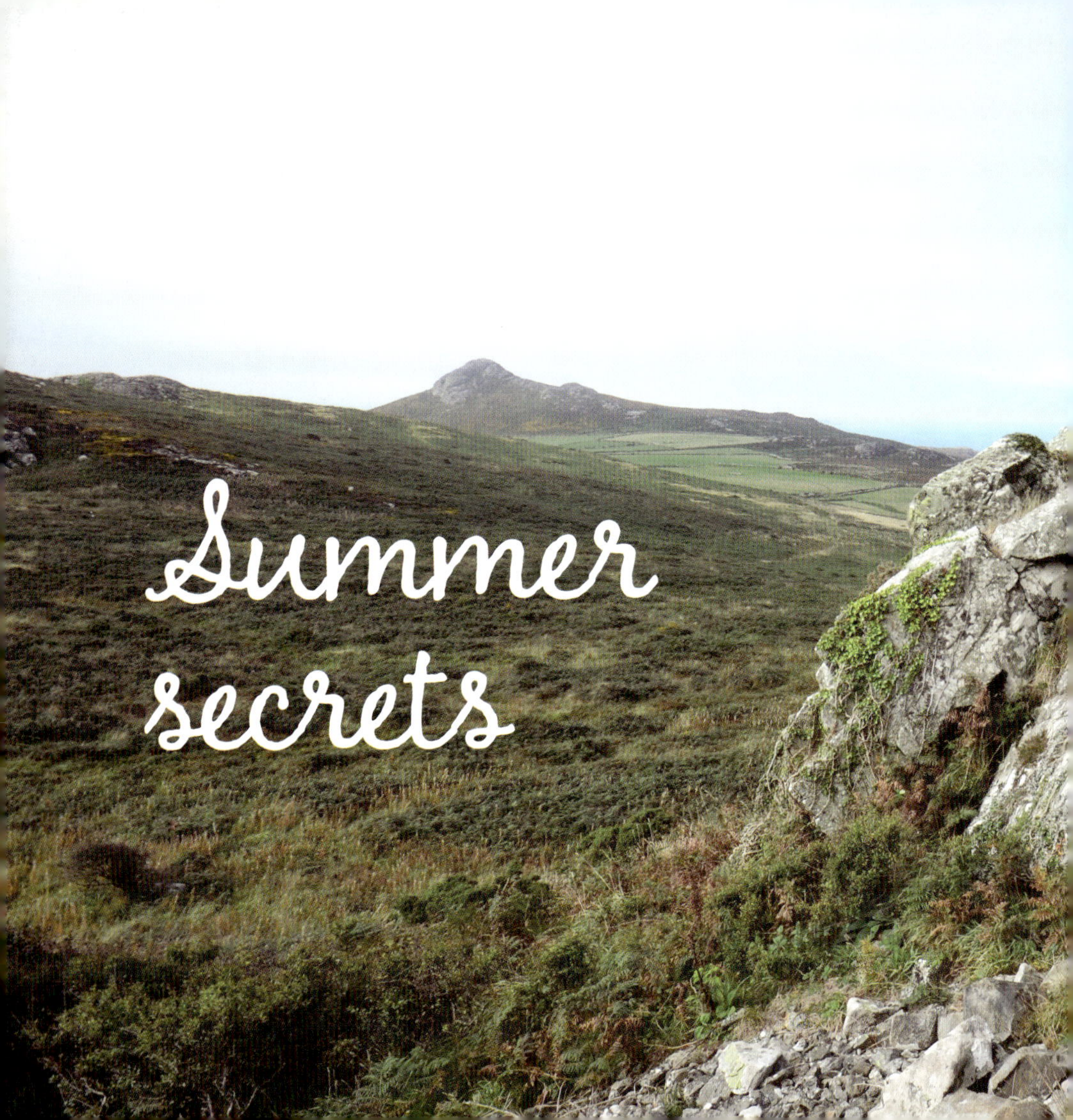
Summer
secrets

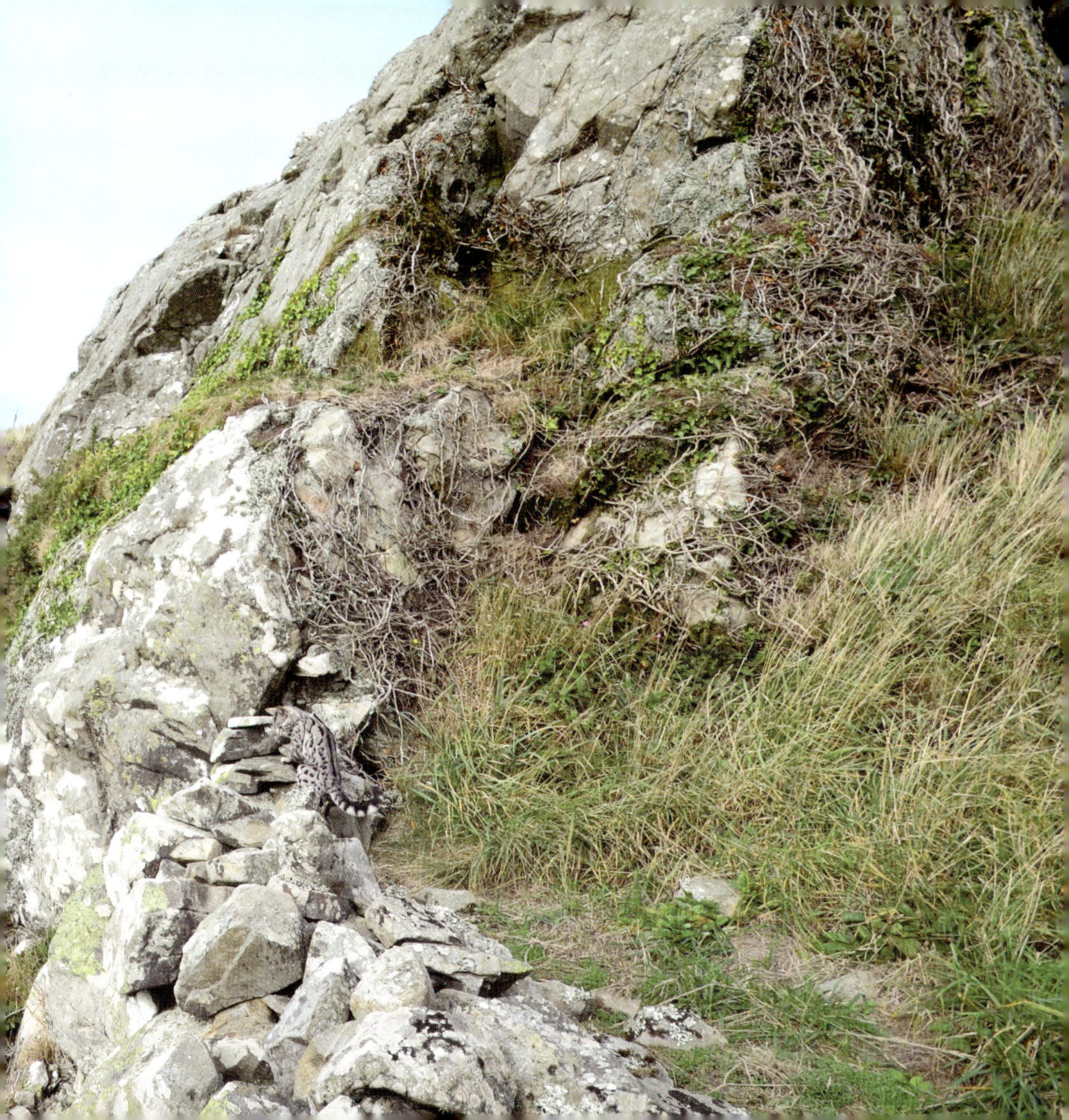

In the summer the path up the hill was as narrow
as a cat, grass a tall tunnel of heavy seed heads.
The two cats would stop for a while to exchange
secrets.

Through the long grass, stalking mice, weaving a
path the width of a small cat, silver in the green.

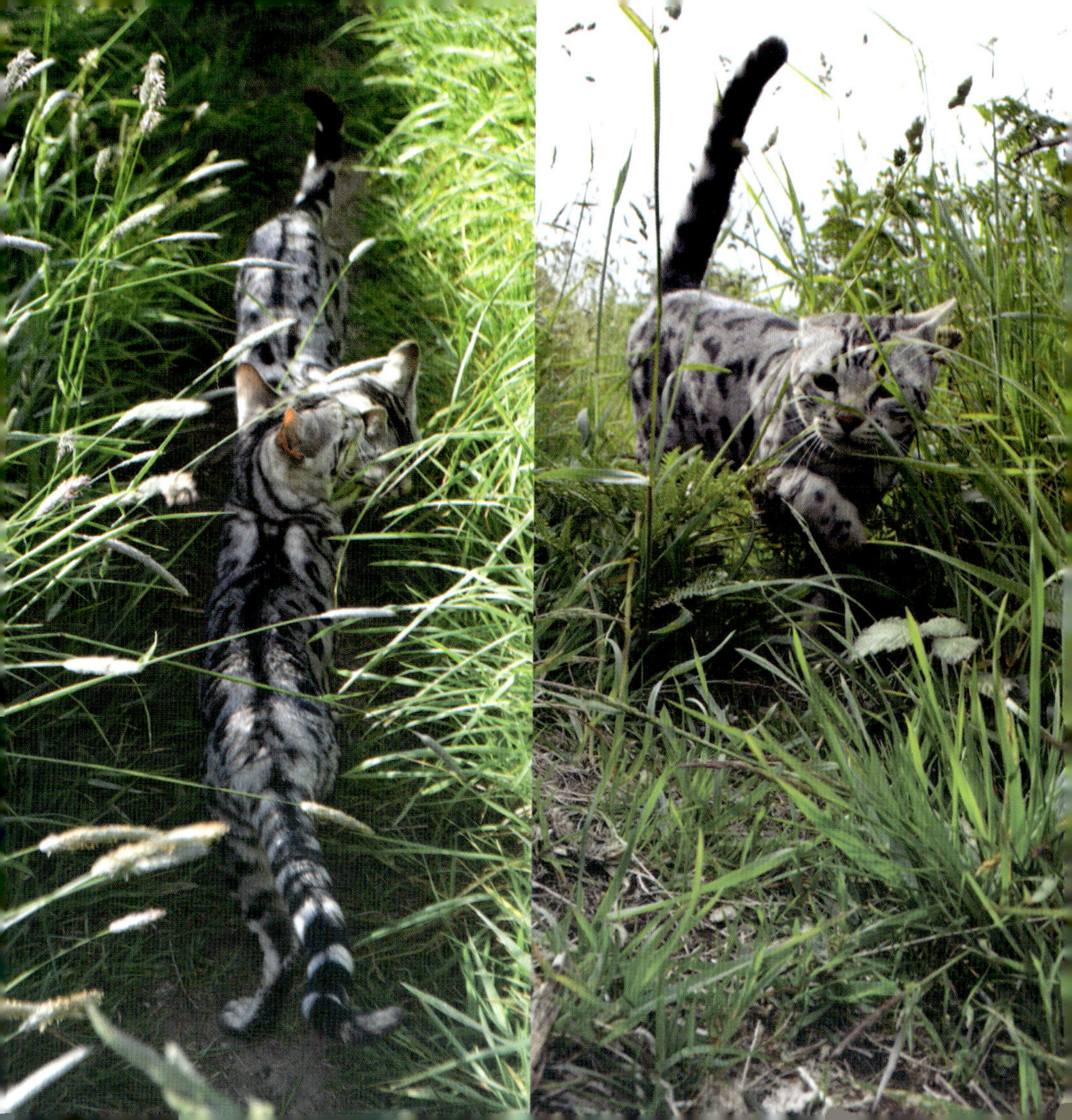

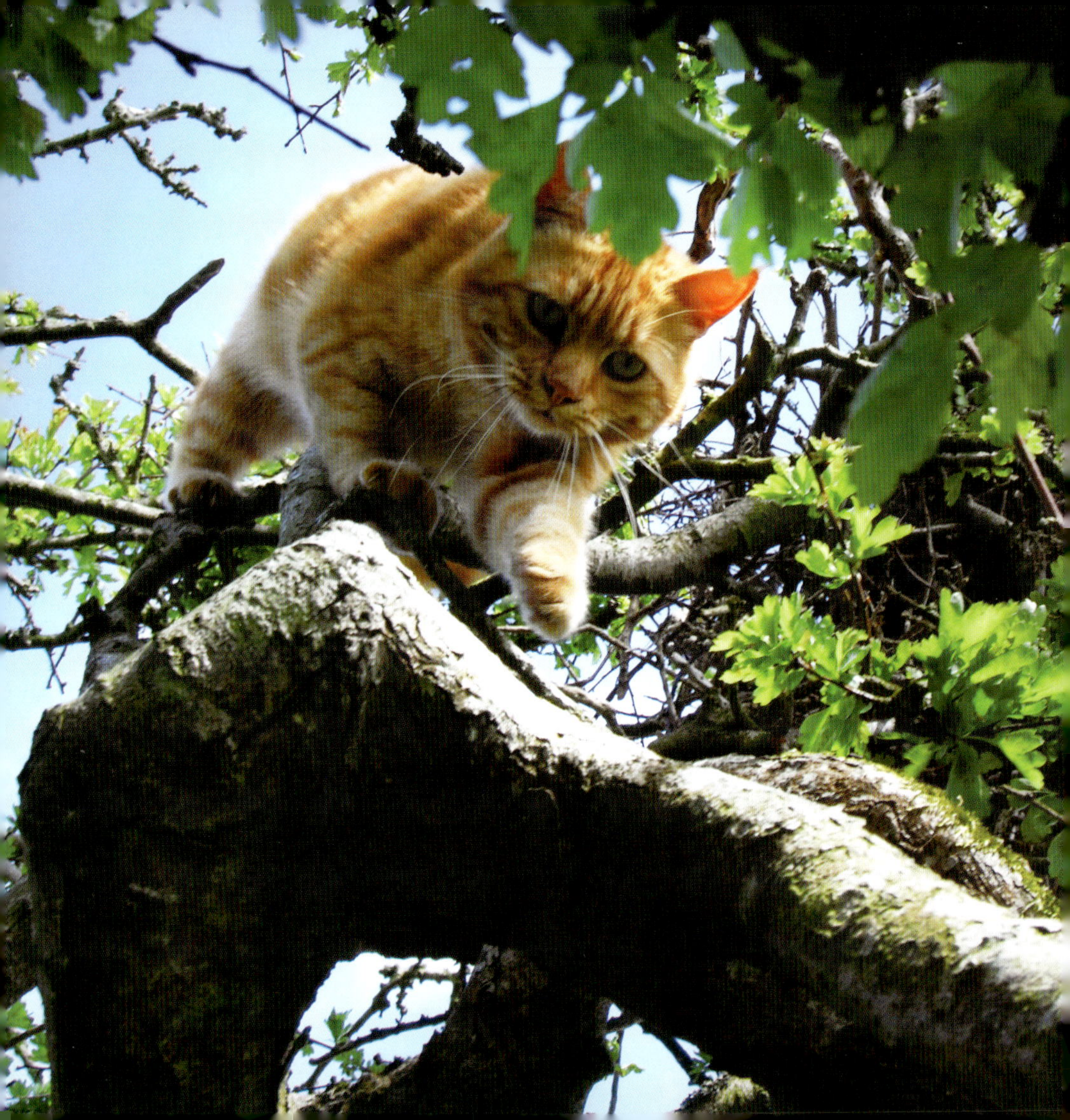

Summer leaves, thick on the thorn tree, hide the
tangled nest of tumbled twigs. A crow's nest.
Every year the crow pair return, raise a brood of
ravenous robber birds. Every year the cats climb
to investigate. But crows are fierce and ginger
cats are brave, but not foolish.

Early morning. The moon is late to rise and makes a translucent hole in a clear blue sky. Cold, for a summer's morning. The cat glows as he hunts, lit by the fresh light of the rising sun.

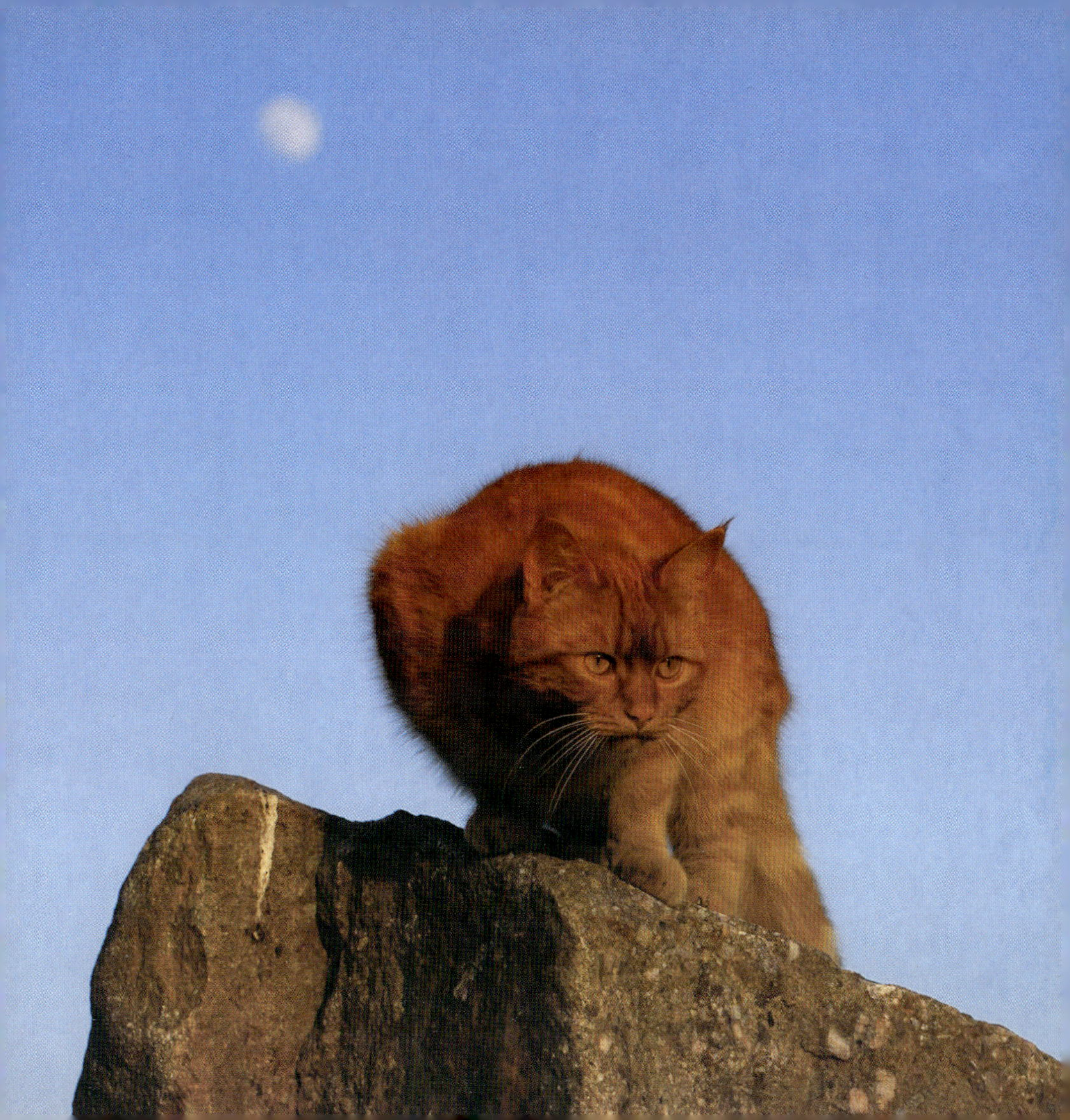

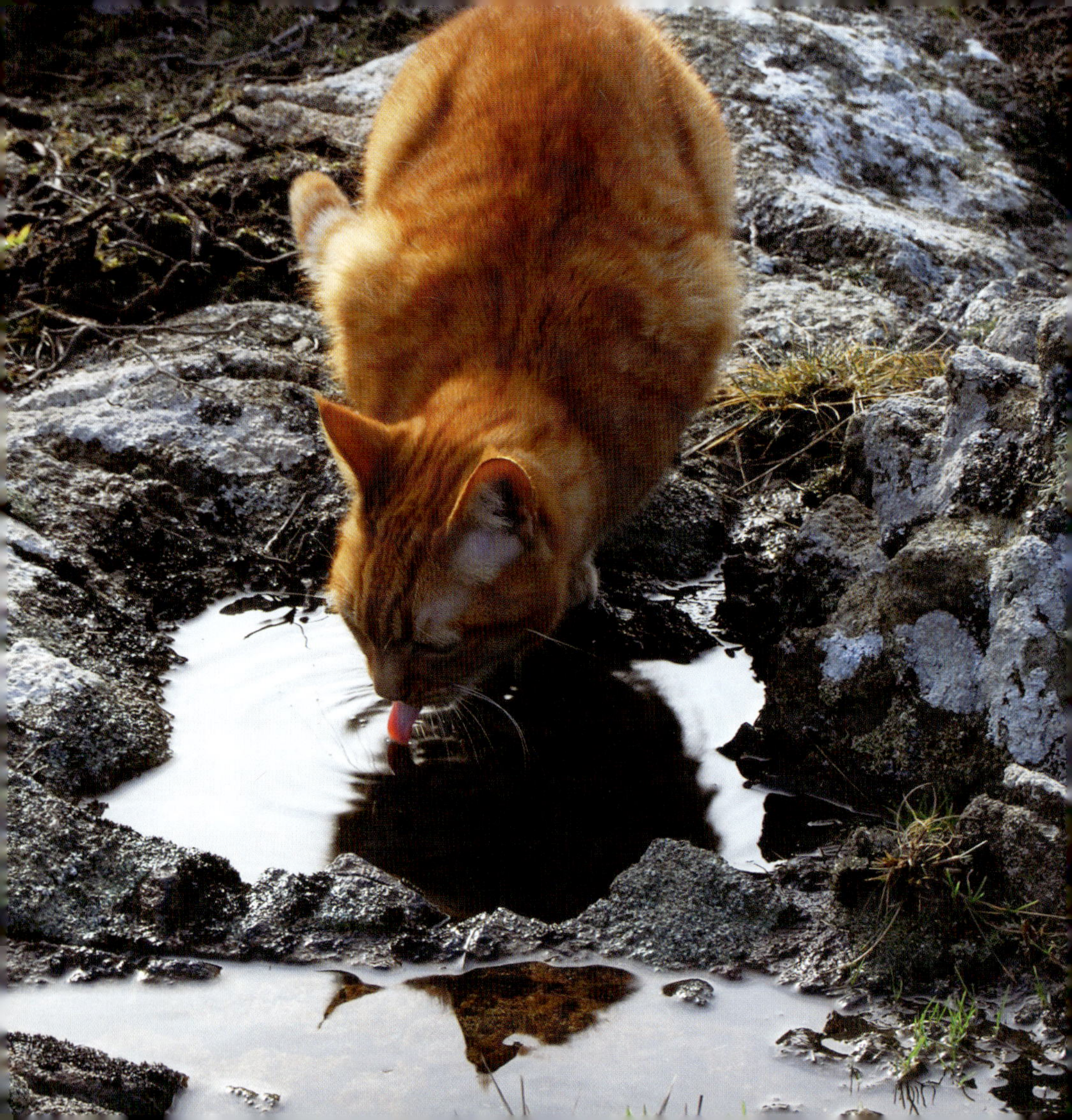

In the heat of a summer's day Pixie lapped from shallow pools of wild rain water caught among the rocks.

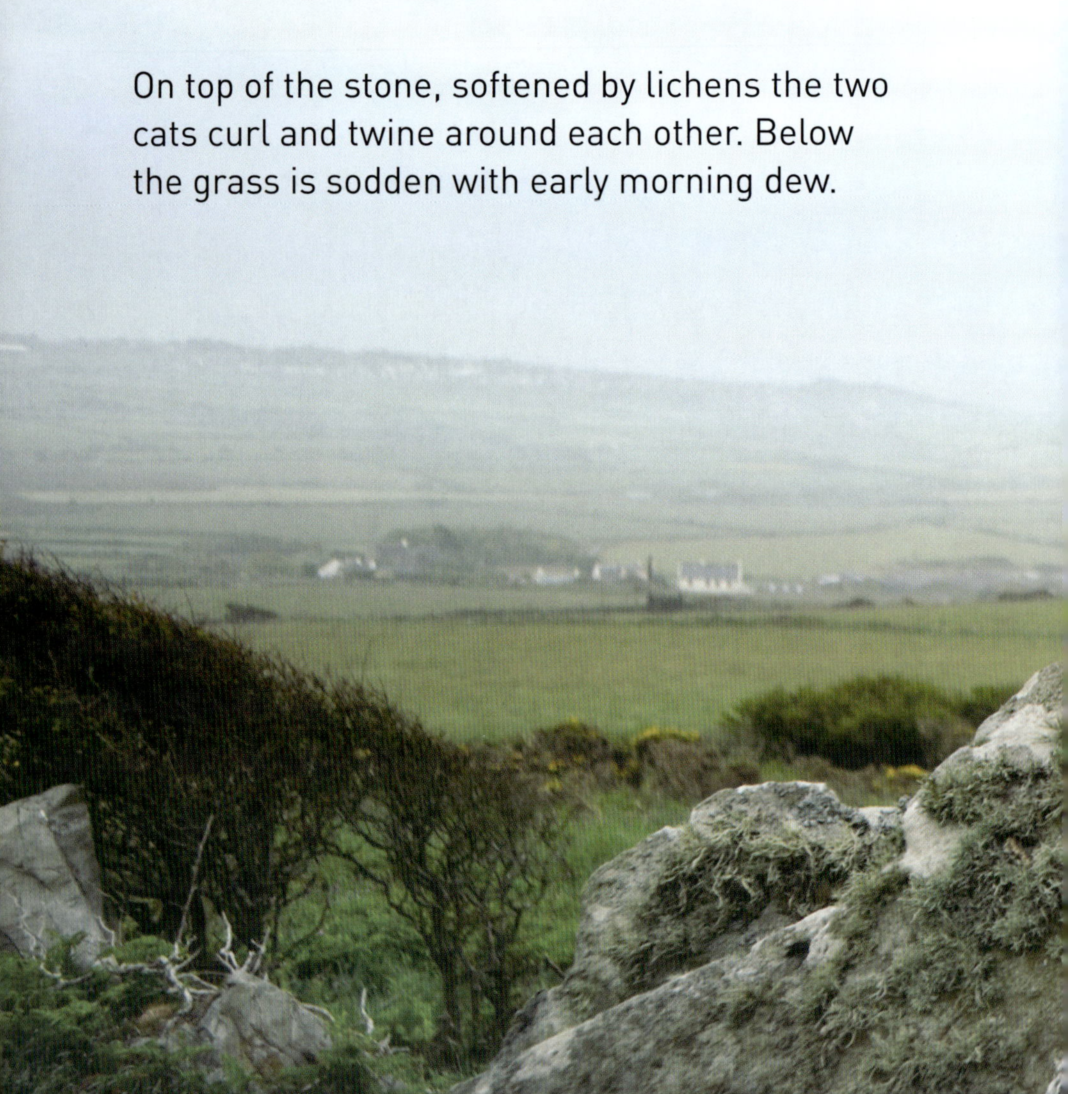

On top of the stone, softened by lichens the two cats curl and twine around each other. Below the grass is sodden with early morning dew.

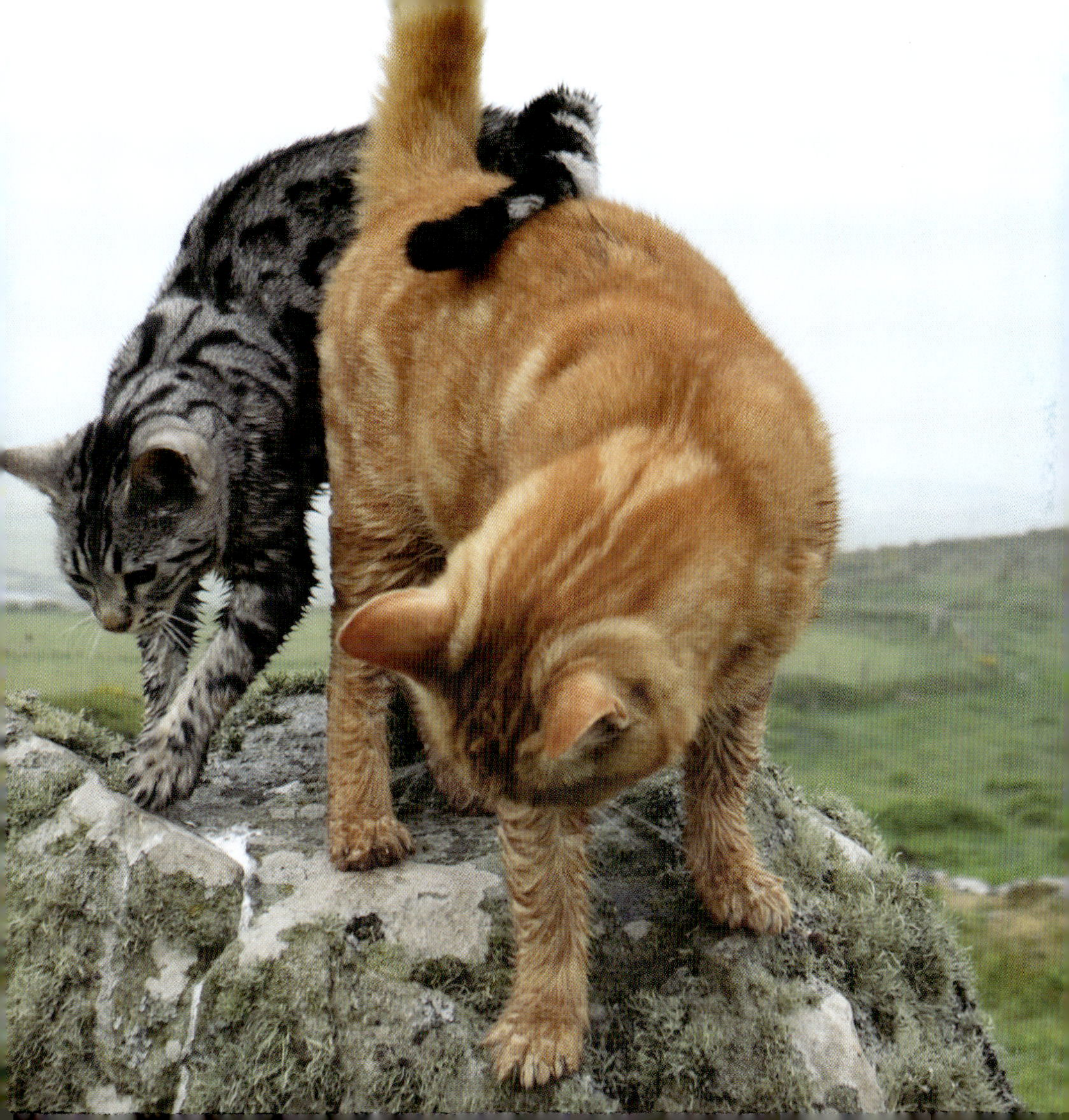

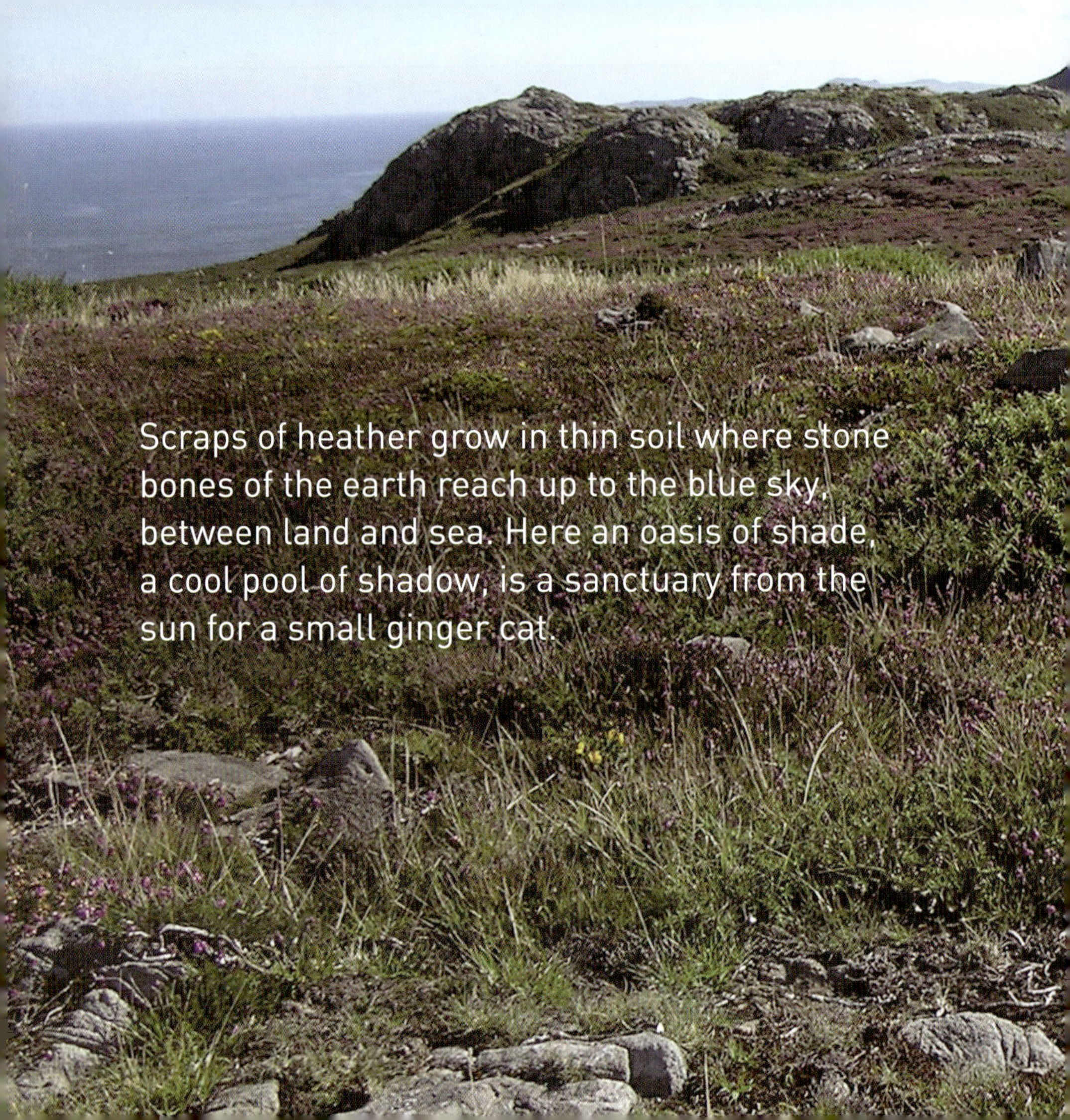

Scraps of heather grow in thin soil where stone
bones of the earth reach up to the blue sky,
between land and sea. Here an oasis of shade,
a cool pool of shadow, is a sanctuary from the
sun for a small ginger cat.

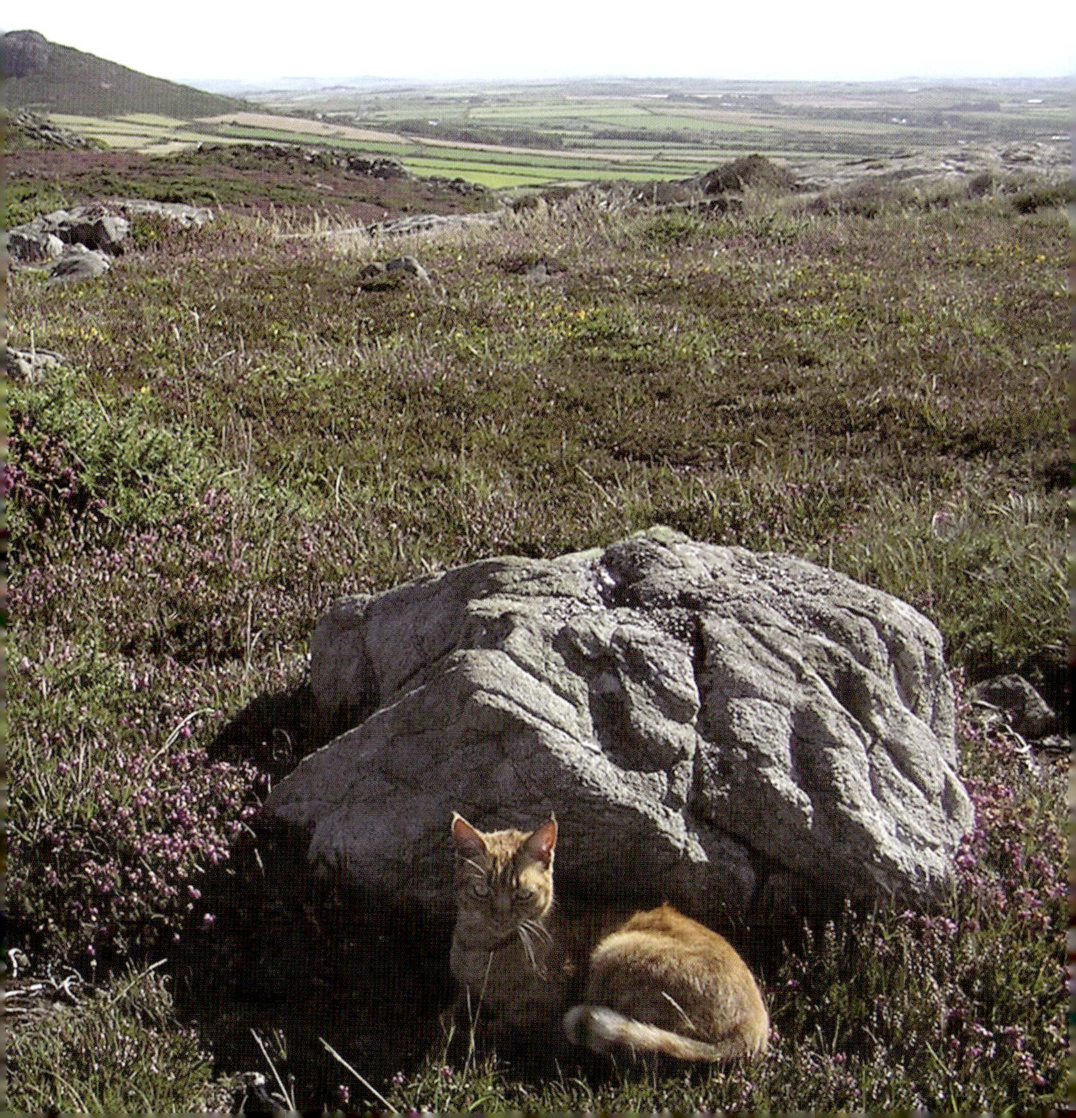

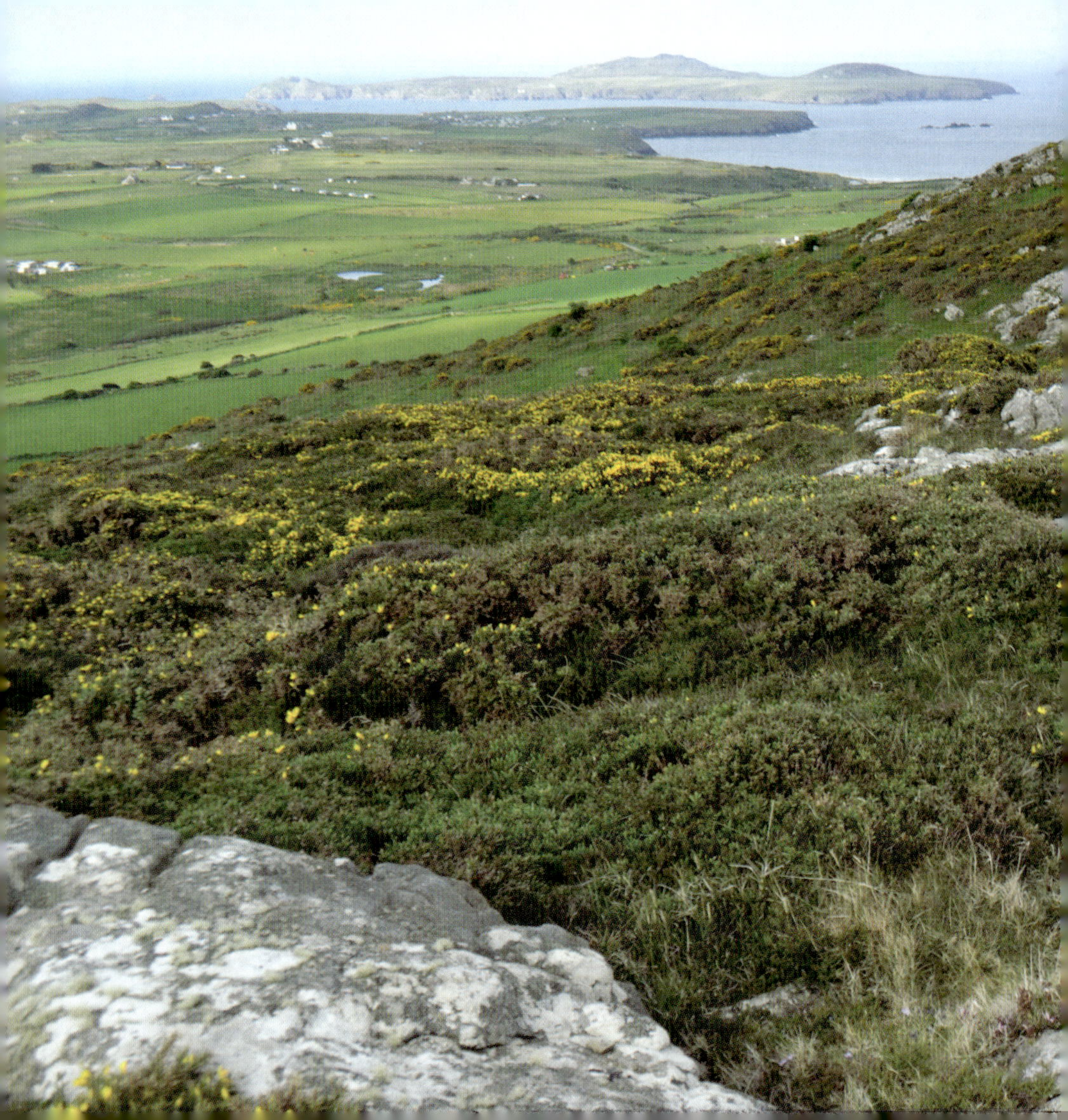

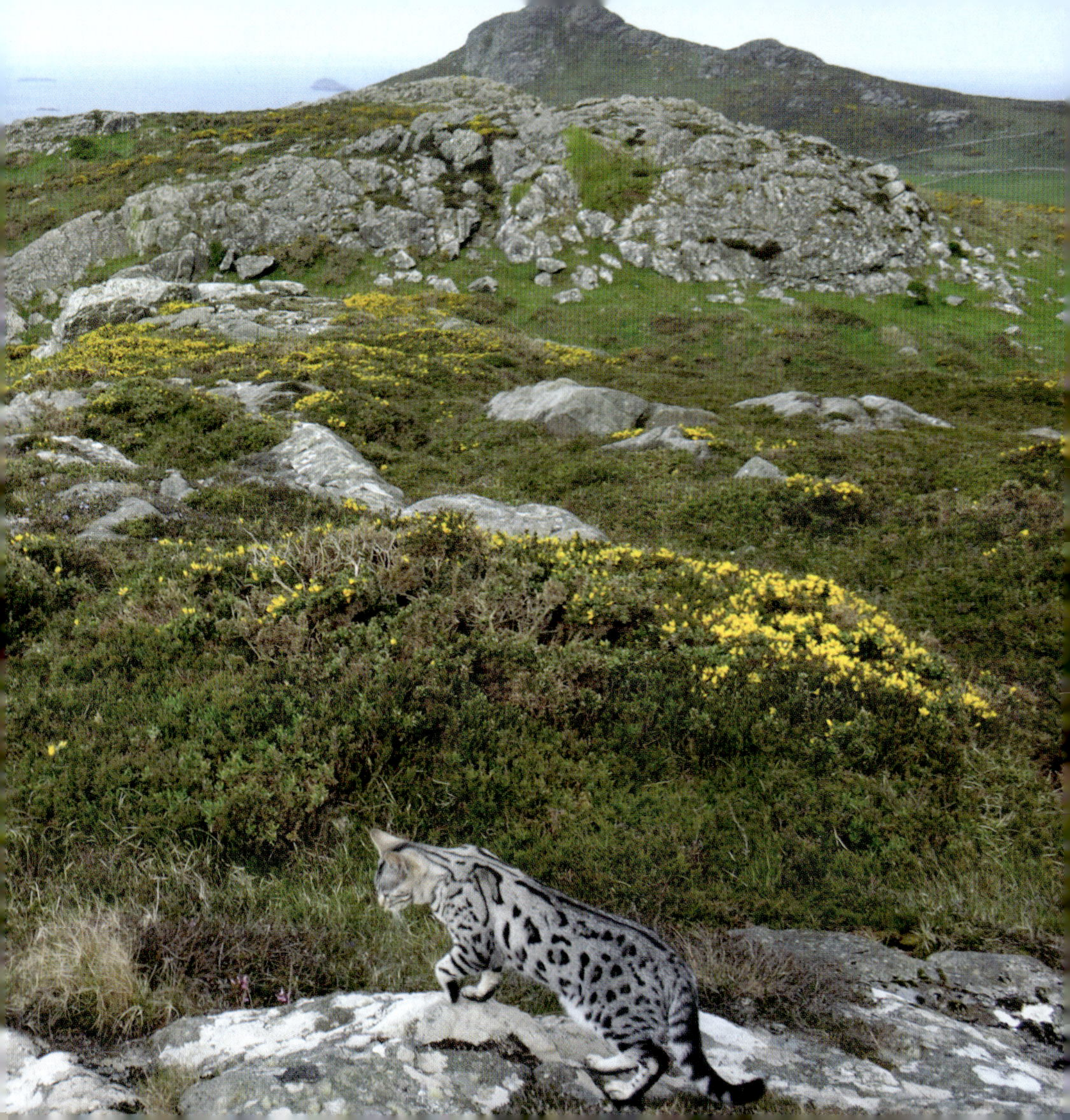

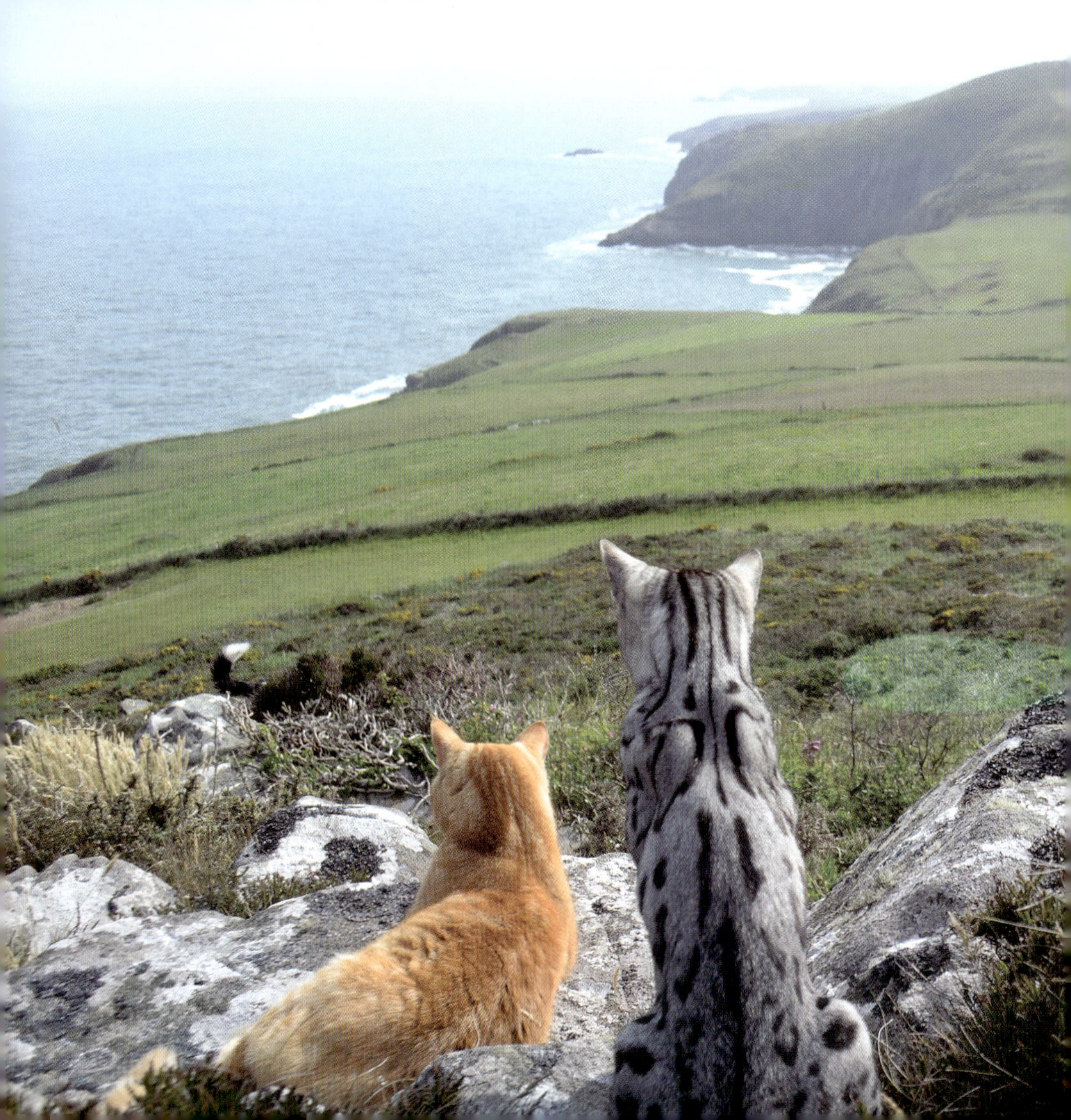

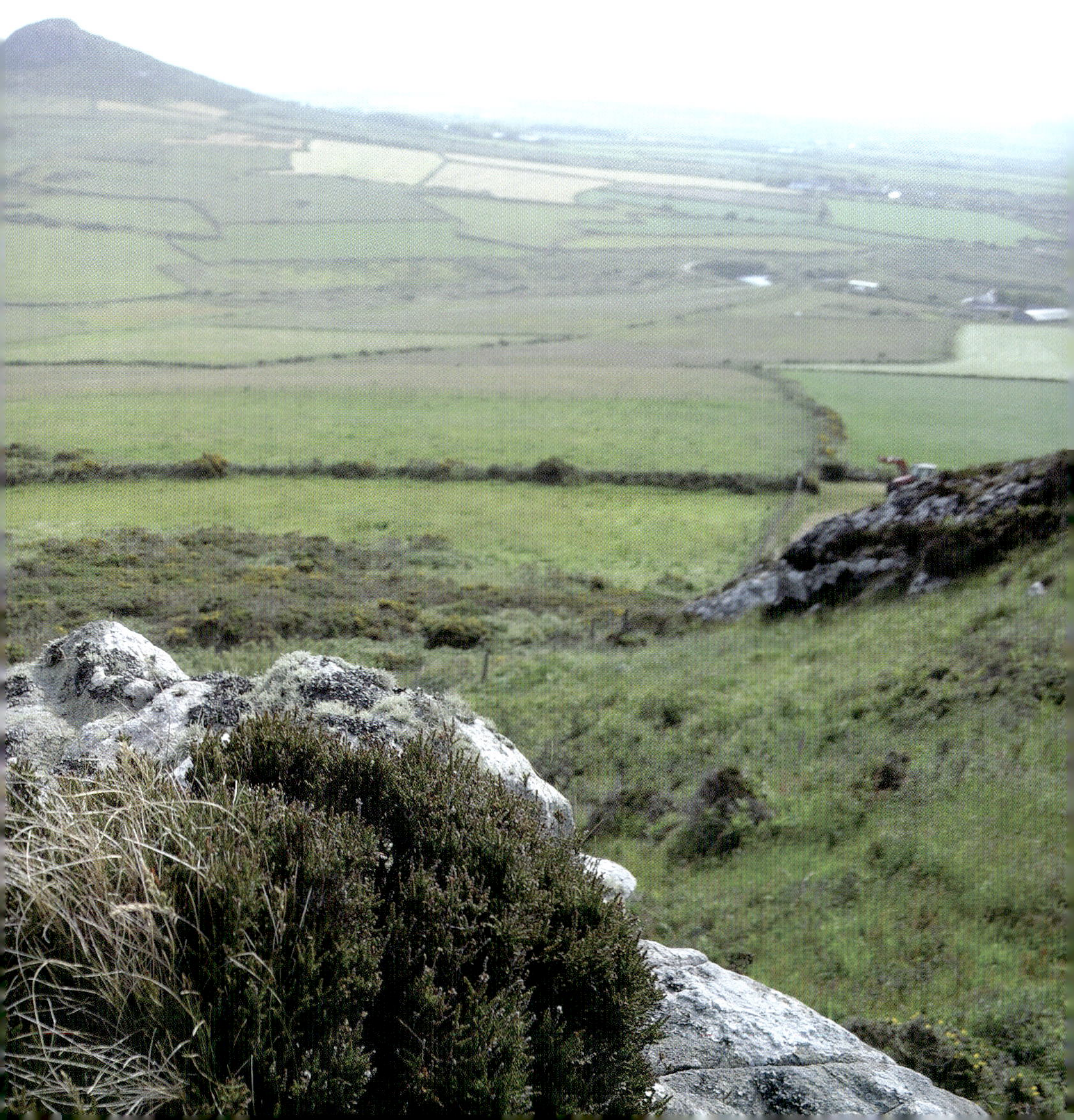

The two cats, brothers, would often sit close,
or walk the lanes with tails entwined.

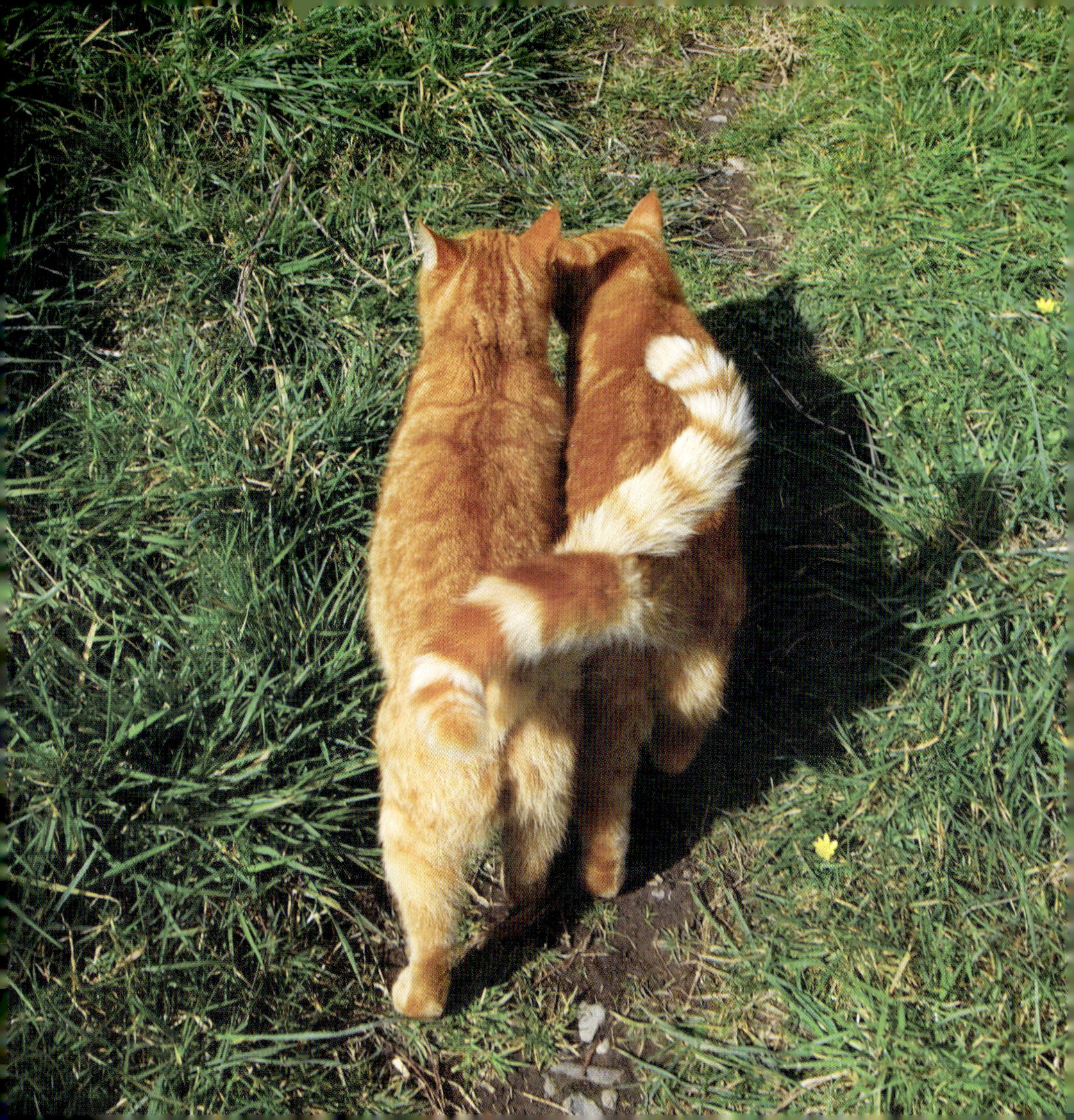

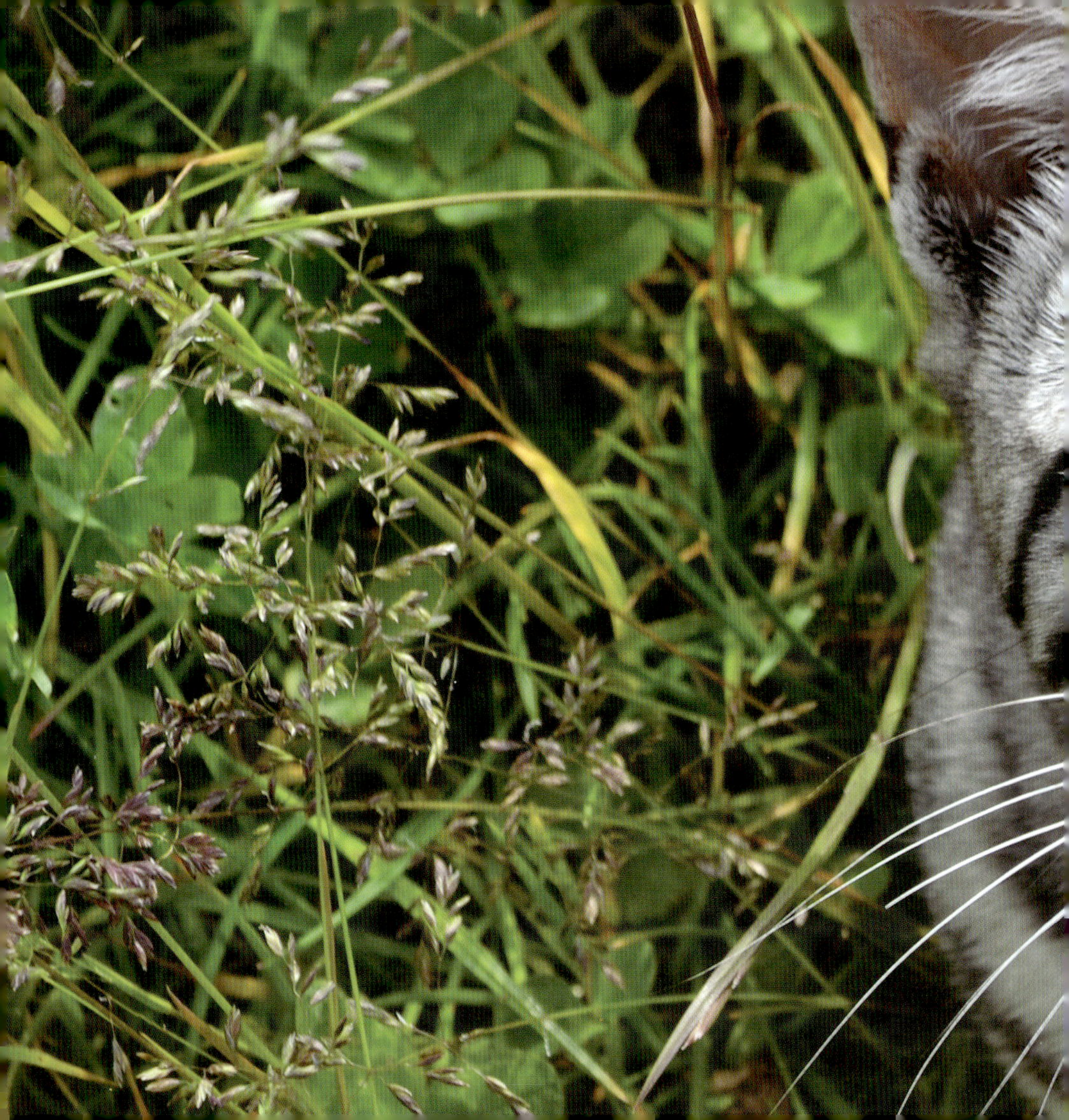

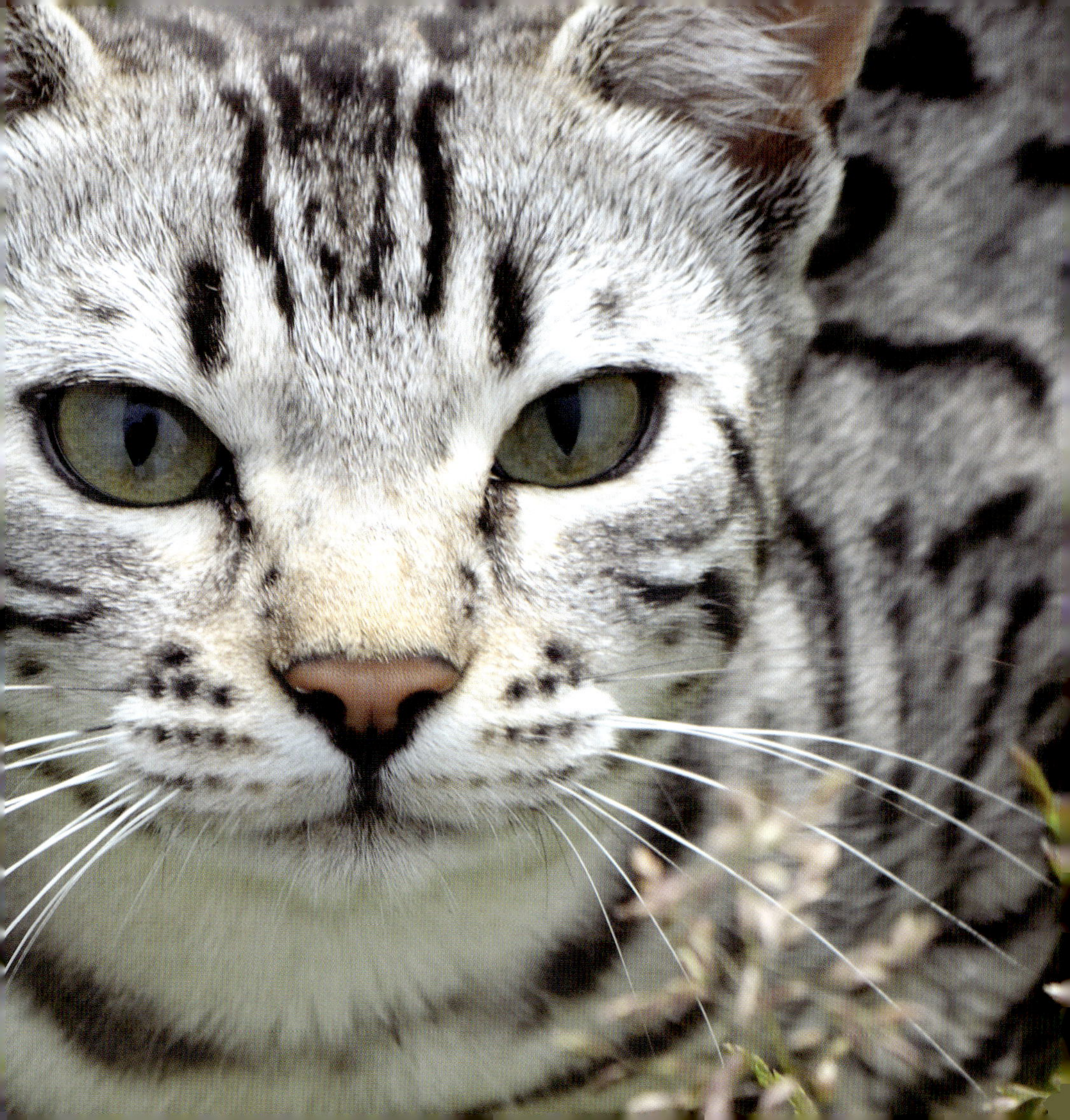

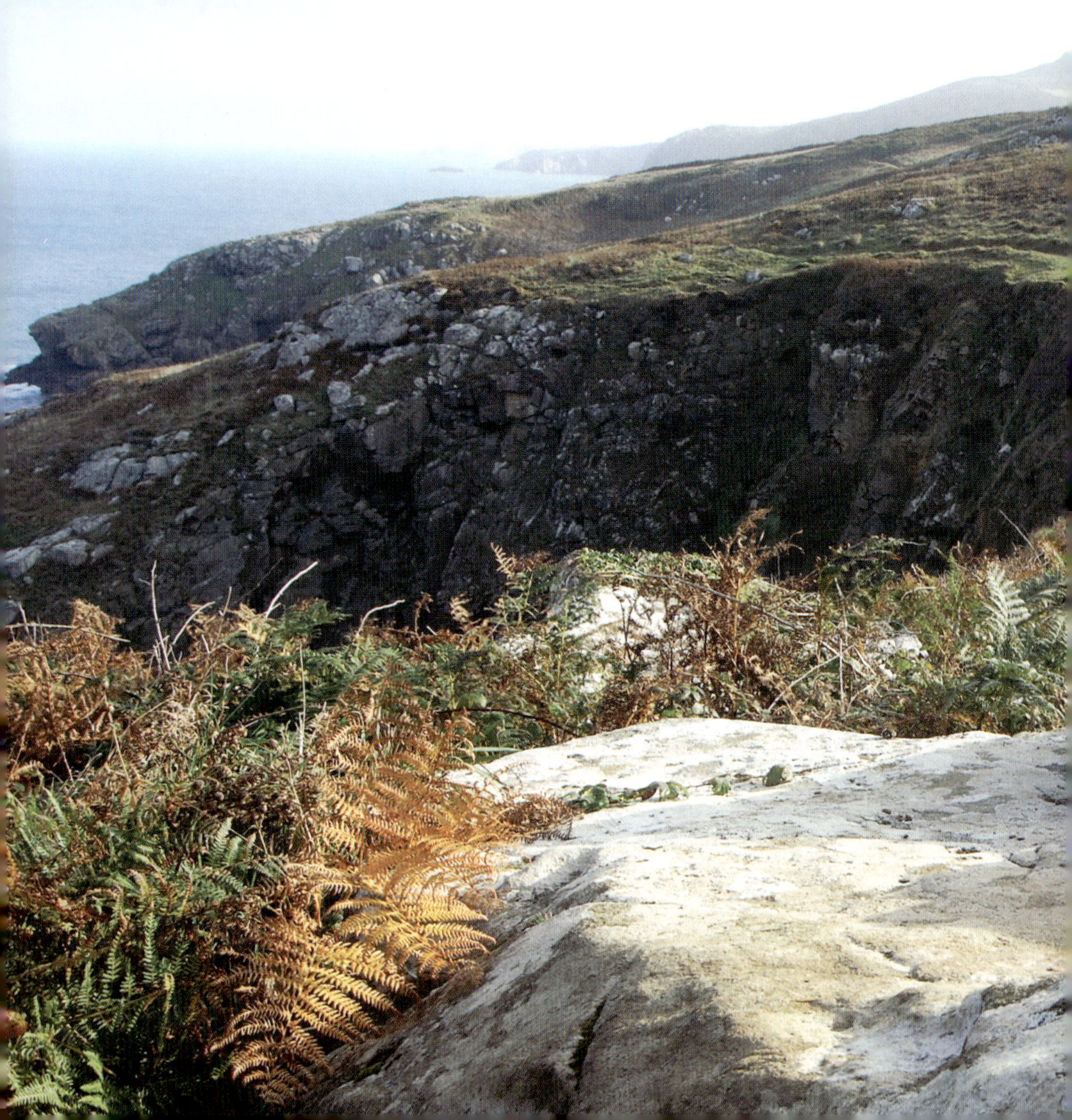

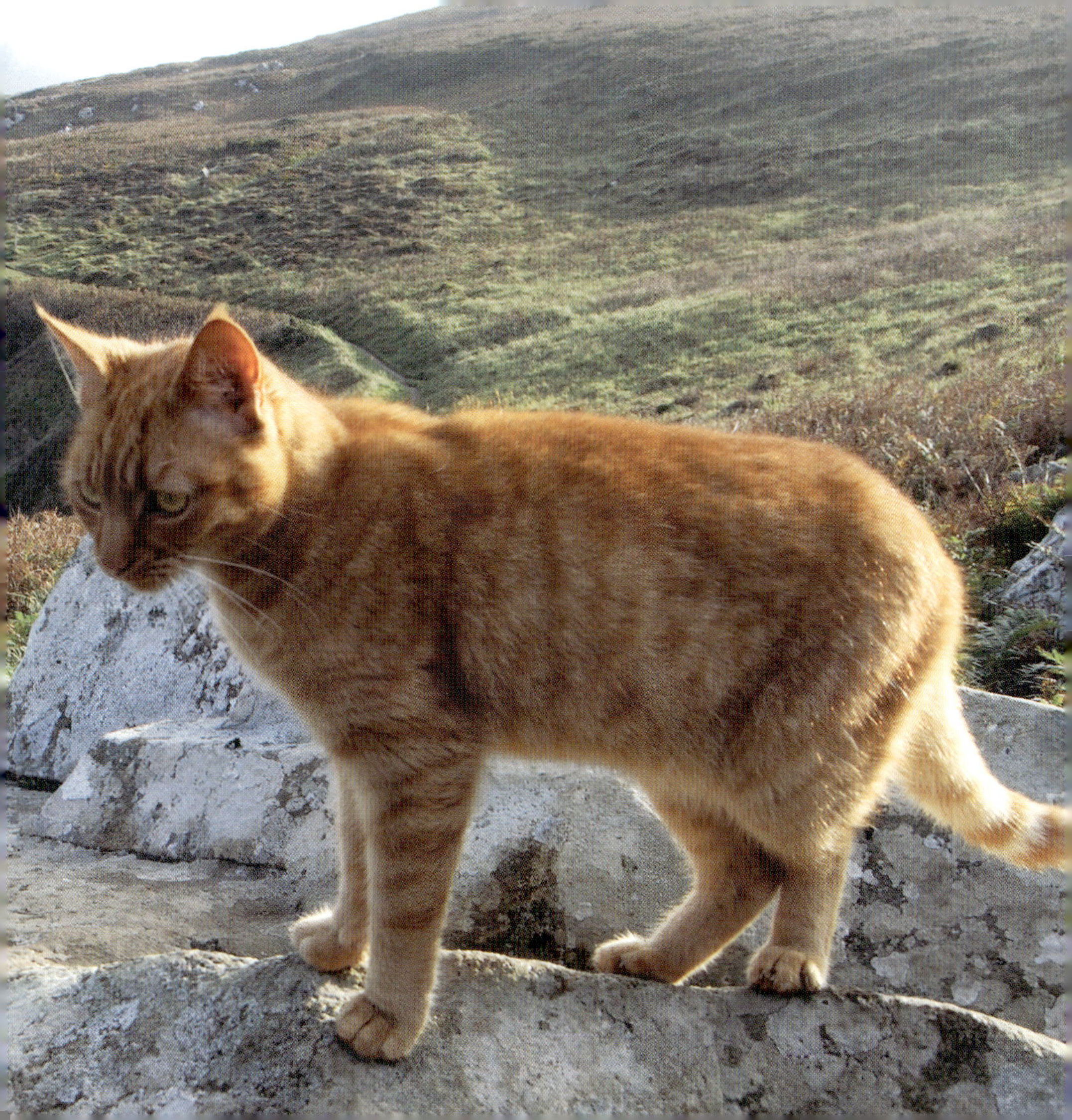

Cats, small in the landscape, inside their heads are giant as tigers, fiercer than lions. On top of the hill they play 'king of the castle' and rest in the long grass.

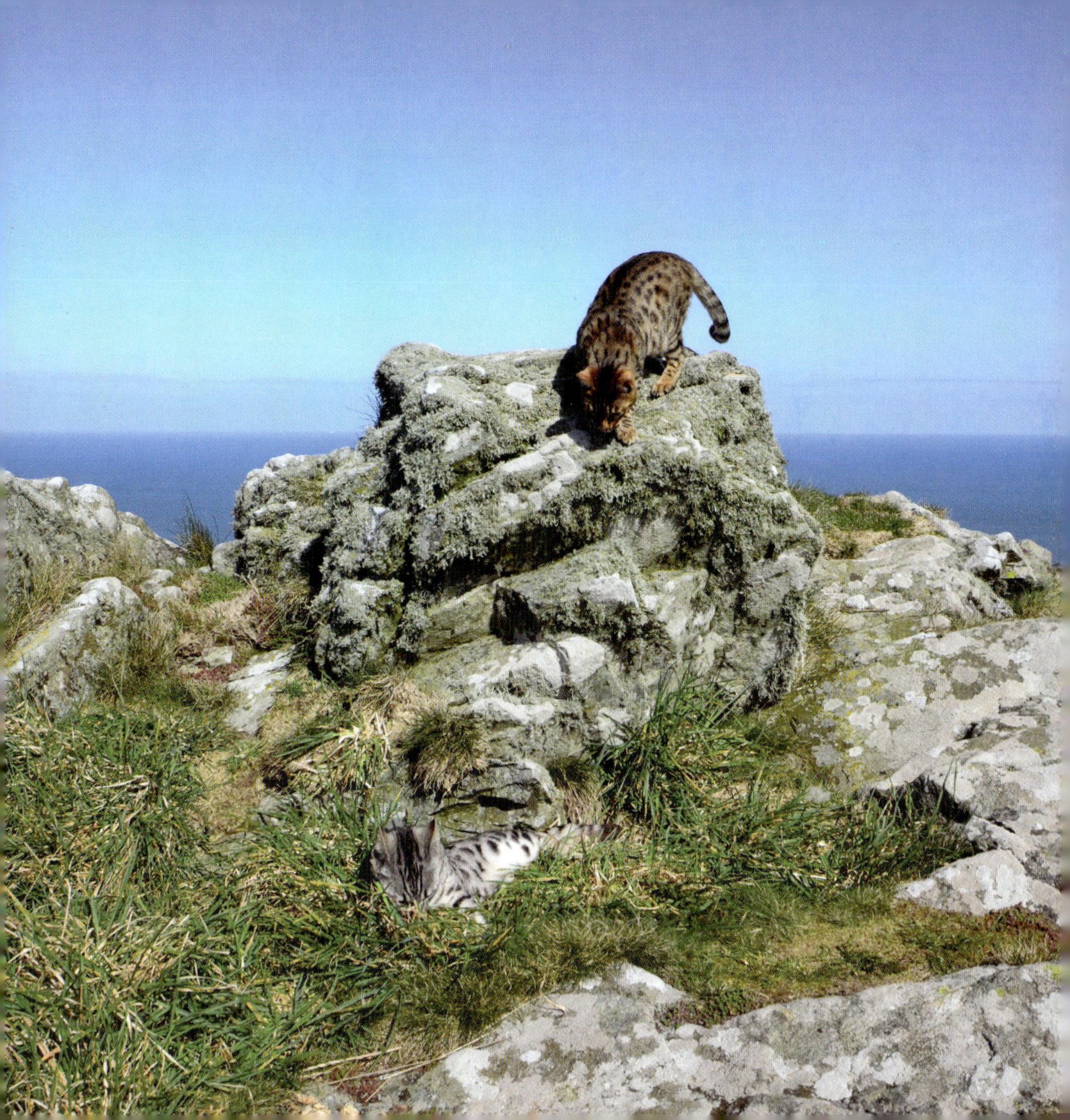

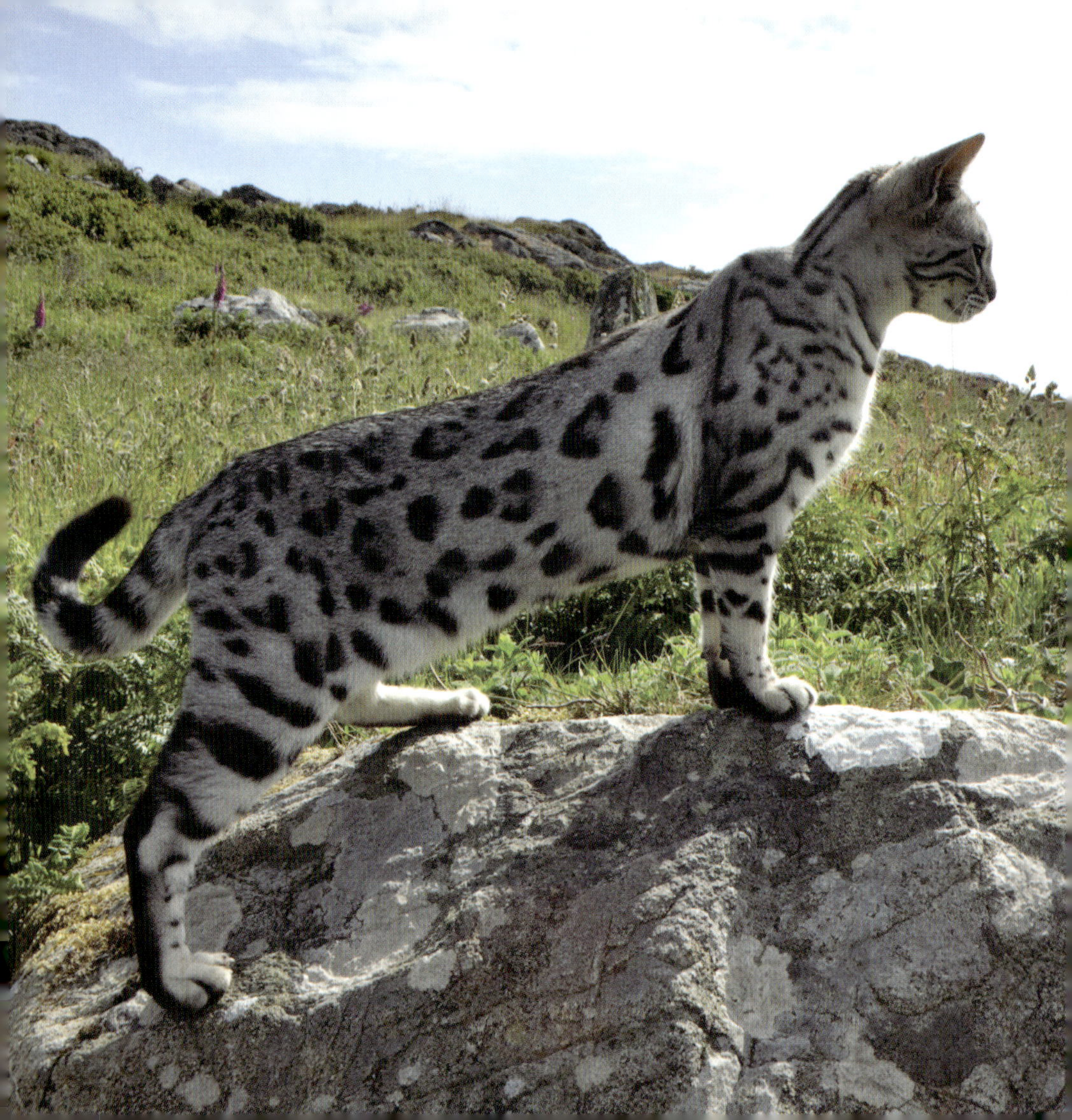

Slender
Dappled
Elegant
Poised
Wild
Silver
Alert
Balanced
Cat

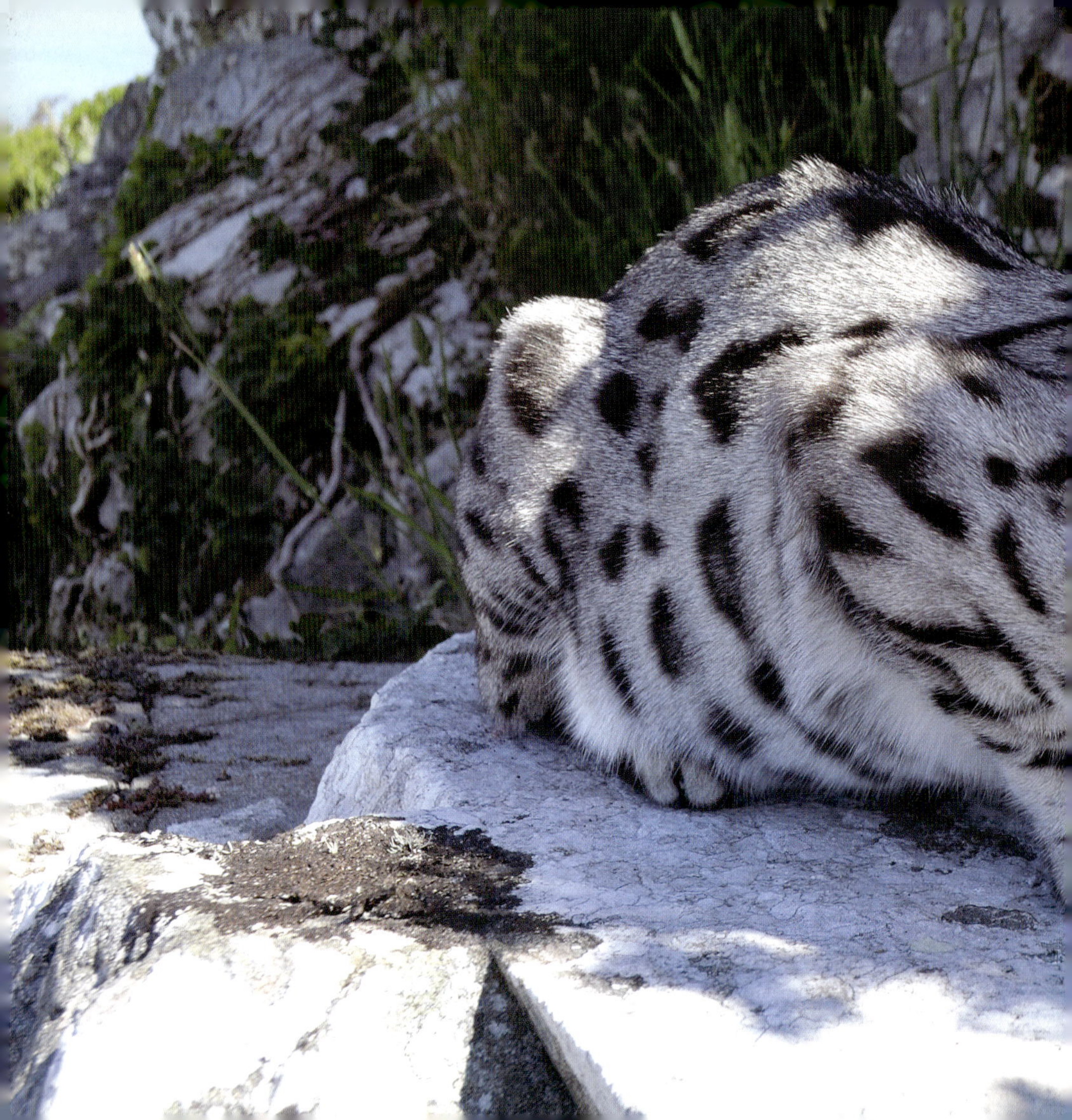

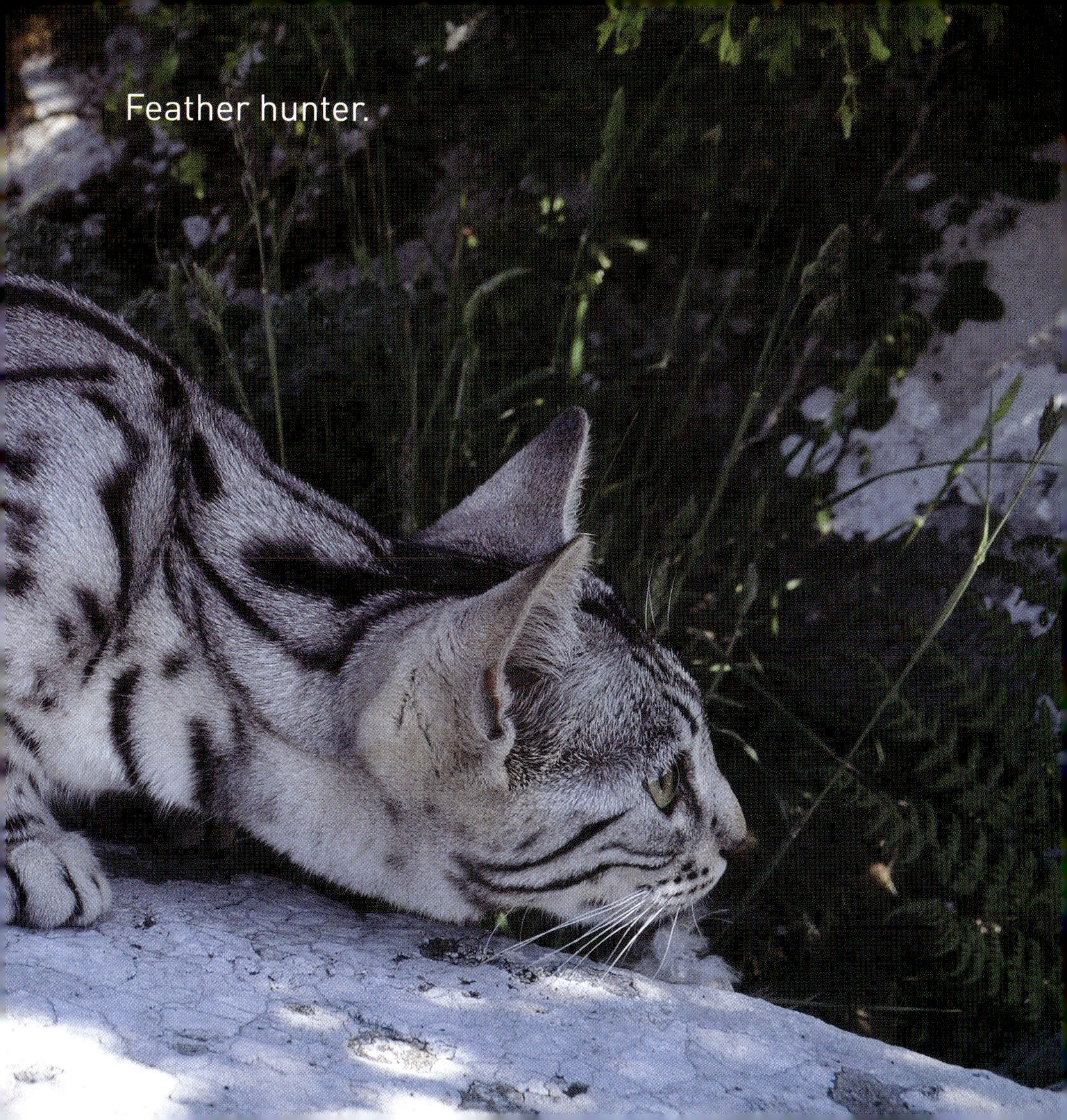
Feather hunter.

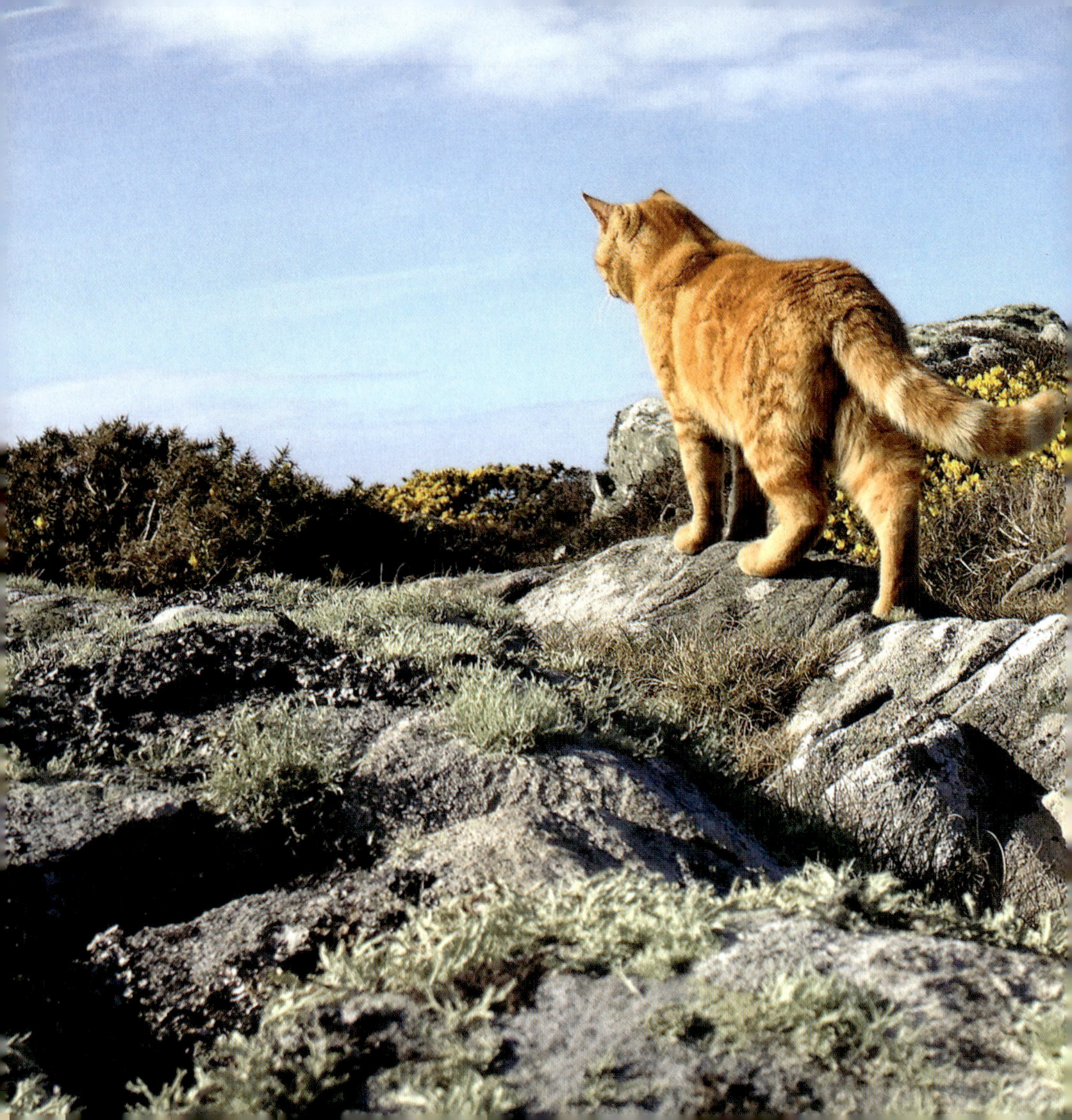

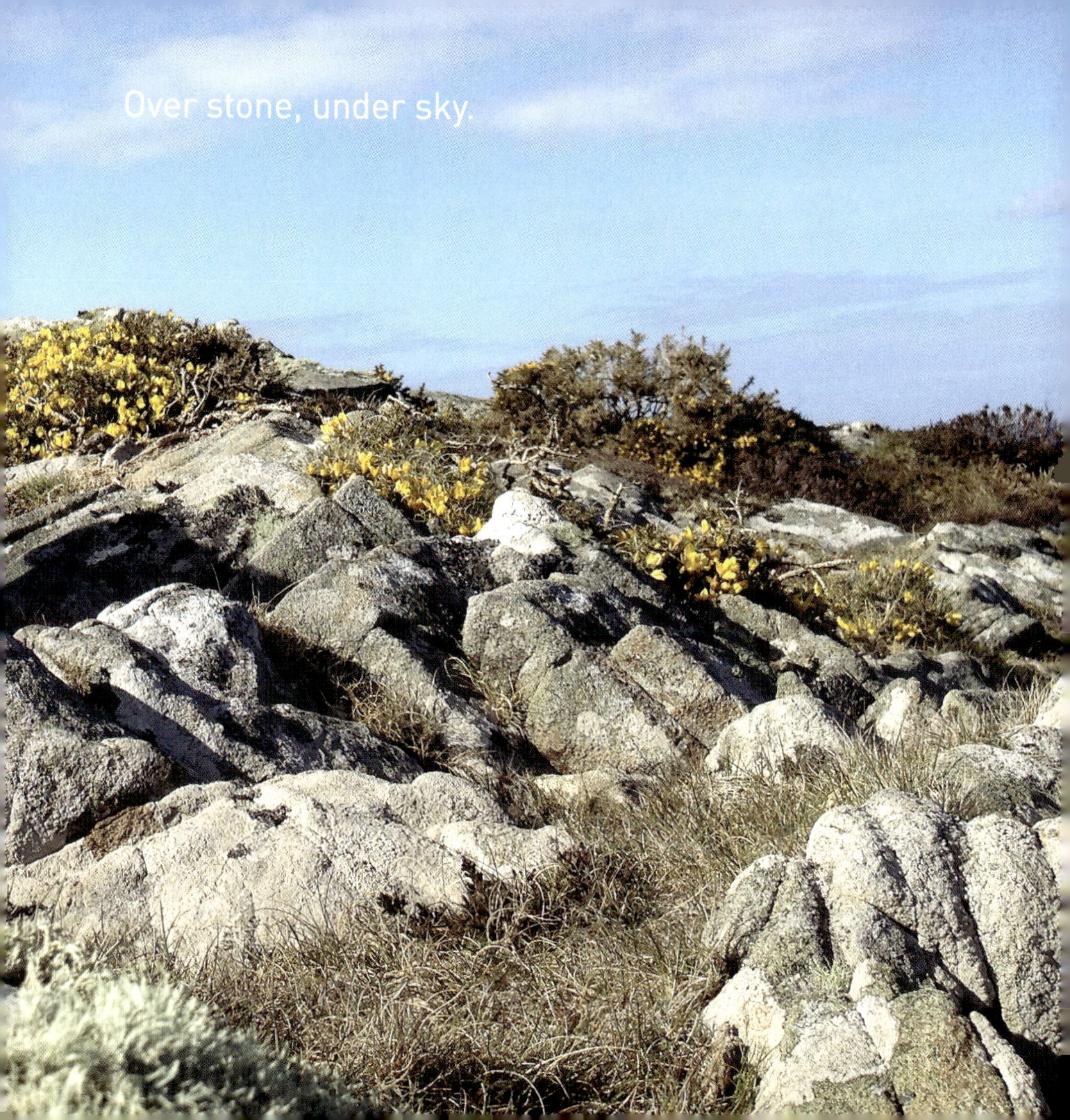
Over stone, under sky.

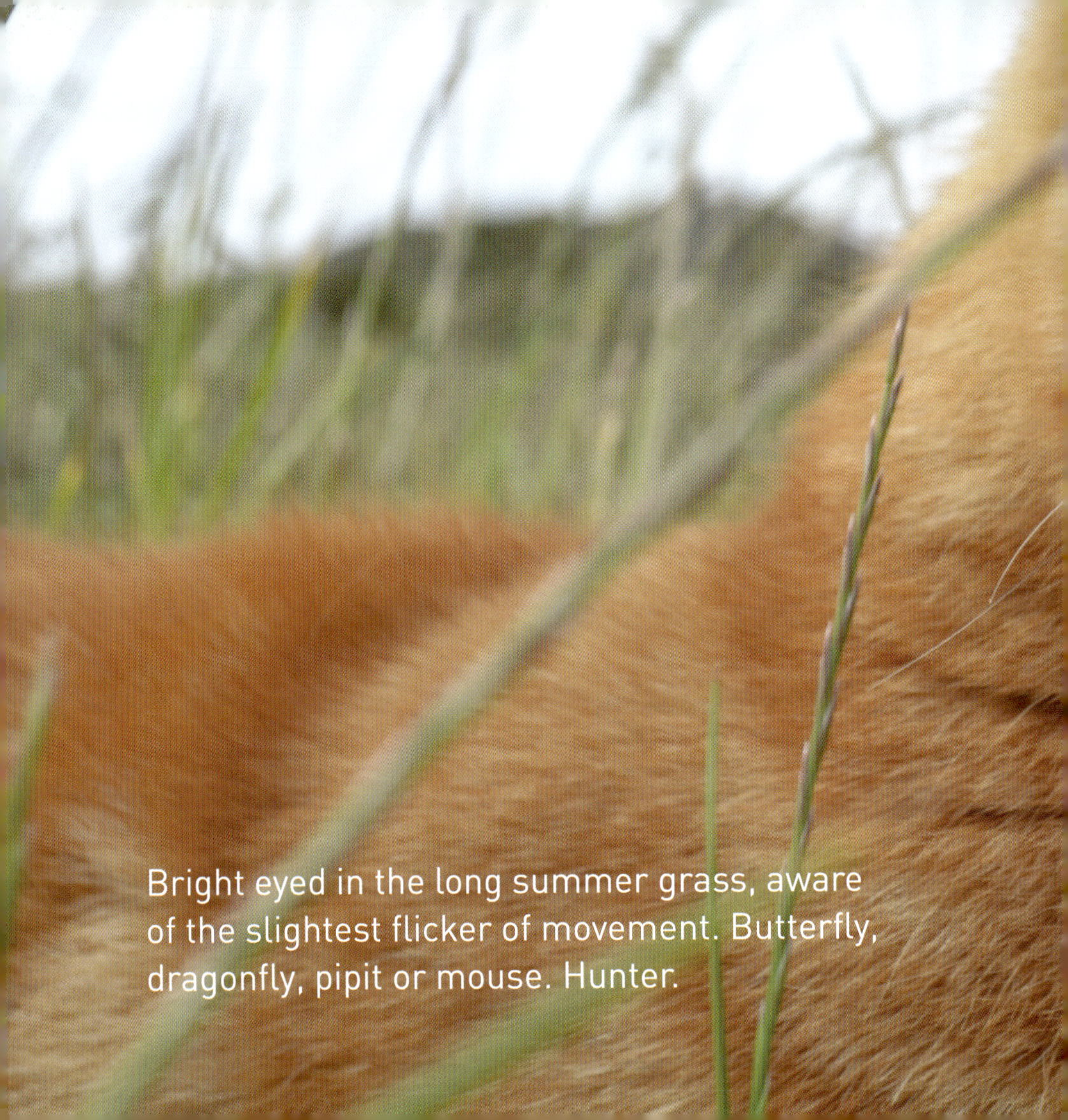
Bright eyed in the long summer grass, aware
of the slightest flicker of movement. Butterfly,
dragonfly, pipit or mouse. Hunter.

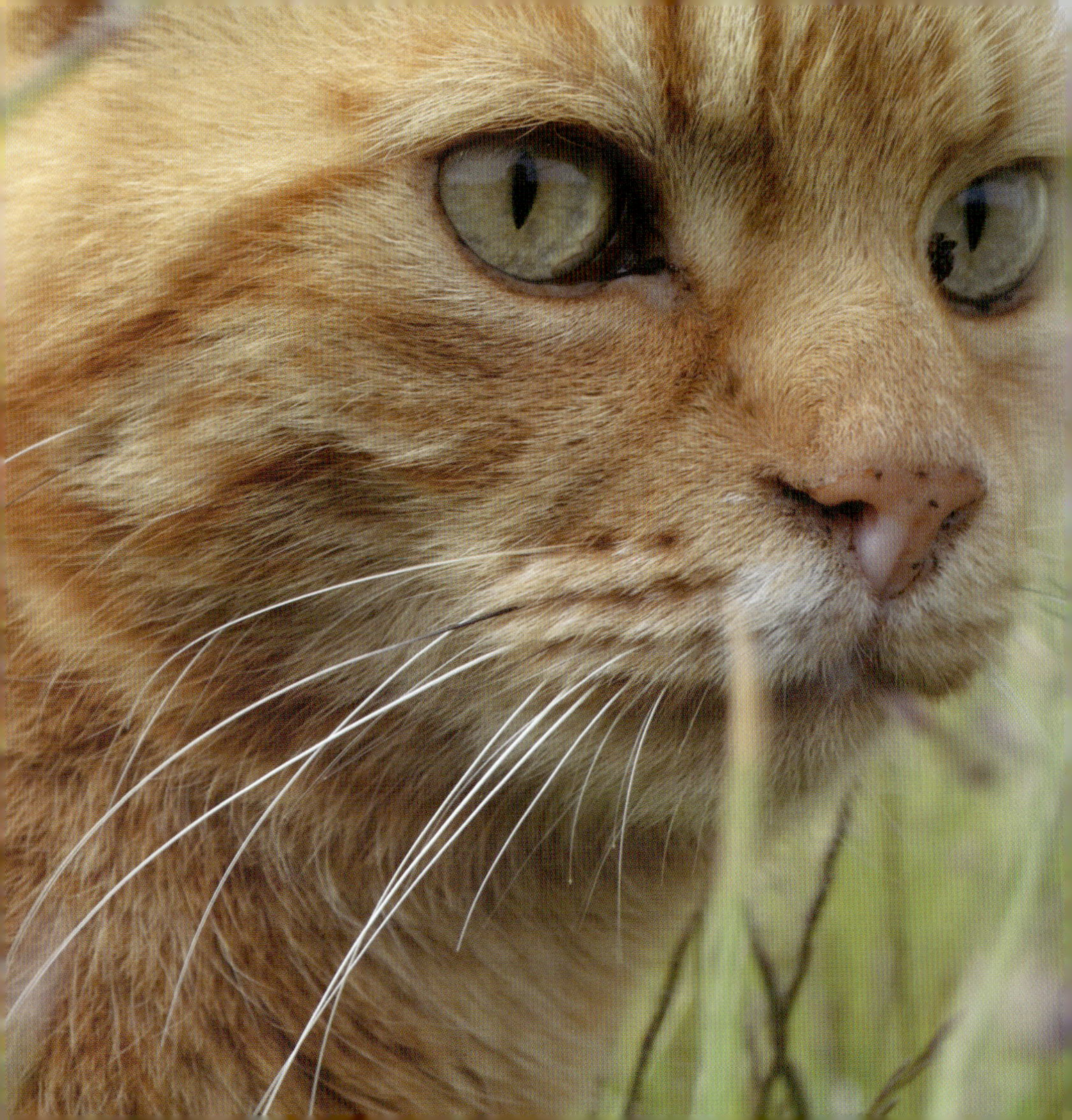

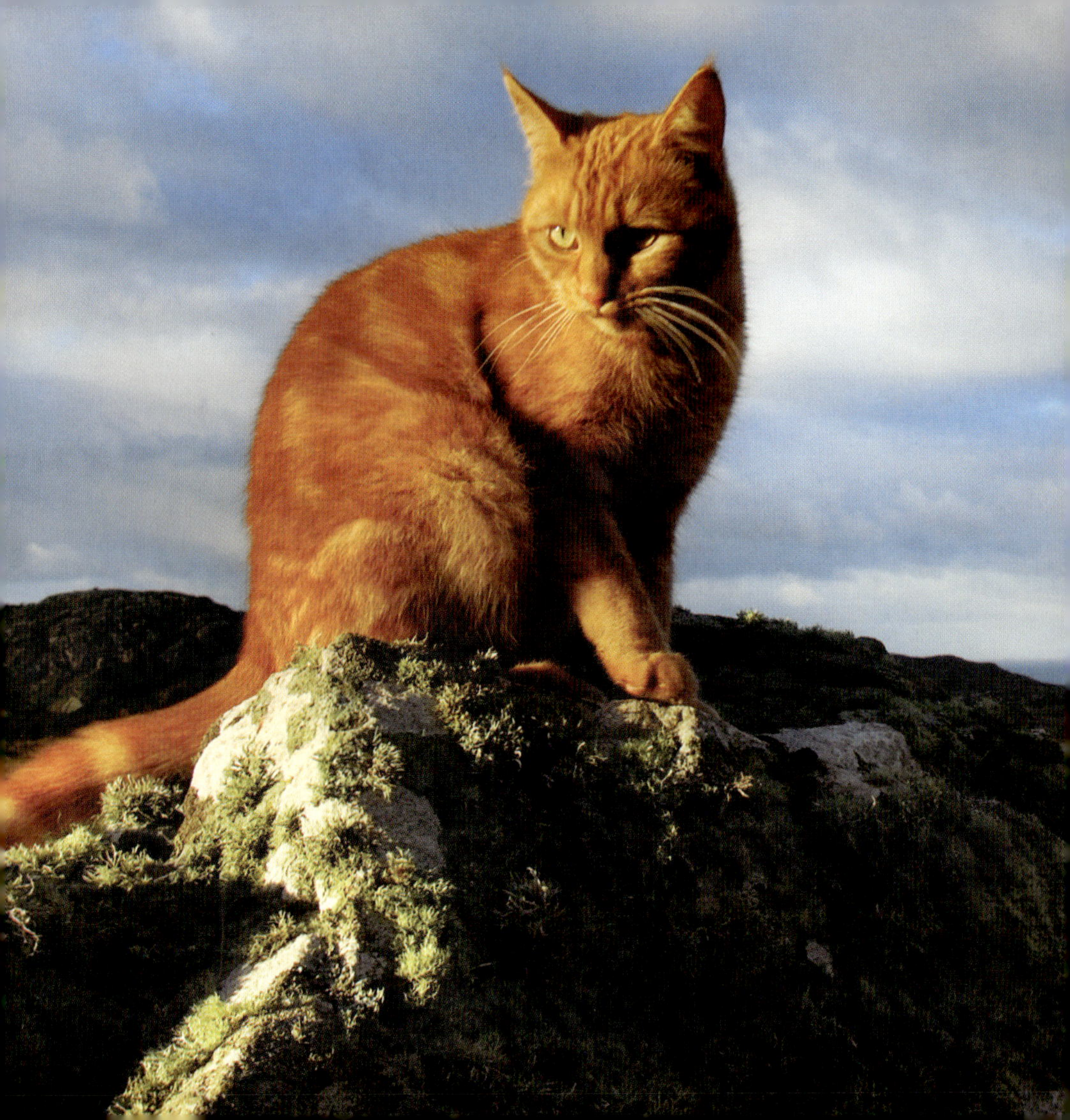

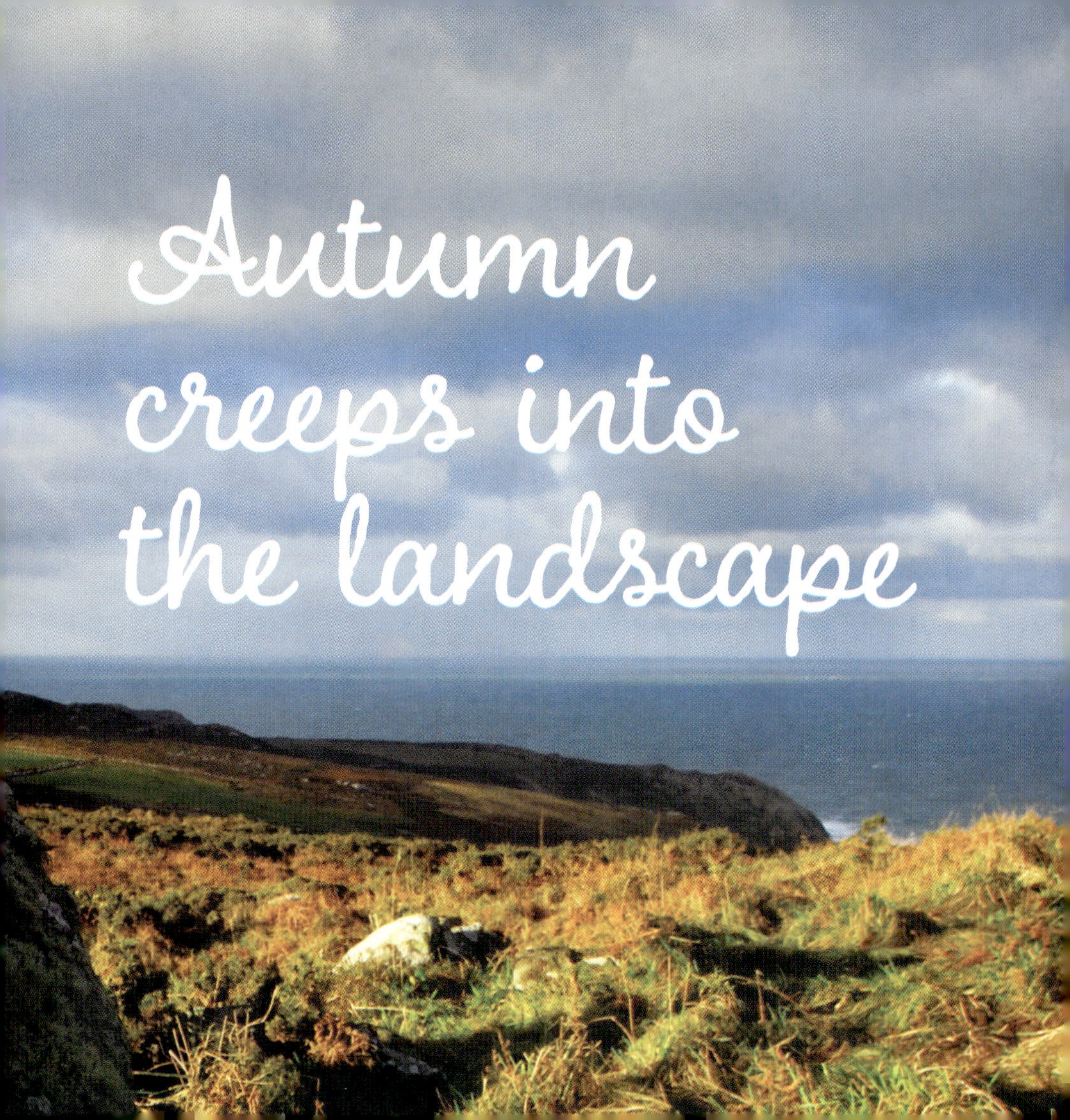

Autumn creeps into the landscape

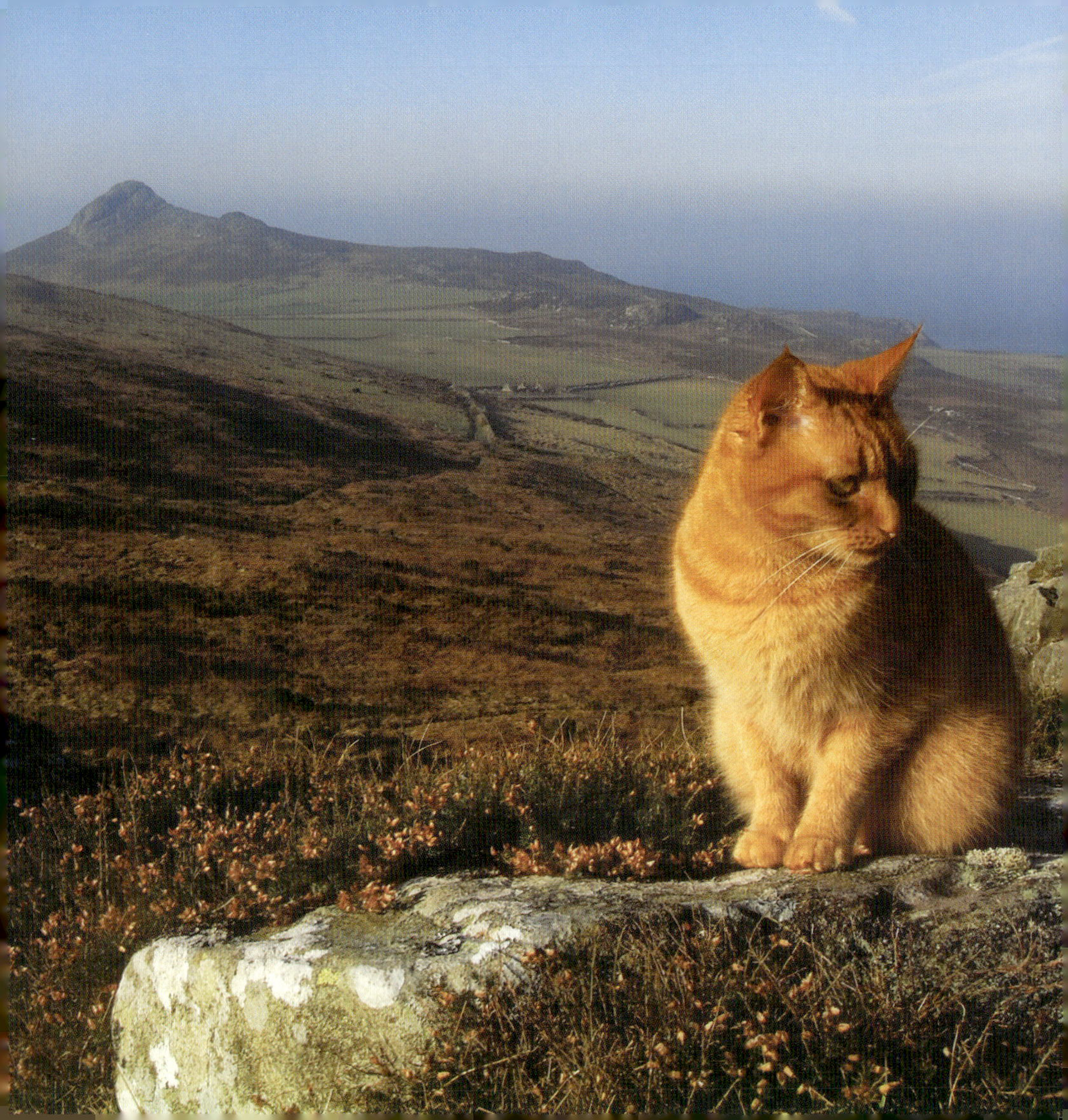

From here you can see the edge of the world.

From here you can hear sweet skylarks sing.

From here you can scent the brackish tang of crushed ferns.

From here you can hear the approach of the wind as it stalks through the rattling brown buds of dead heather.

From here you can taste the salt sea carried on the wind's hands.

From here you can watch the raven's flight, lifted skyward in the wind's arms.

From here you can watch the white specks wheel, gannets over porpoise at the sea's edge.

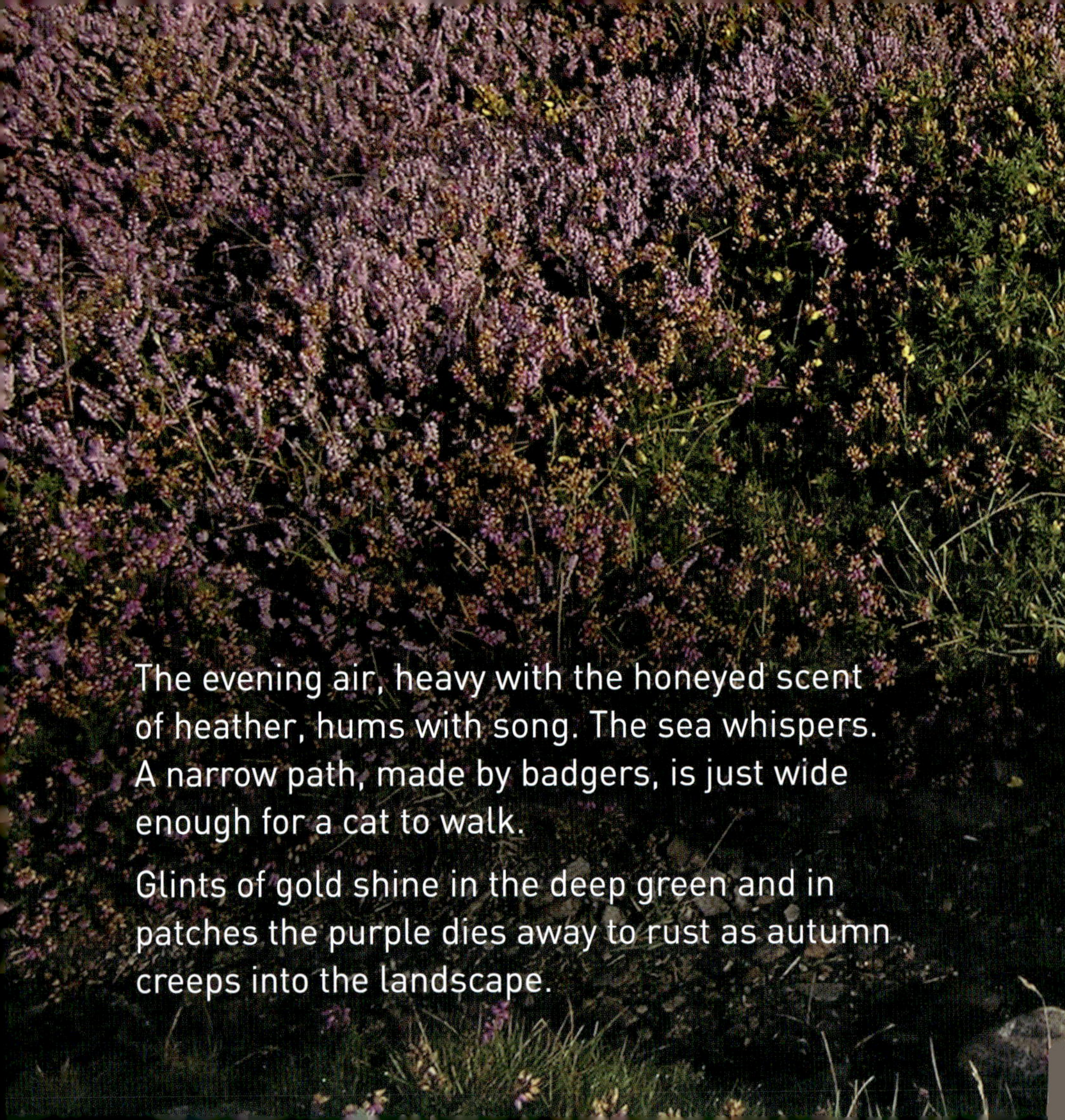

The evening air, heavy with the honeyed scent of heather, hums with song. The sea whispers. A narrow path, made by badgers, is just wide enough for a cat to walk.

Glints of gold shine in the deep green and in patches the purple dies away to rust as autumn creeps into the landscape.

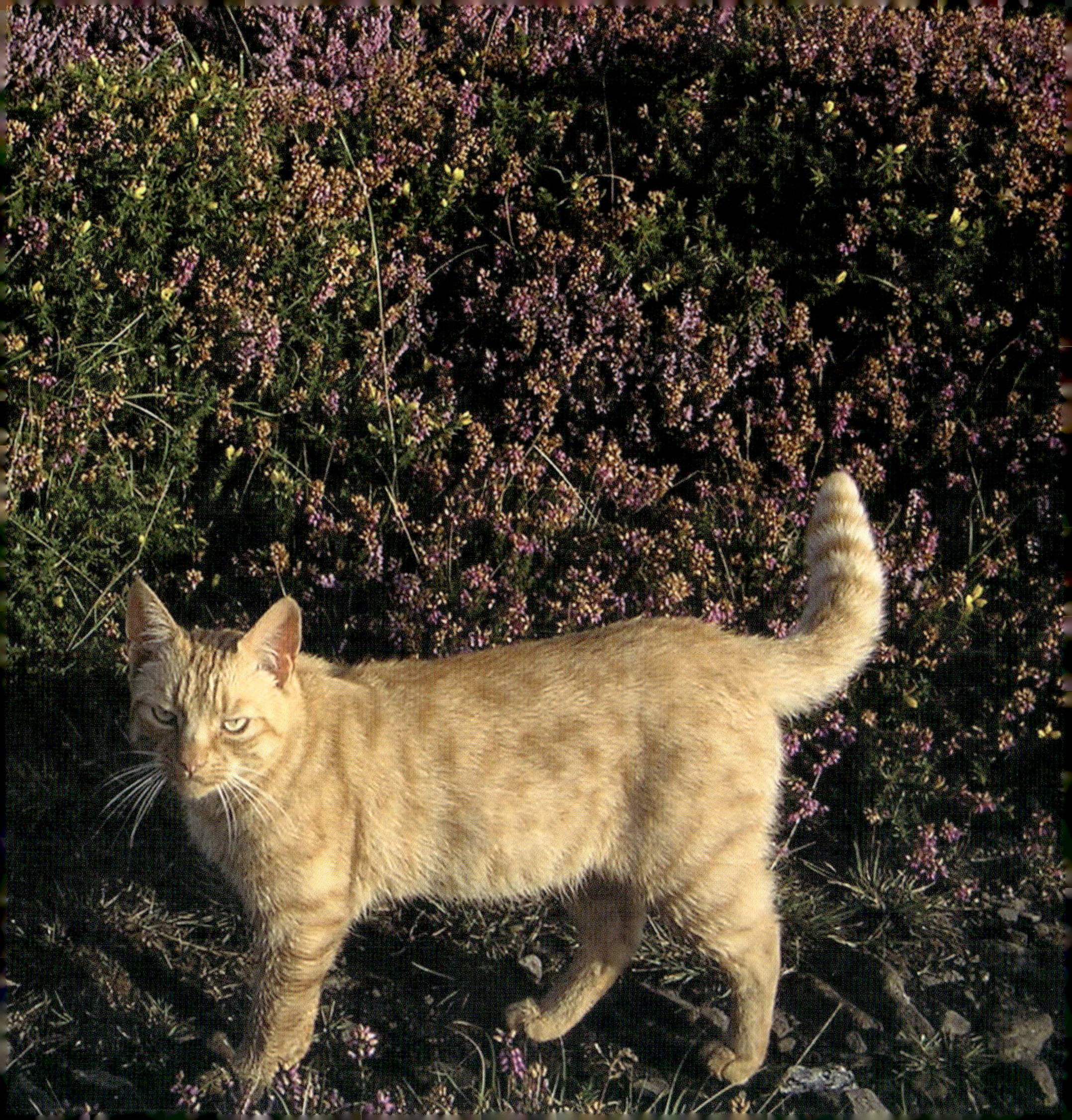

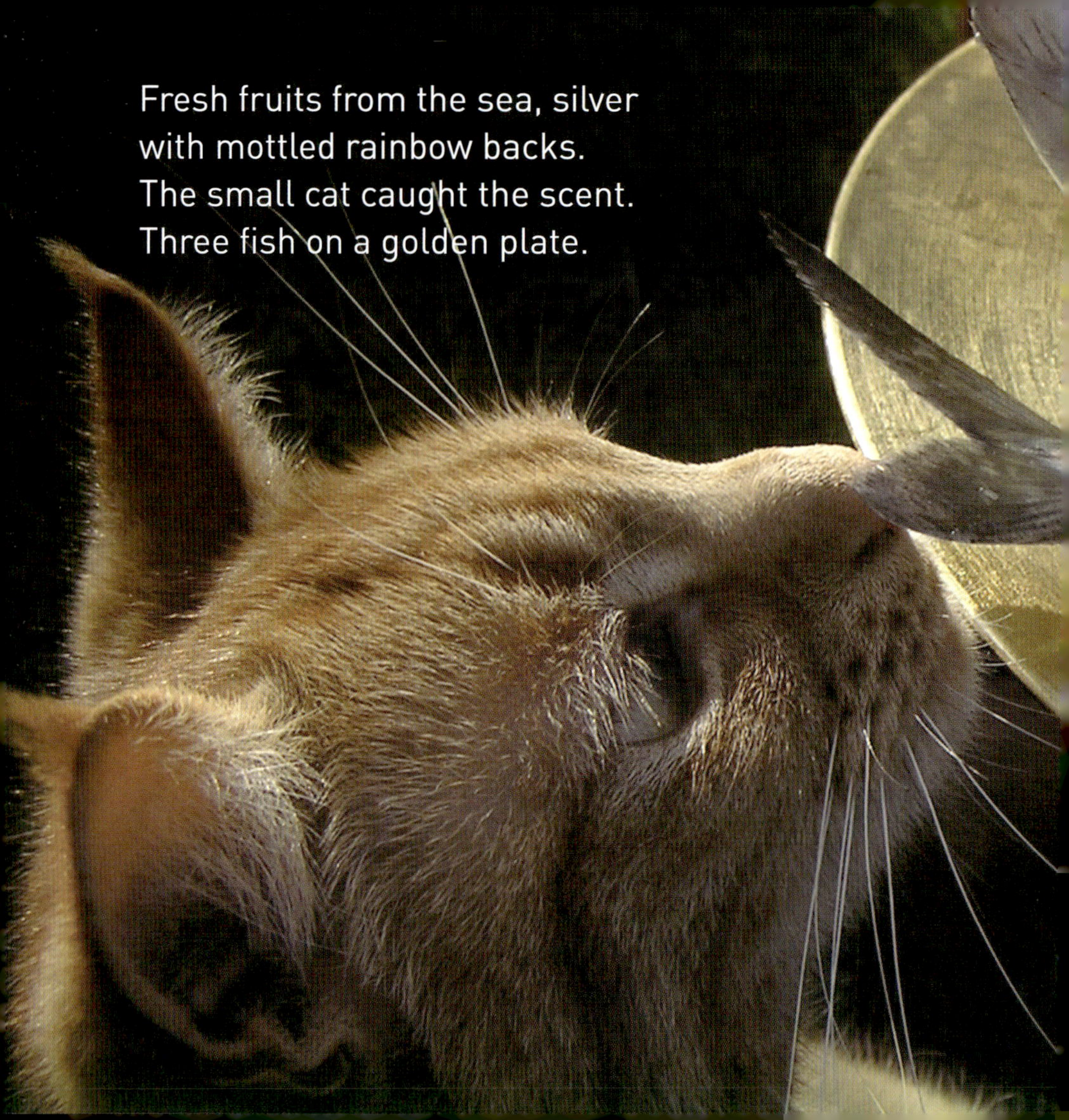
Fresh fruits from the sea, silver
with mottled rainbow backs.
The small cat caught the scent.
Three fish on a golden plate.

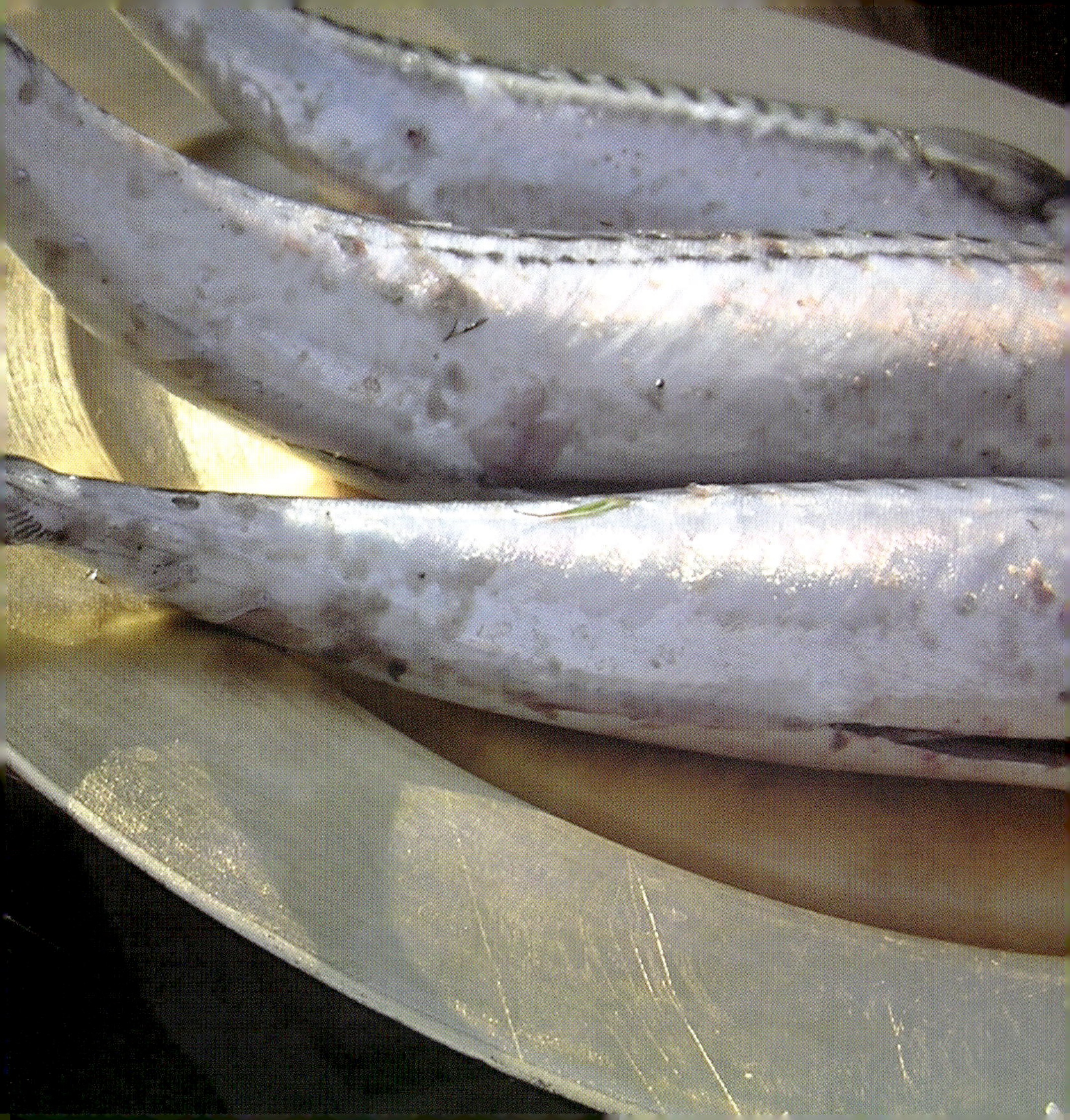

The old thorn tree had grown over centuries from
a crack in the boulders. All blossoms were now
stripped and a fresh blush of green leaves grew
on its clawed branches. Sunlight, stone, cat.
A moment of watchfulness caught in time.

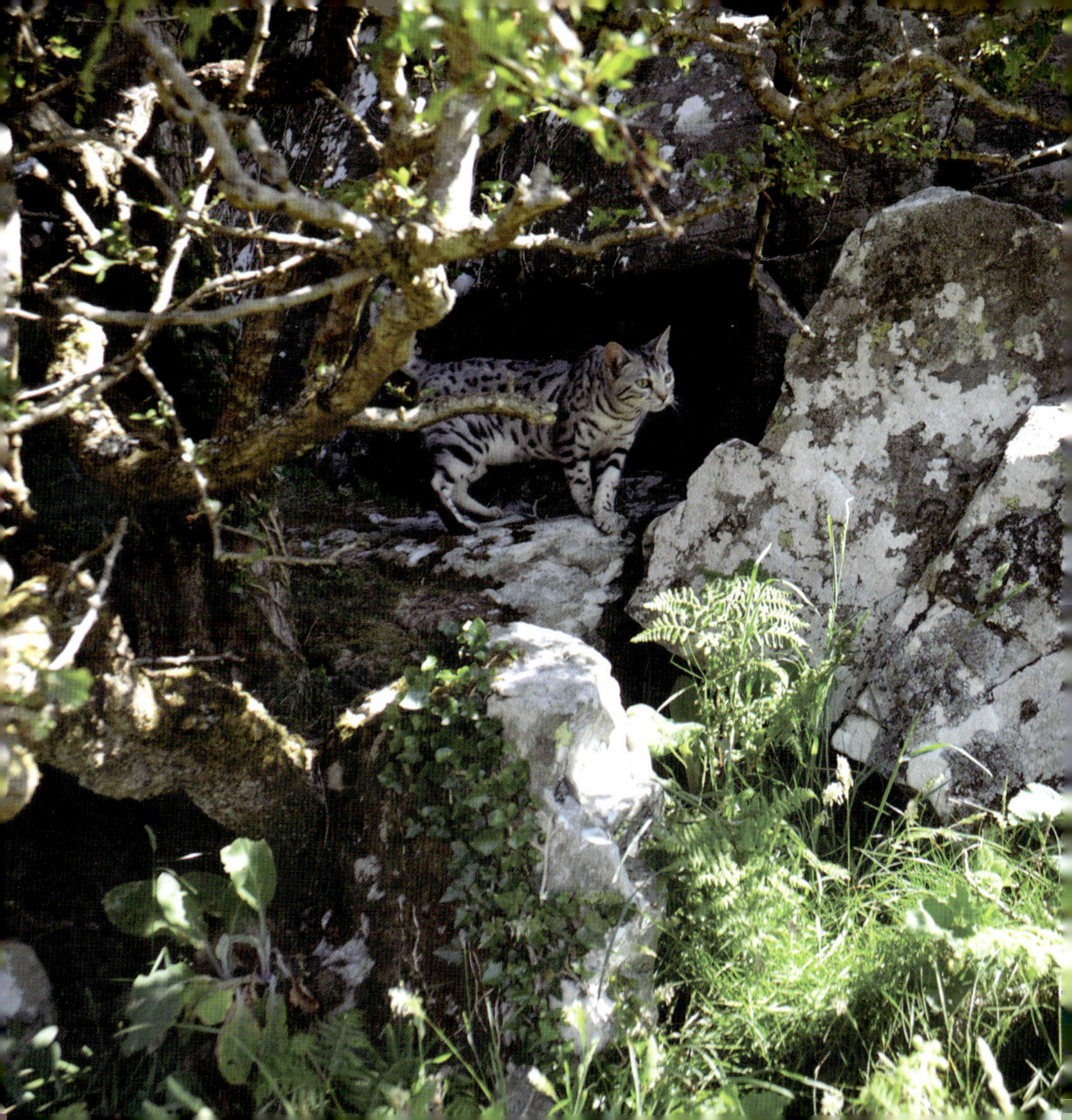

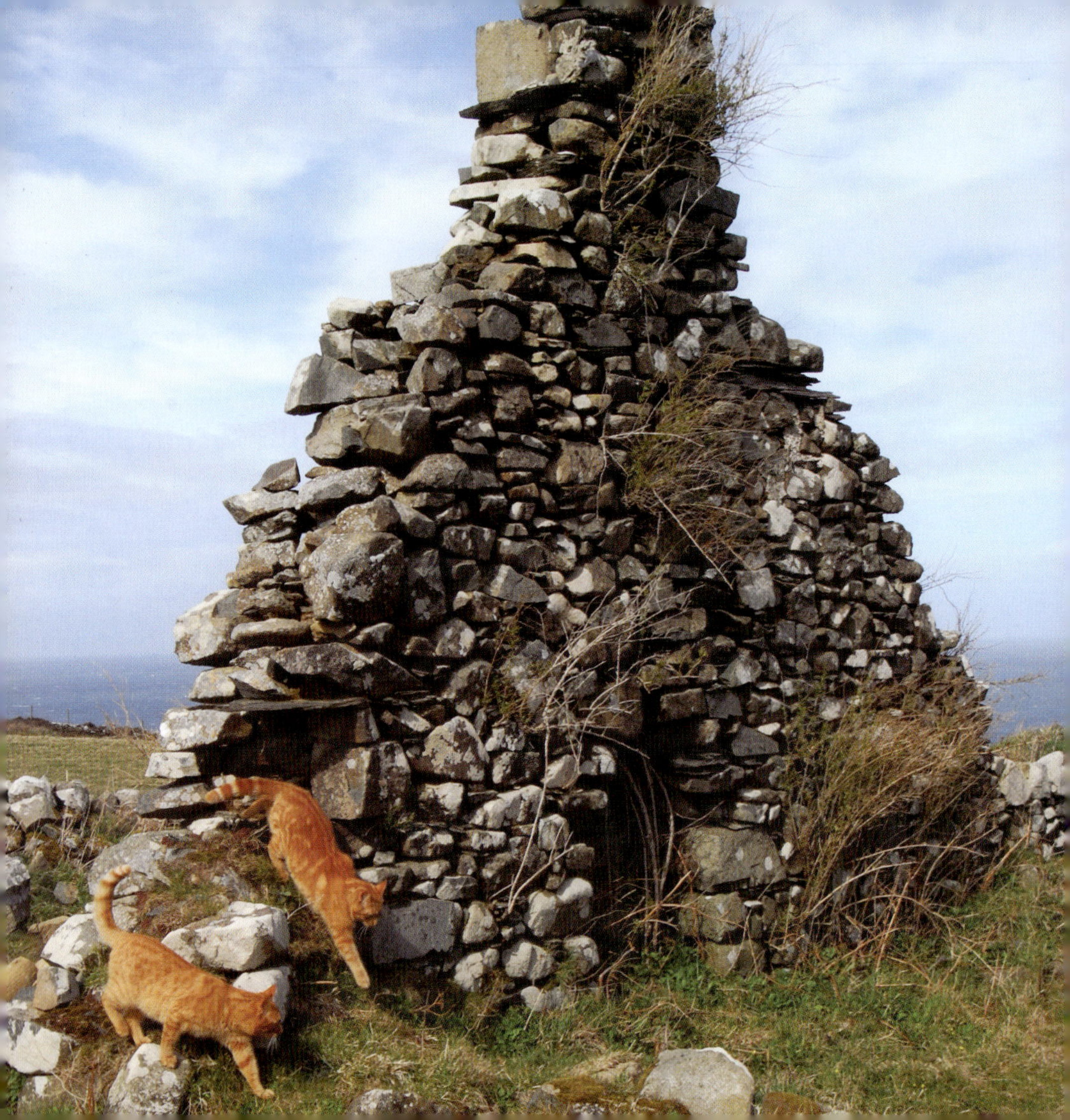

On a November day, when snipe were calling from the hillside, the cats walked over the cold stones of the ruined house.

Winter winds and rains and storms had stolen away stones and tumbled the walls, but for a while the sky was blue and the cats glowed bright in winter sunlight.

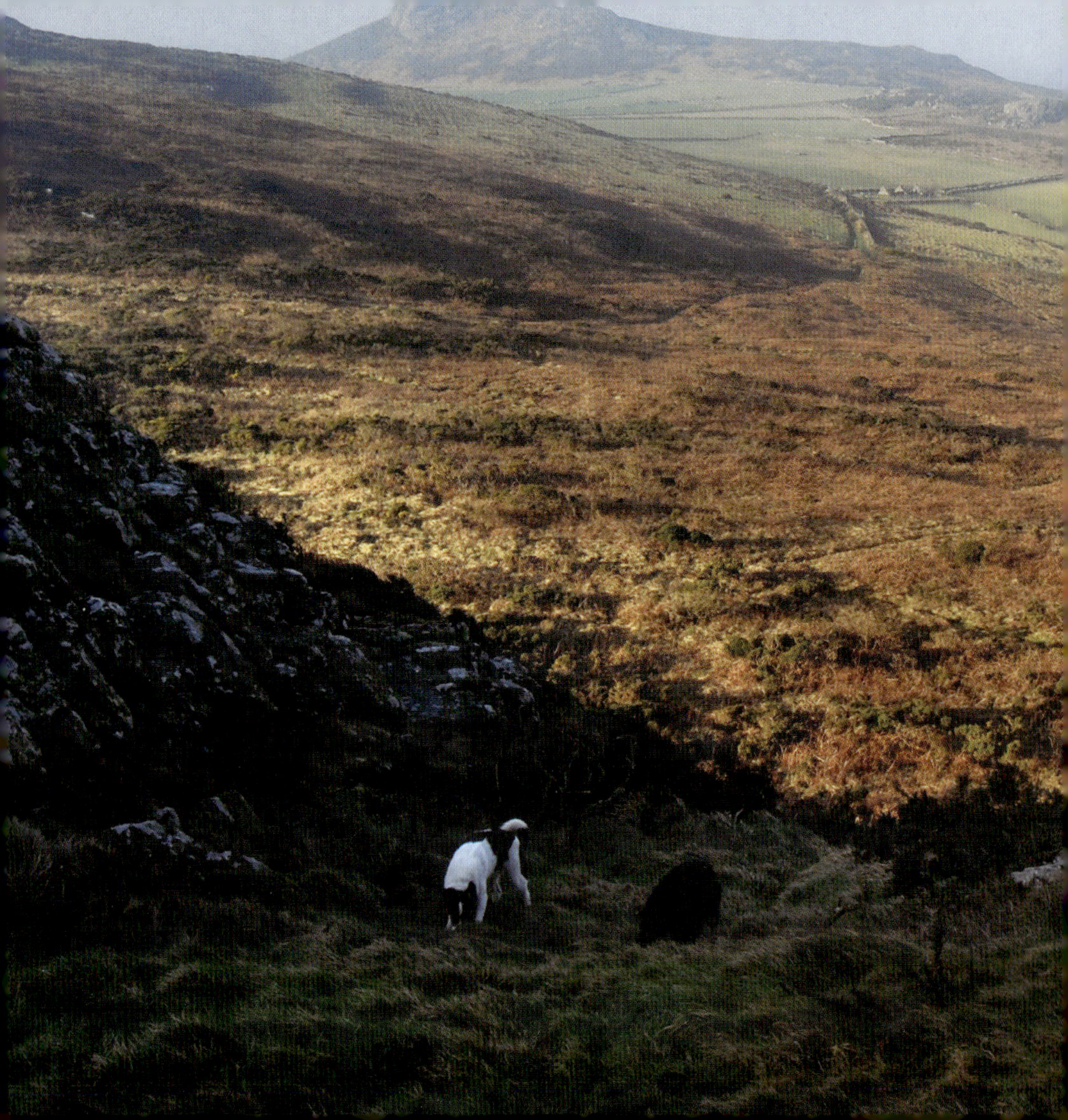

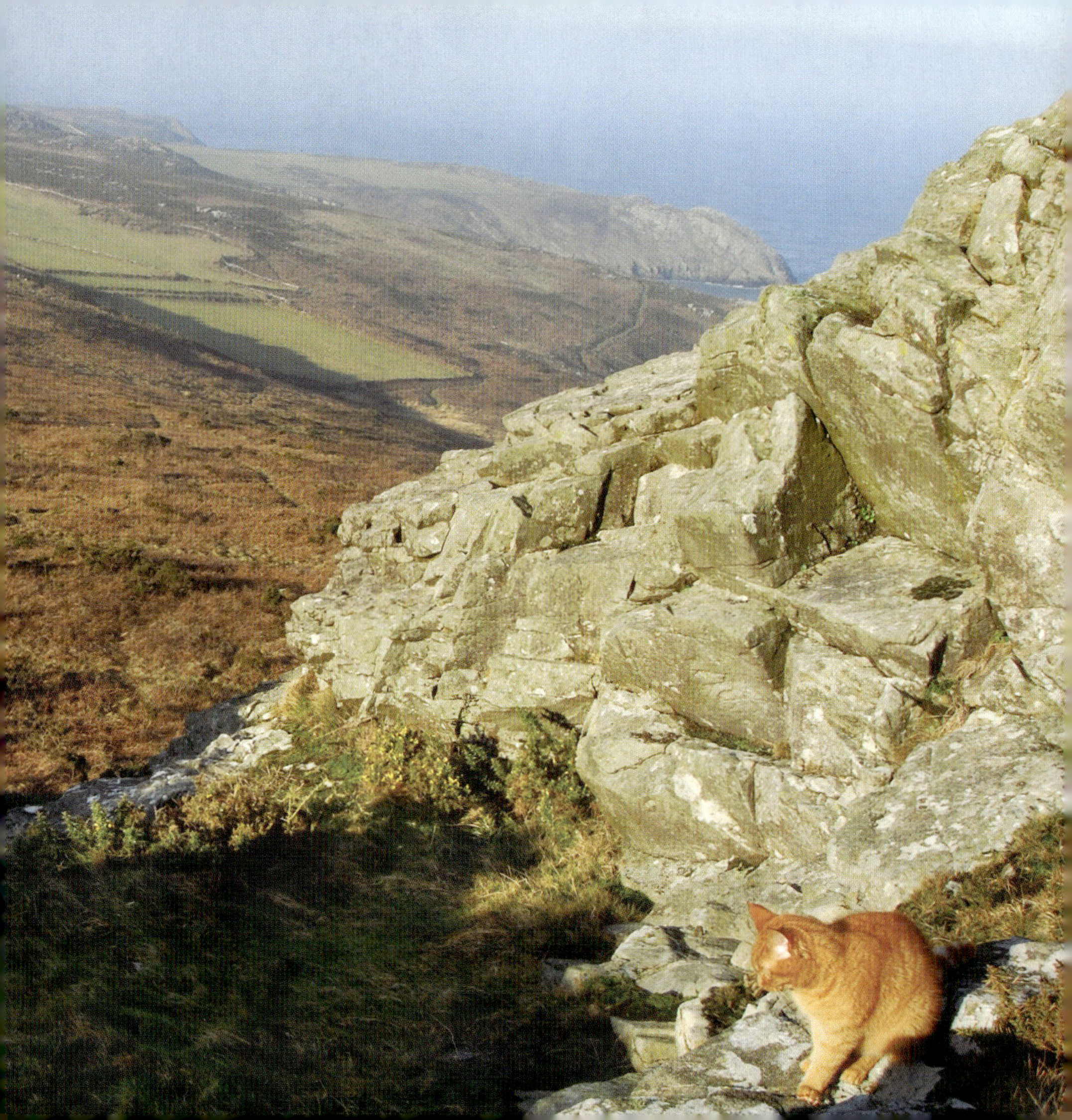

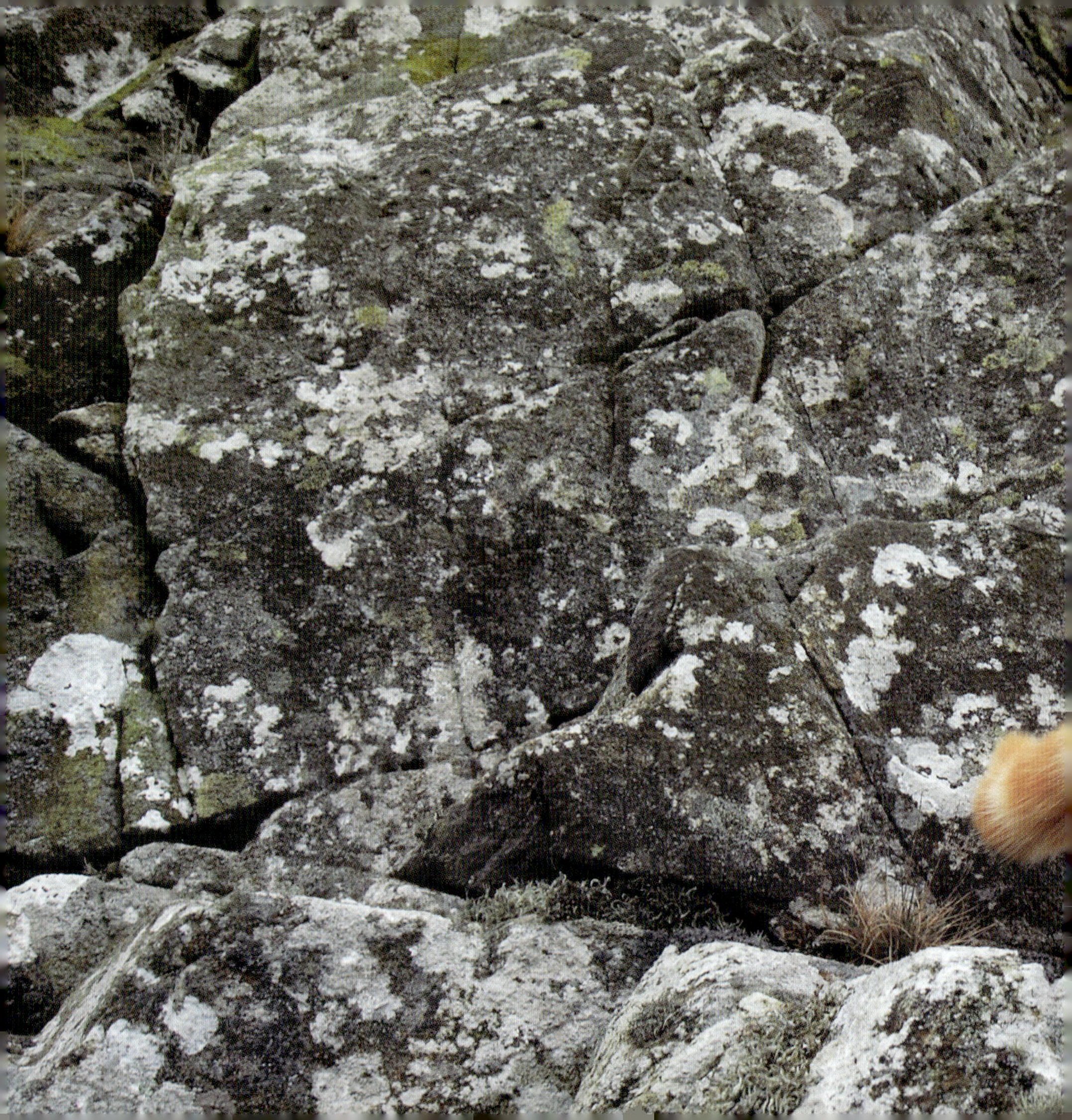

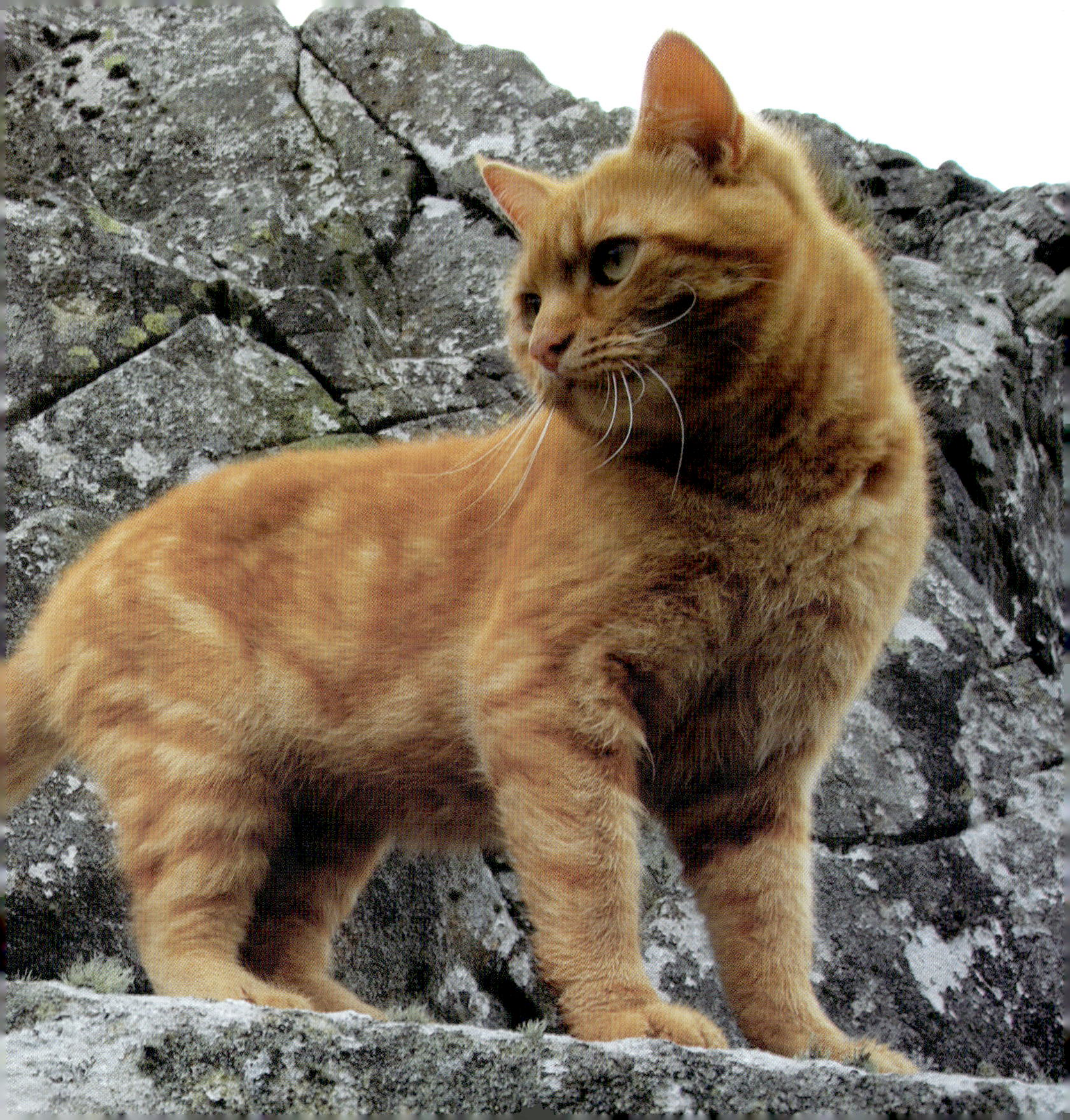

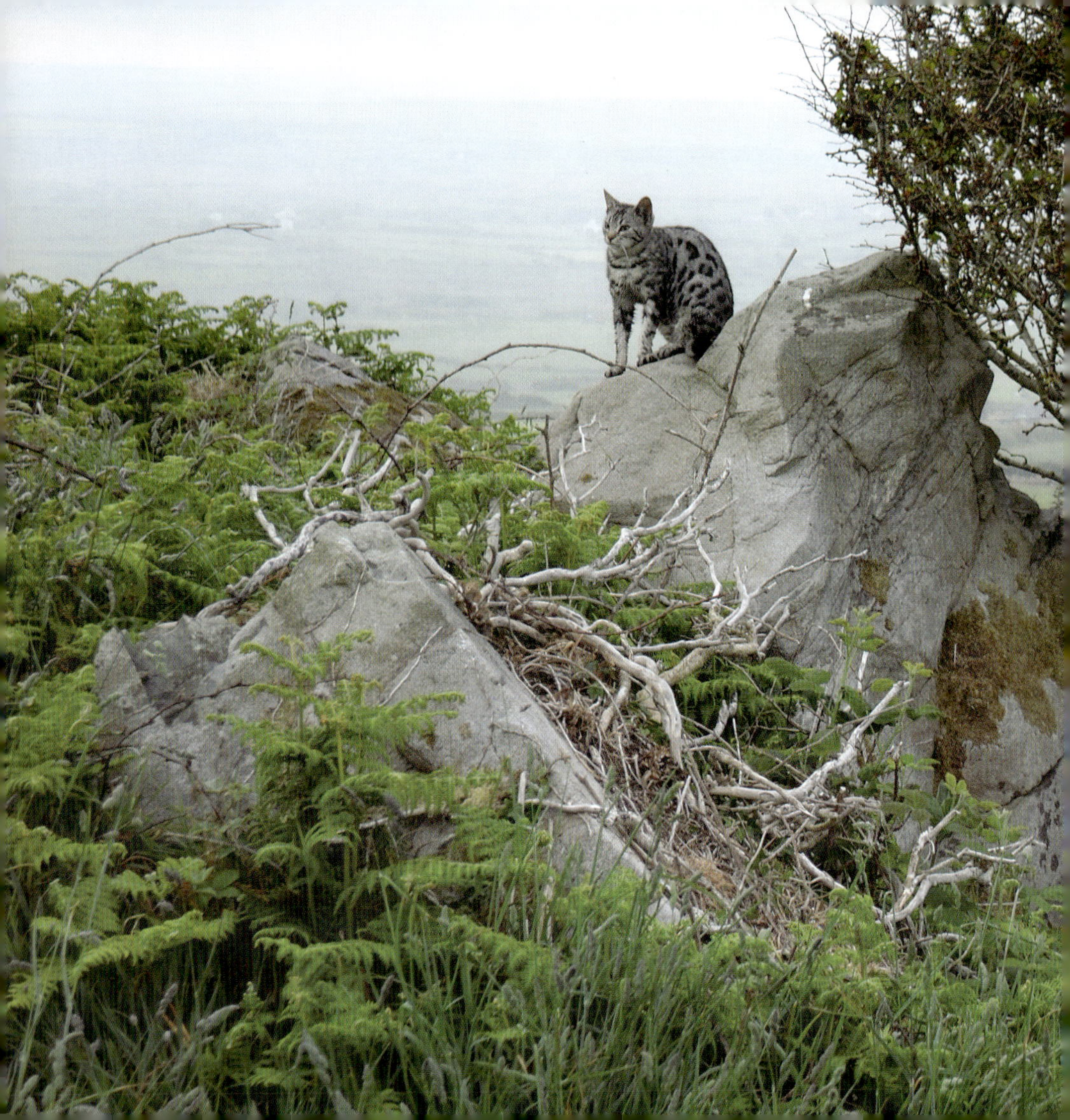

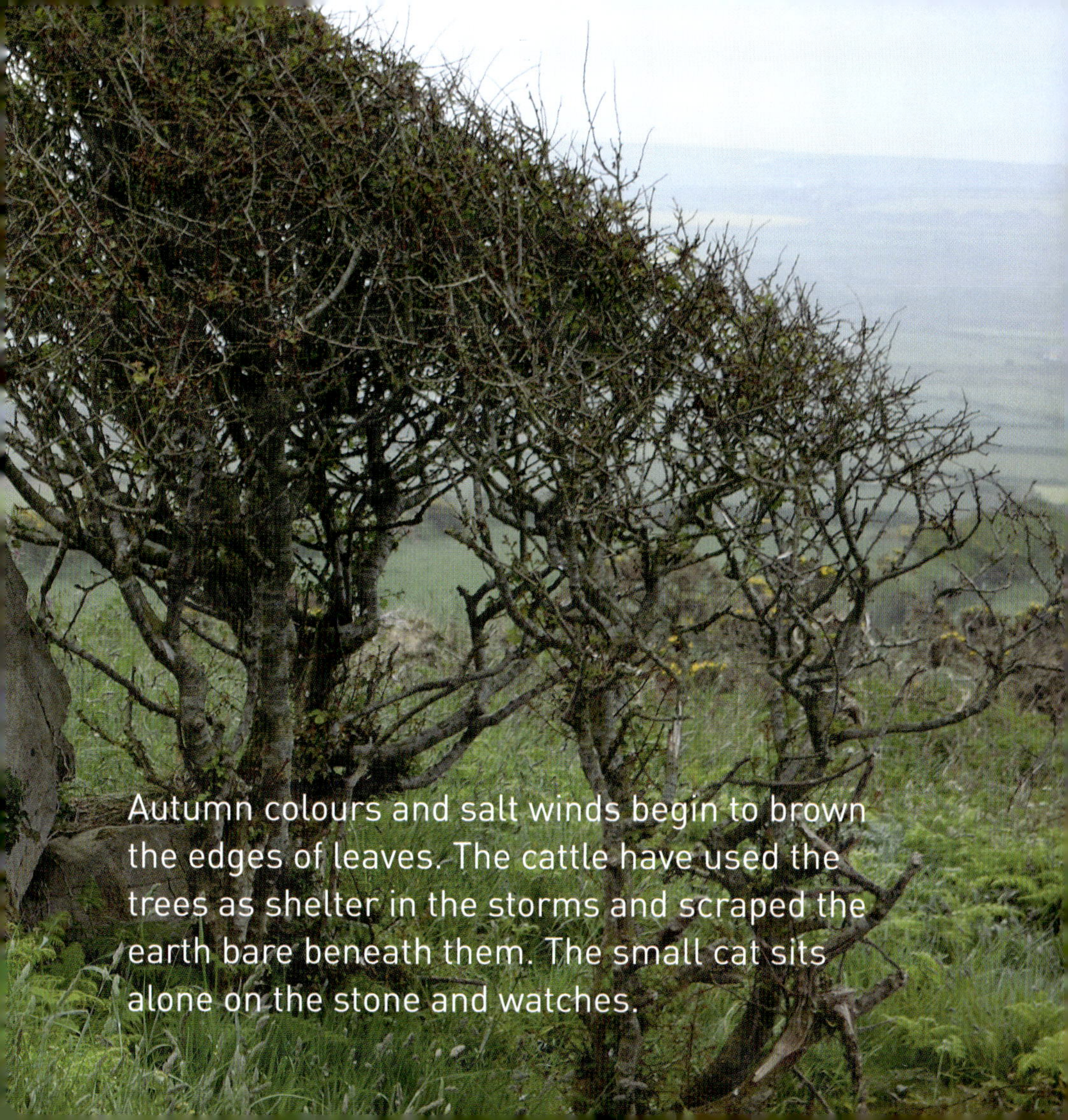
Autumn colours and salt winds begin to brown the edges of leaves. The cattle have used the trees as shelter in the storms and scraped the earth bare beneath them. The small cat sits alone on the stone and watches.

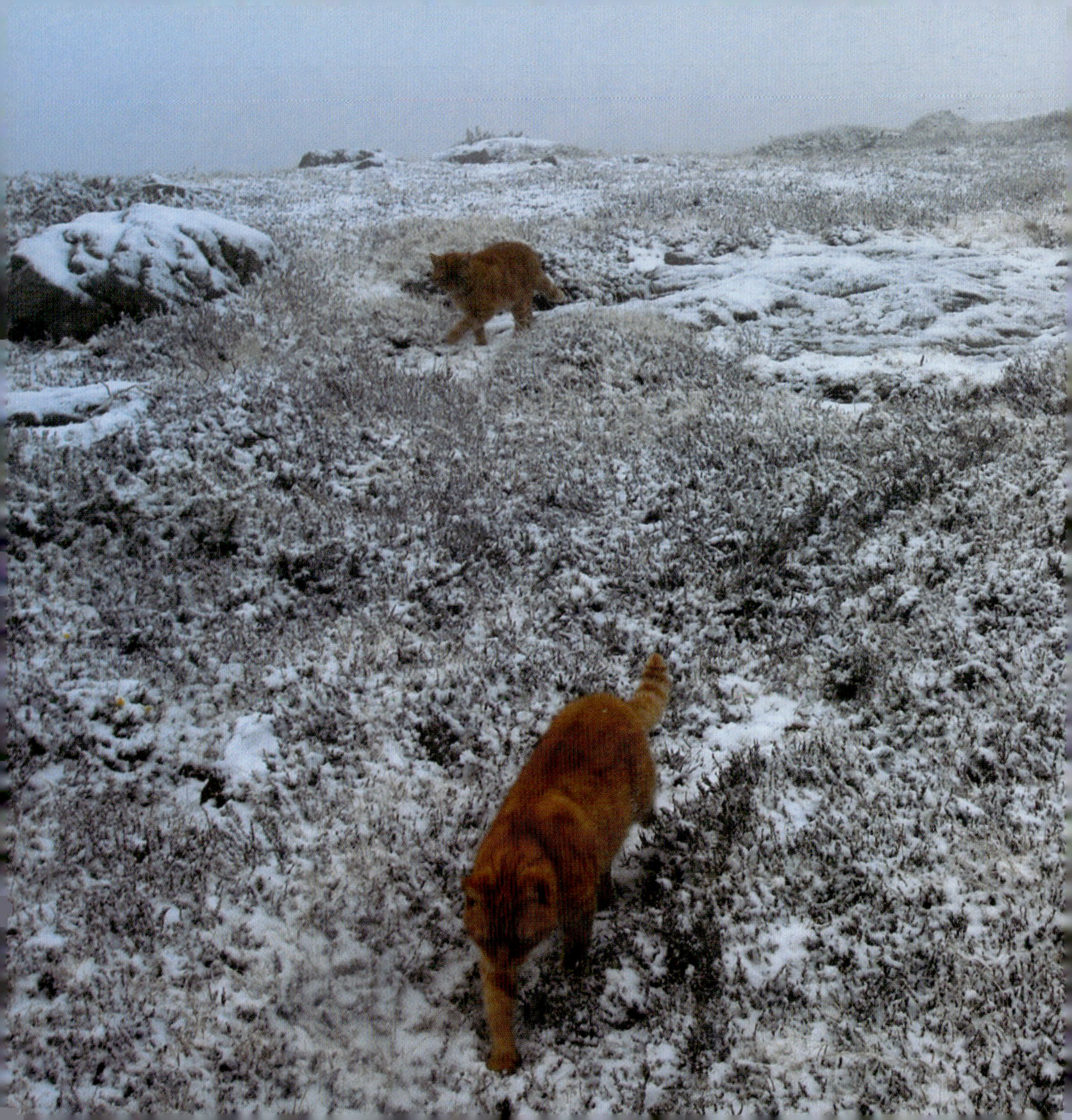

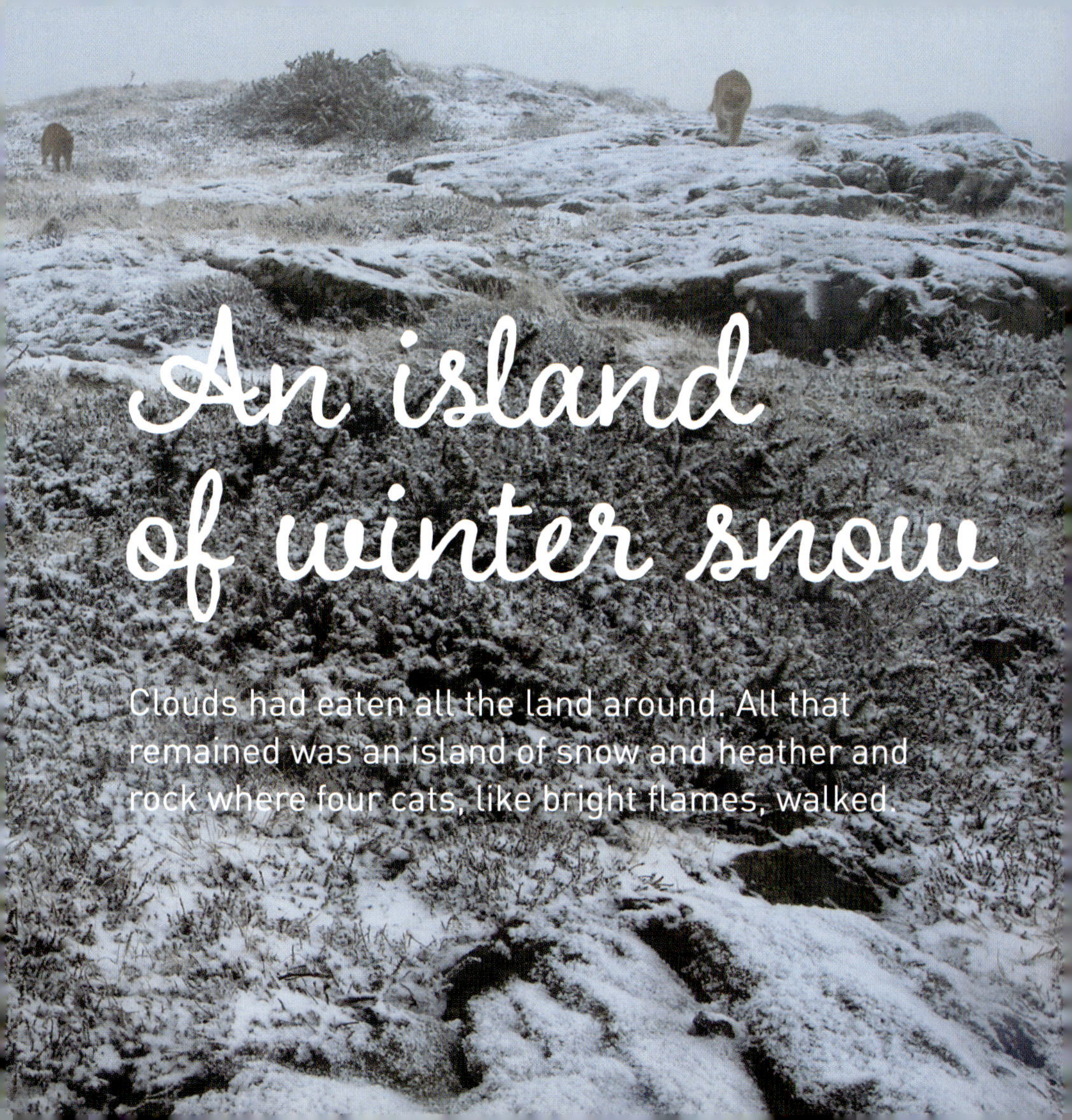


An island
of winter snow

Clouds had eaten all the land around. All that
remained was an island of snow and heather and
rock where four cats, like bright flames, walked.

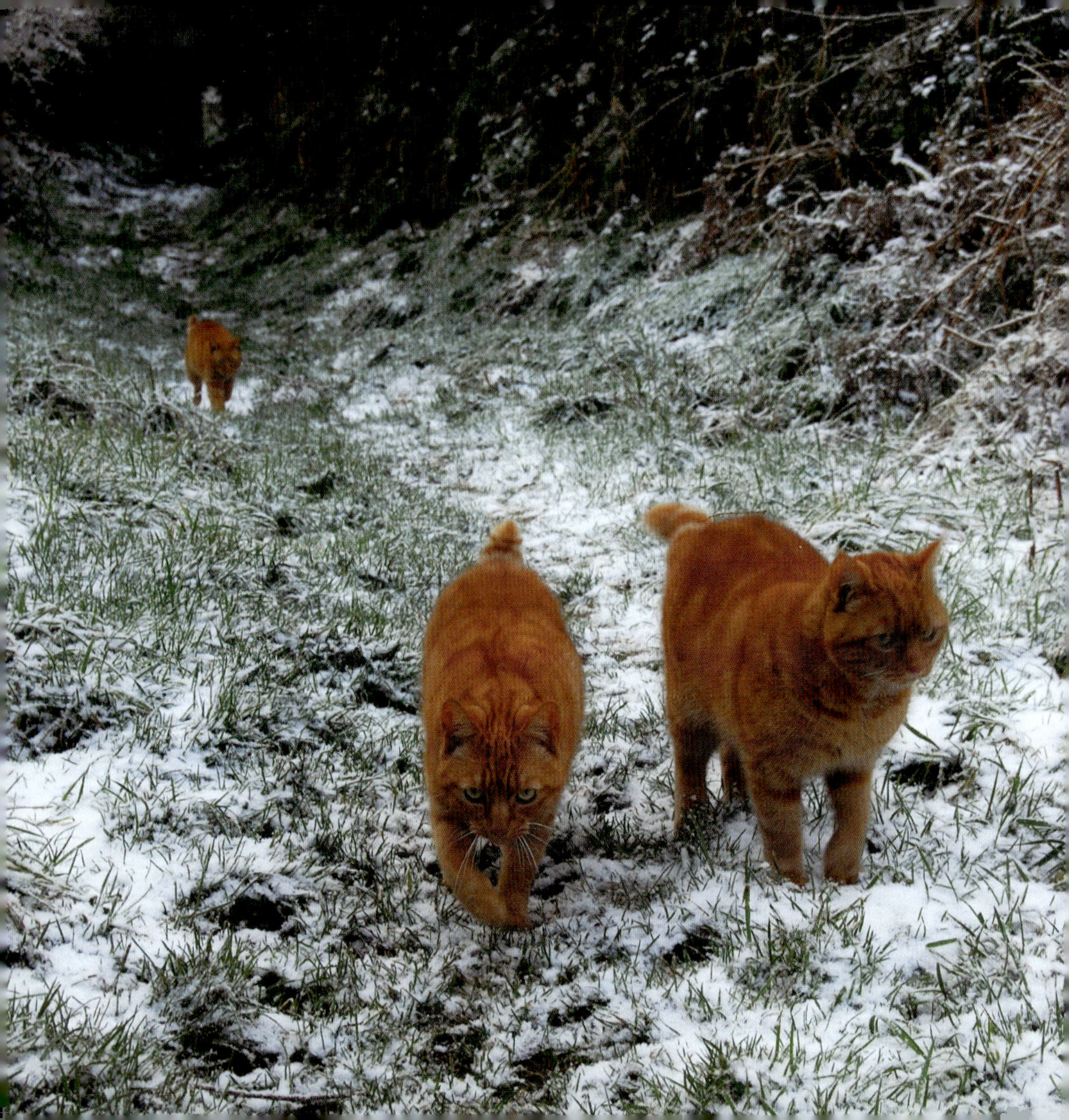

And then one morning they all awoke to find a world changed by snow. Just a light dusting in the green lane that leads to the high hill. Blackthorn branches and hedgebanks had kept the path sheltered from snowflakes' fall.

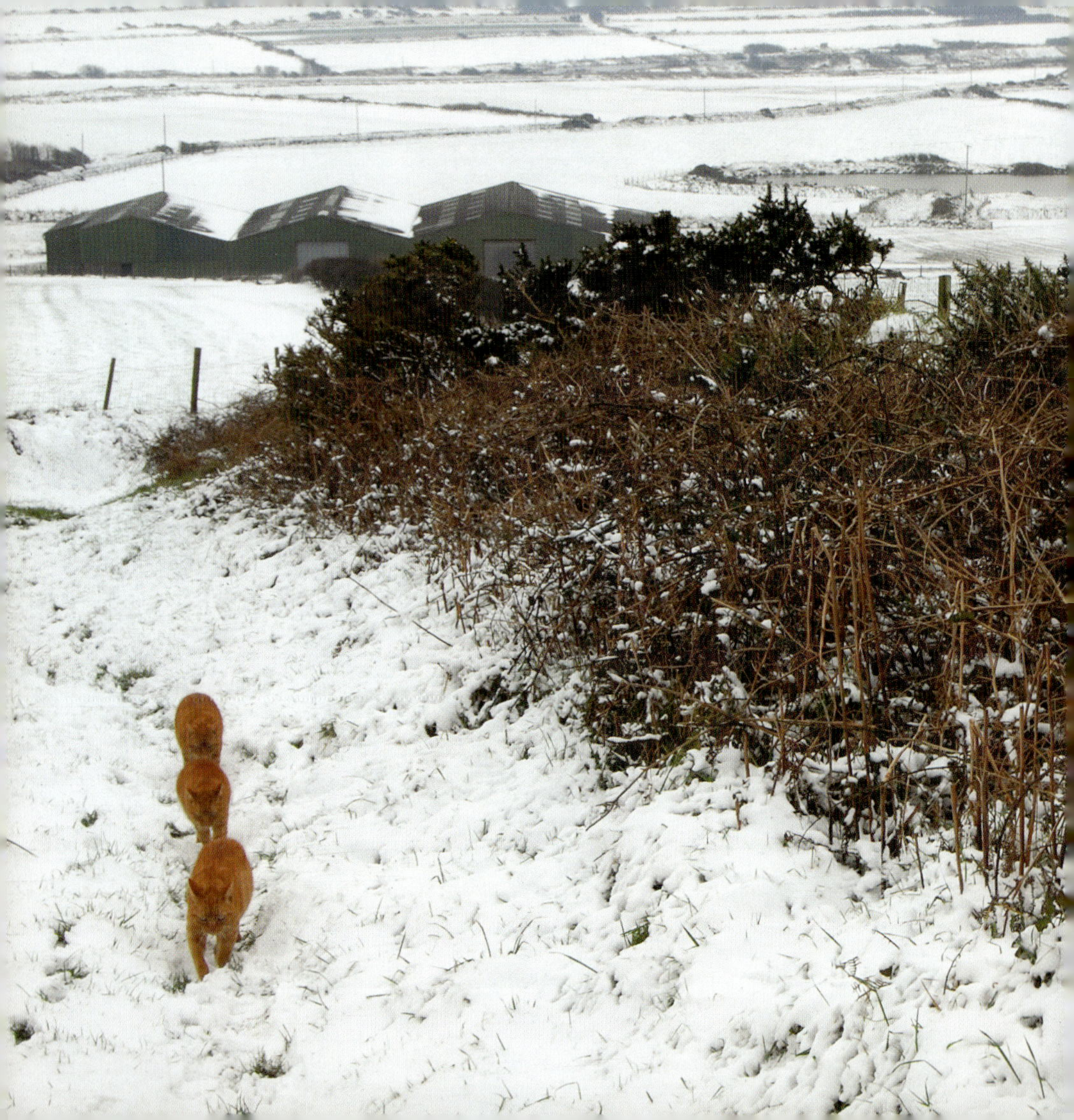

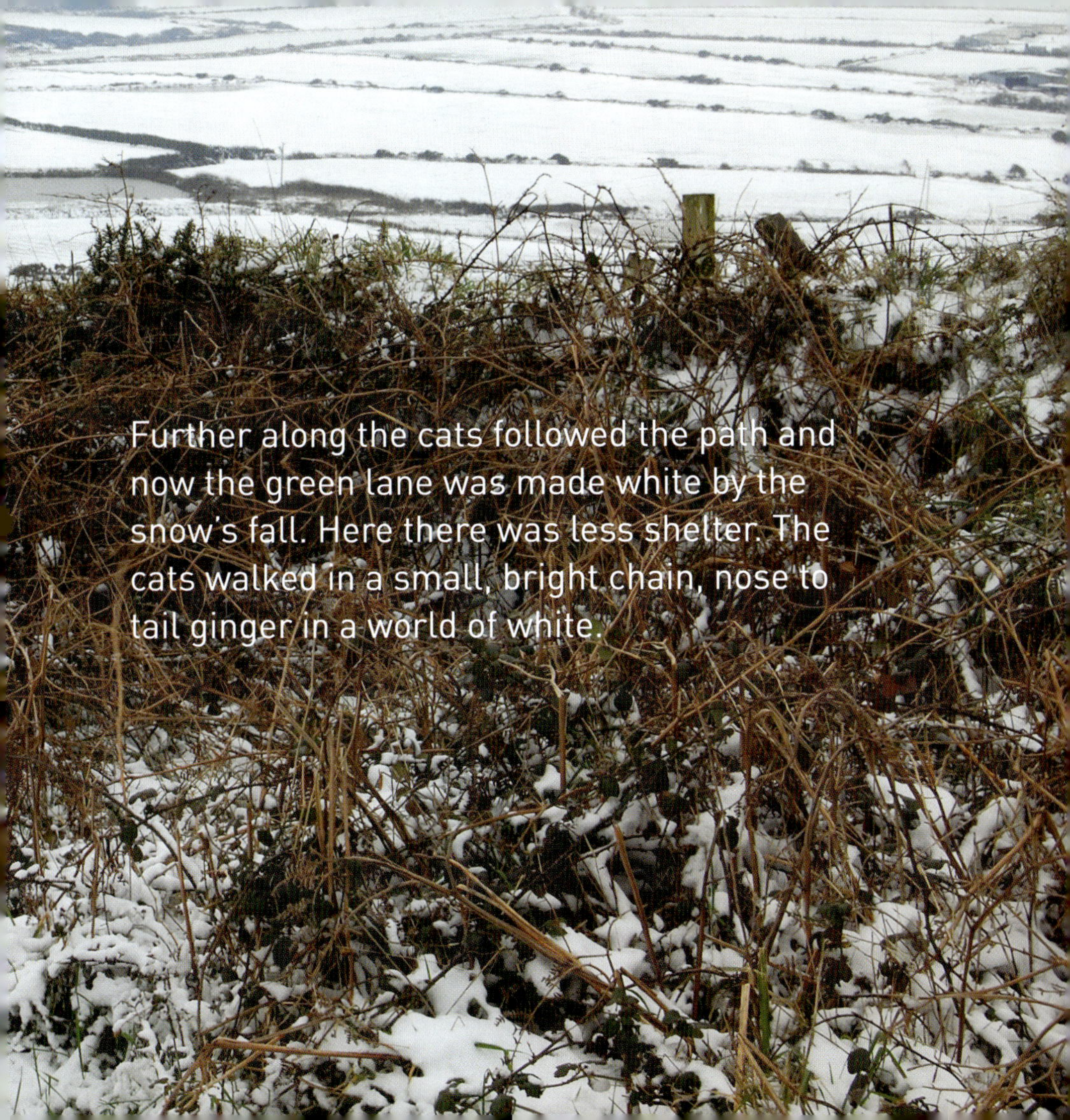

Further along the cats followed the path and now the green lane was made white by the snow's fall. Here there was less shelter. The cats walked in a small, bright chain, nose to tail ginger in a world of white.

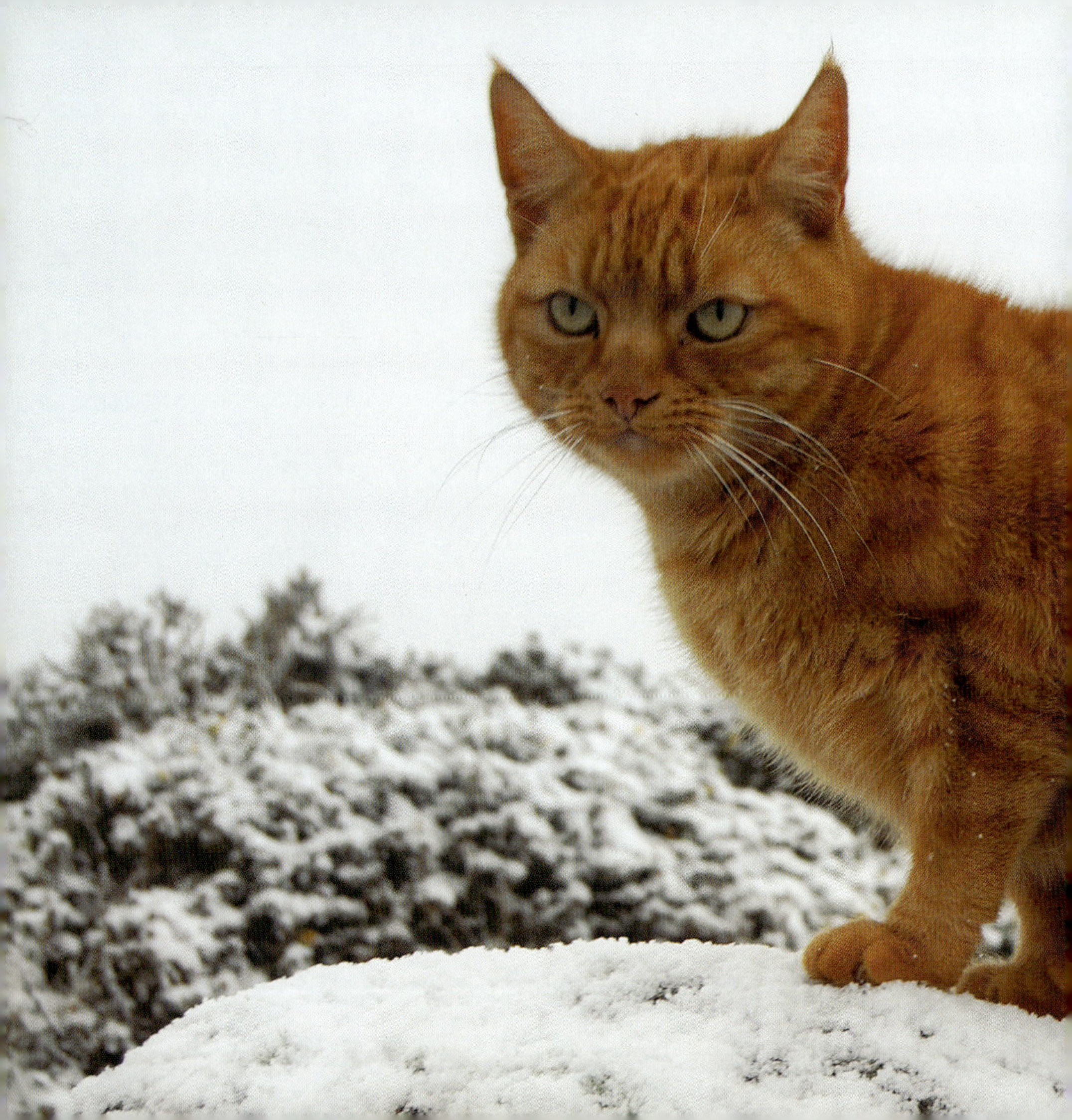

On top of the hill the air was freezing, nothing but ice and cold and the cats fluffed up their fur, a trick learned from the birds who will fluff up their feathers to catch warm air between each fine filament.

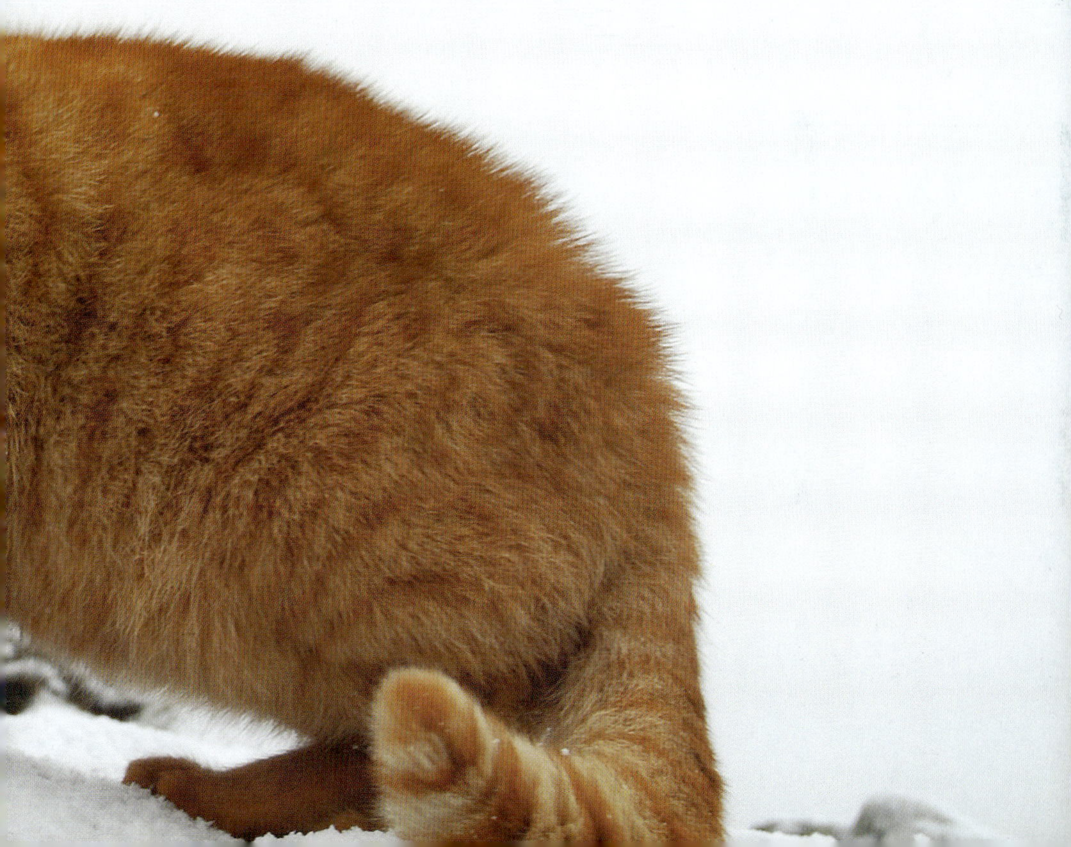

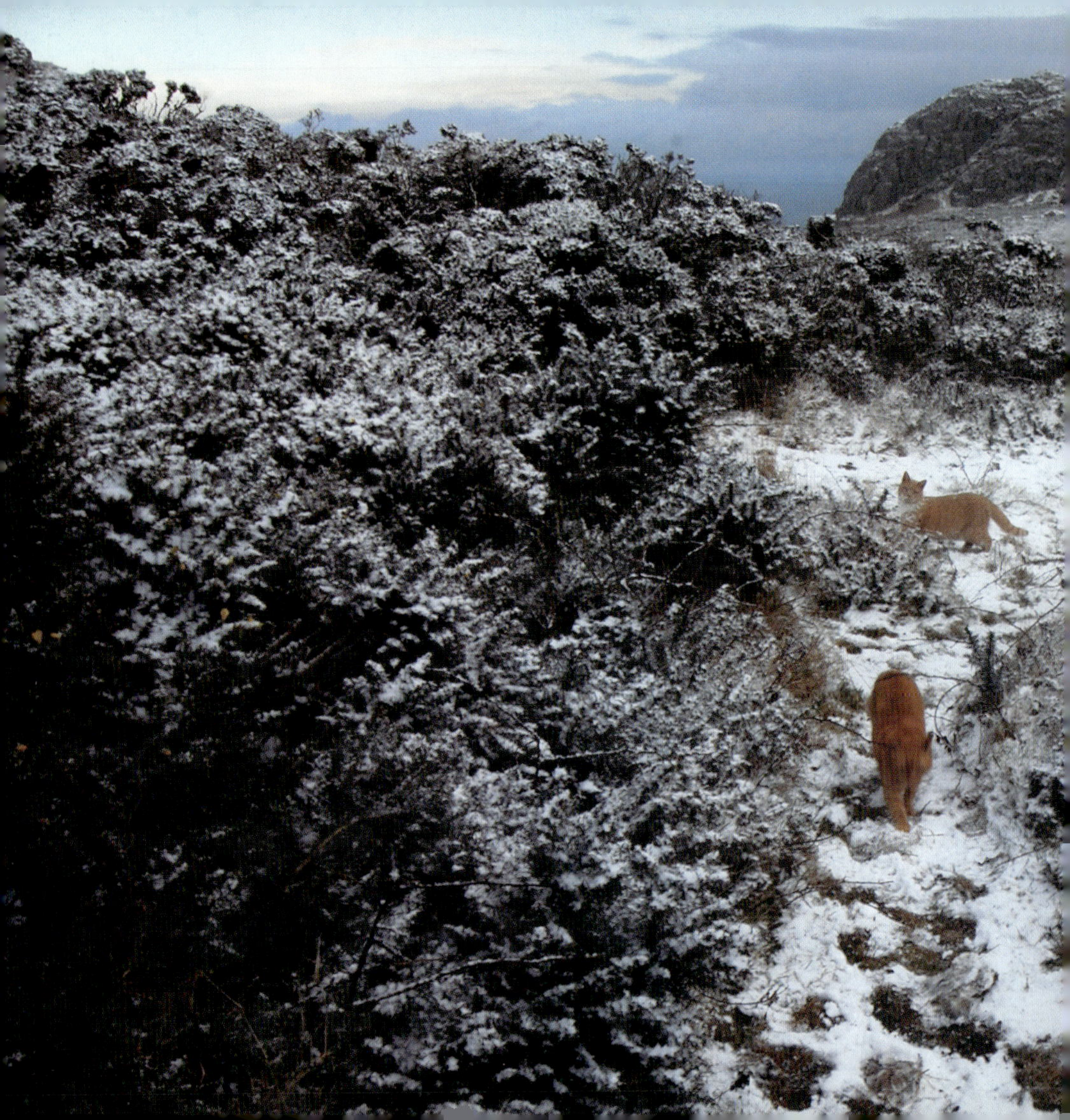

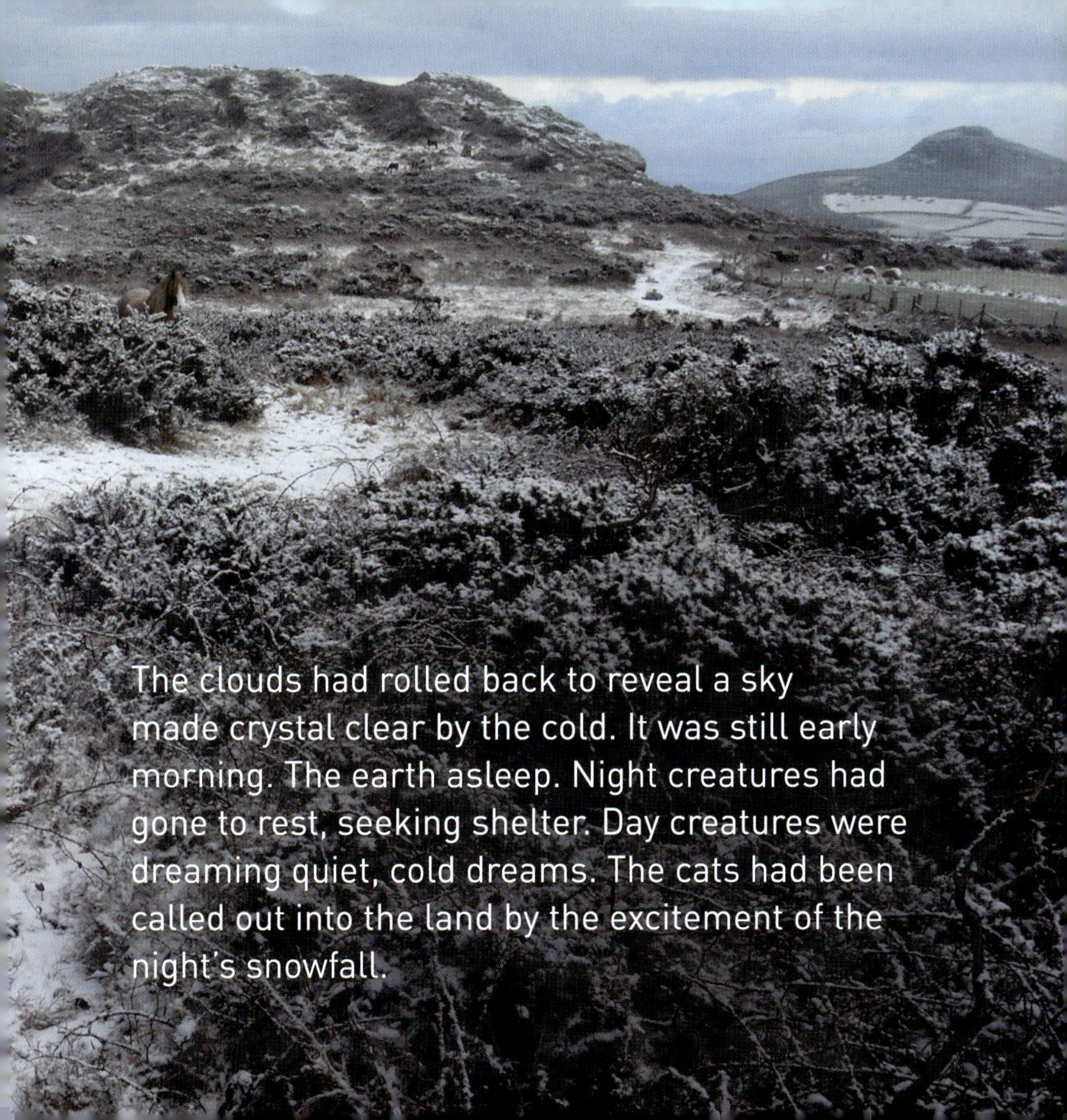

The clouds had rolled back to reveal a sky
made crystal clear by the cold. It was still early
morning. The earth asleep. Night creatures had
gone to rest, seeking shelter. Day creatures were
dreaming quiet, cold dreams. The cats had been
called out into the land by the excitement of the
night's snowfall.

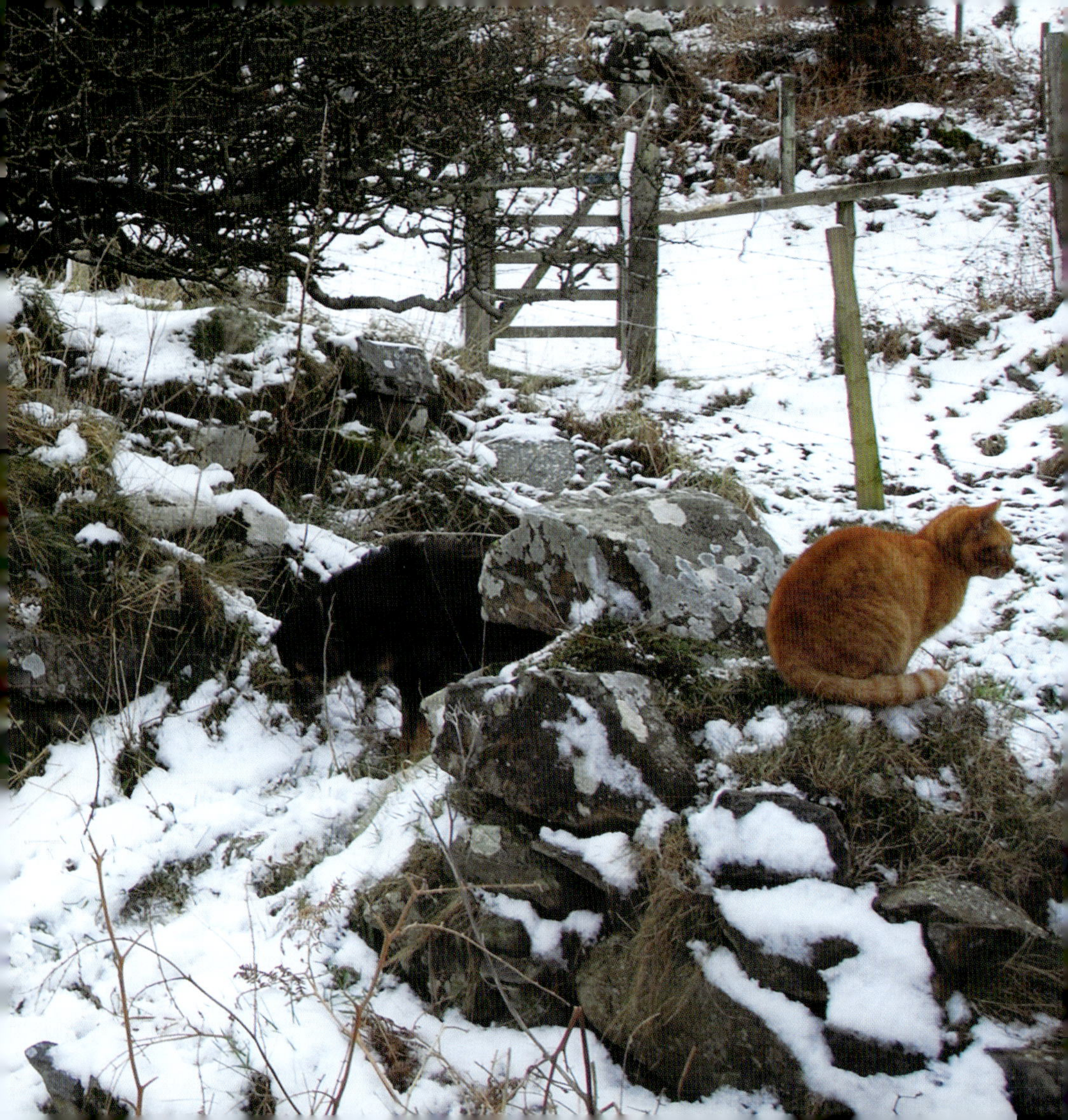

They walked to the old village, silent in the snow. Once, other cats had sat here, dreaming cold dreams beside driftwood fires, sunning themselves on sunny window ledges. Now the chimney fawr had fallen, and snow was the only carpet to cover the floor. Each year a few more stones would tumble from the cottage walls, pushed by wind and weather. Each year a few more ghosts would wander the pathways, in and out of empty windows, open doorways.

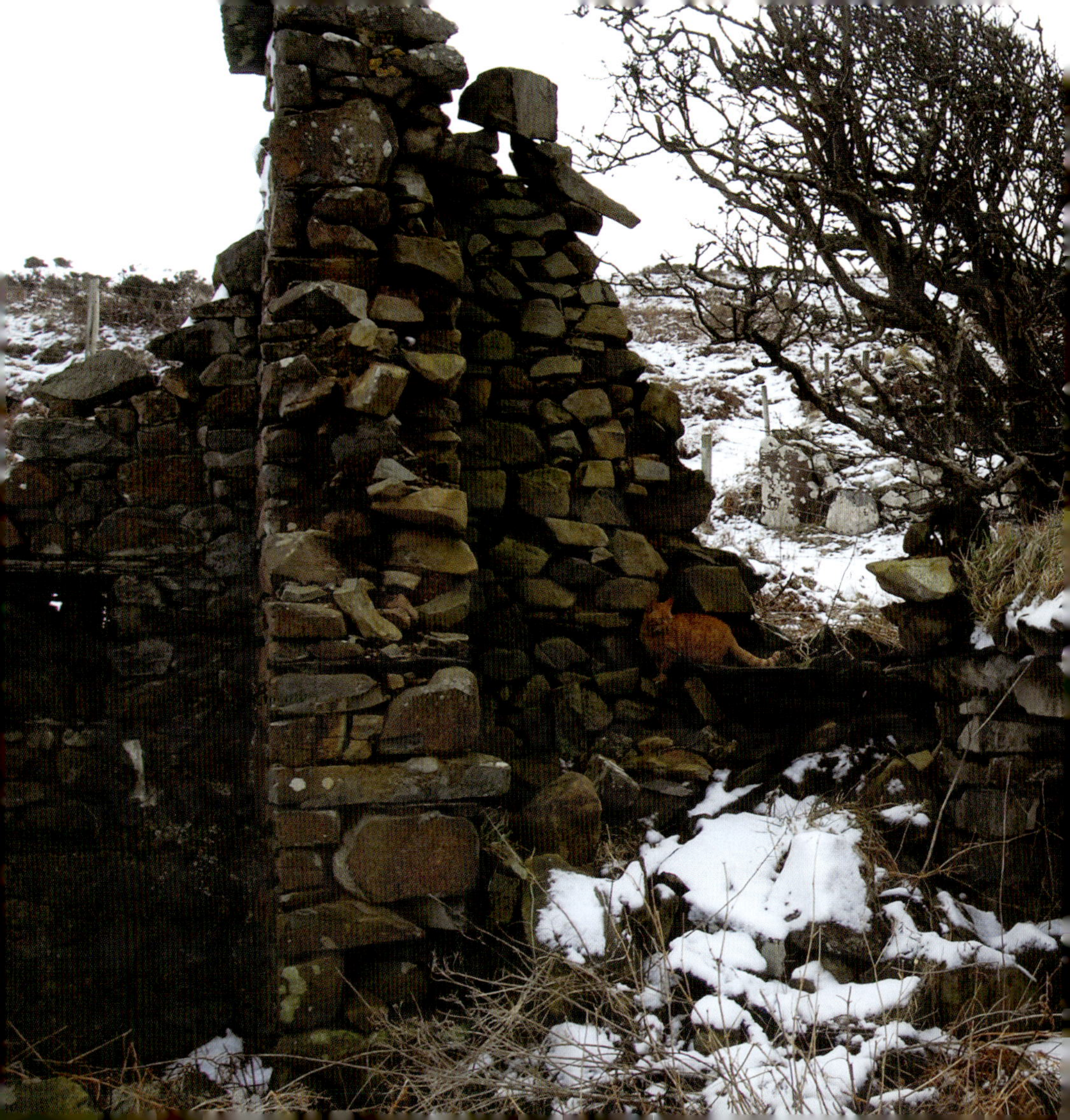

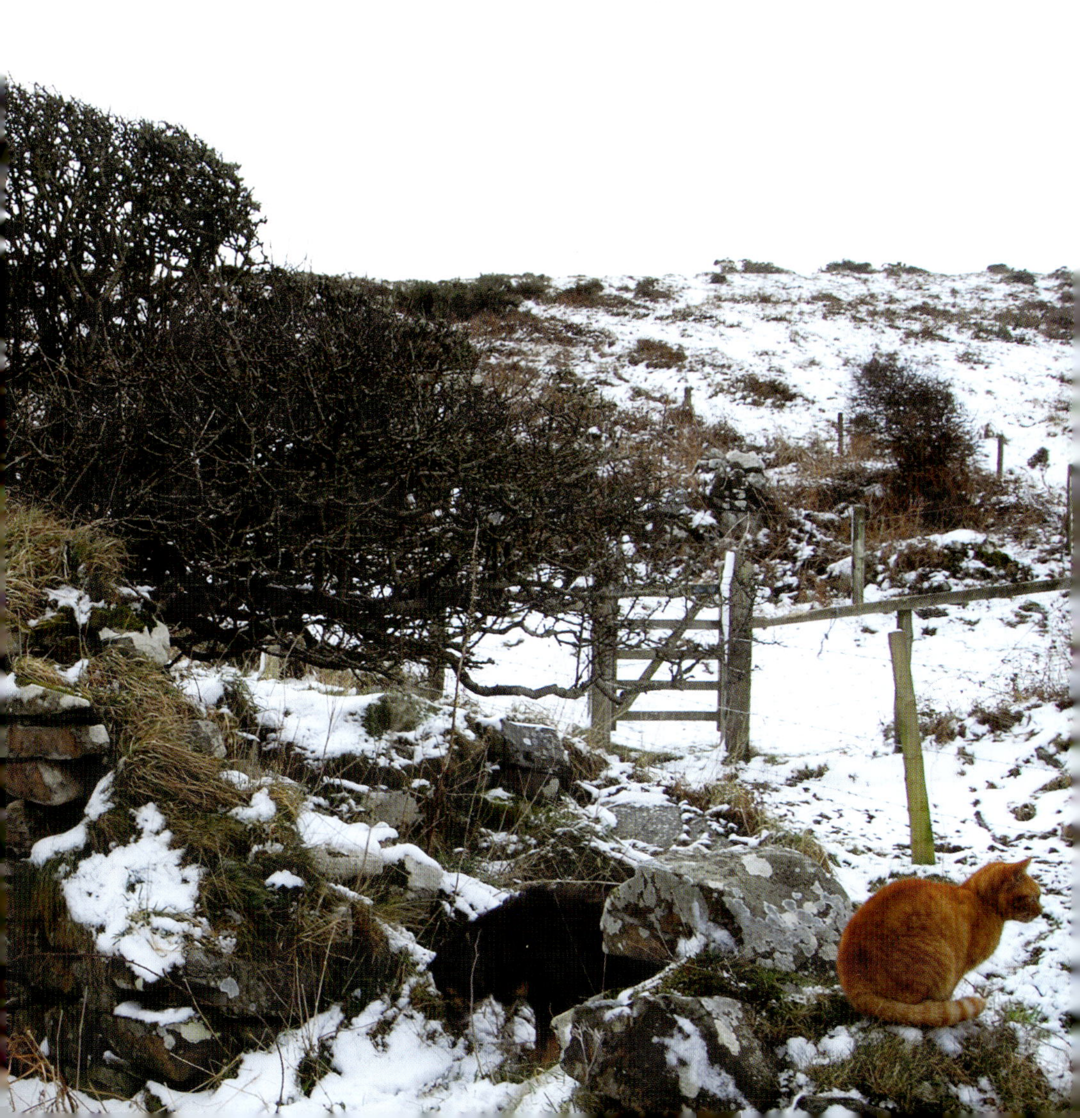

Snow dusted the old tumbled fieldstone walls of the ruined village. There was some shelter. The old ones knew how to build, and where. The hawthorn tree that grew beside the empty window had broken the snow's fall.

The cats always walked carefully here, not wishing to disturb the rest of the ancient ghost cats who had once sat and warmed their bones on the window ledge, or moved closer to the driftwood fires that burned with salty witchfire flames in old hearths. It was quiet on that day. Even the birds were too cold to sing.

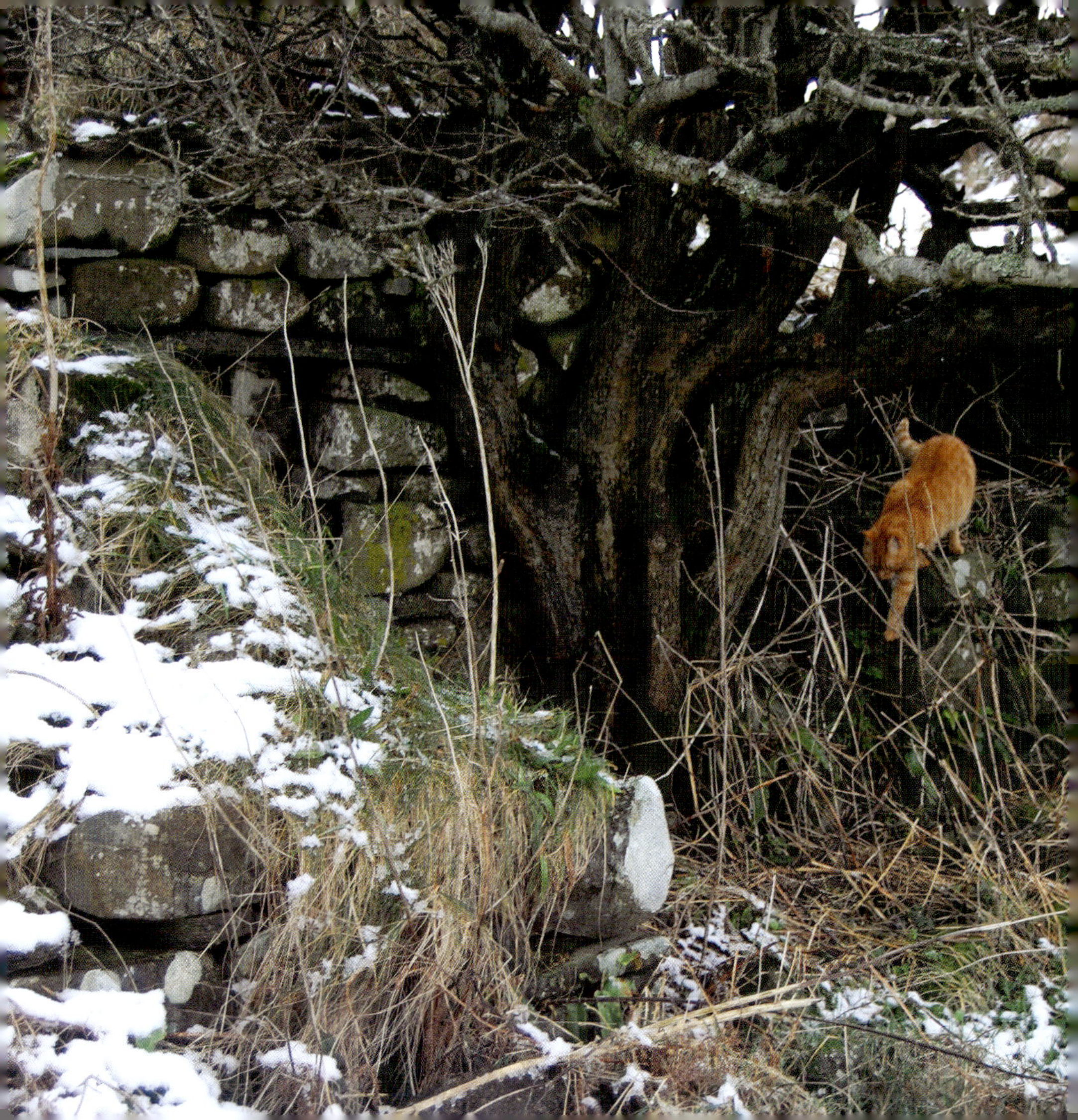

The contrast of pale sky and snow covered fields
brought out the colours in the fieldstone of the
ruined cottage walls. Green, rust, grey, blue, and
on top of it all one small orange cat, surveying
the land, excited by the soft, cold snowfall.
He searched the sky for birds, but all was still.
It seemed as if the earth was waiting.

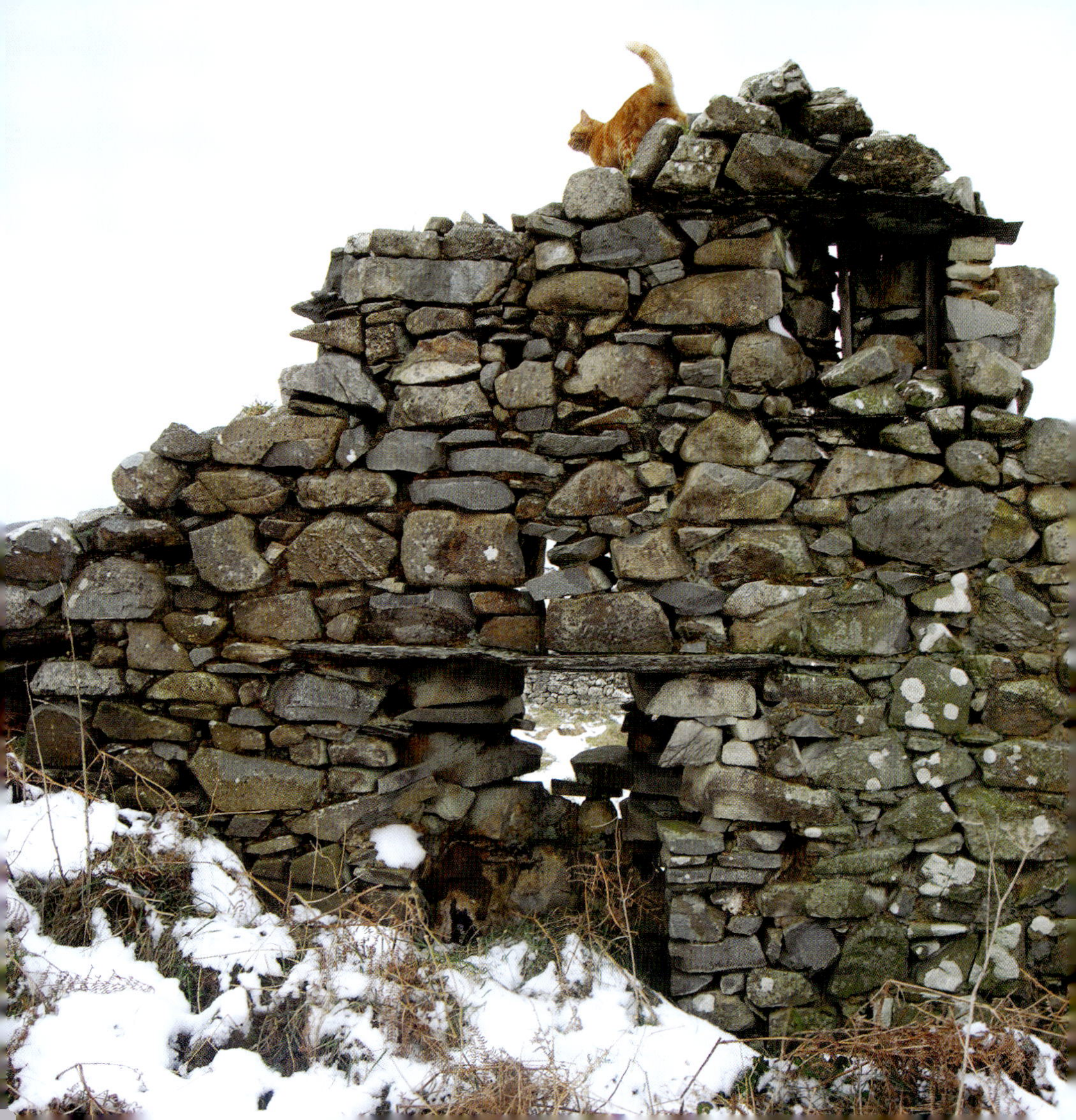

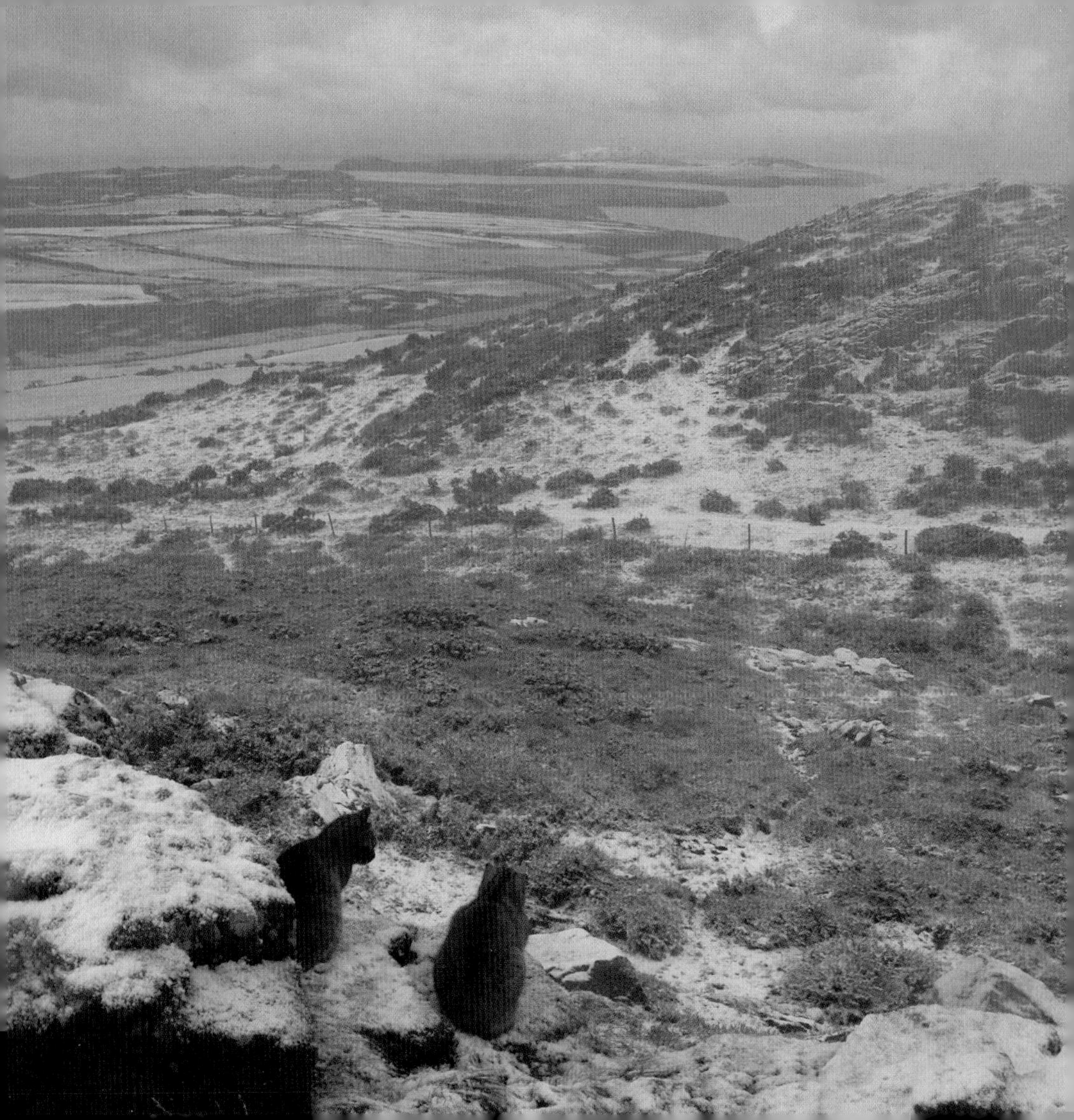

They moved on. For a while the small cats sat and rested, watching the world beneath them. Clouds built on the horizon. There might be more snow to come.

They could smell it. And all around it seemed that the colour had been pulled from the land, that the world was redrawn in monochrome shades of pencil, that the only colour was the bright ginger sparks shaped like cats.

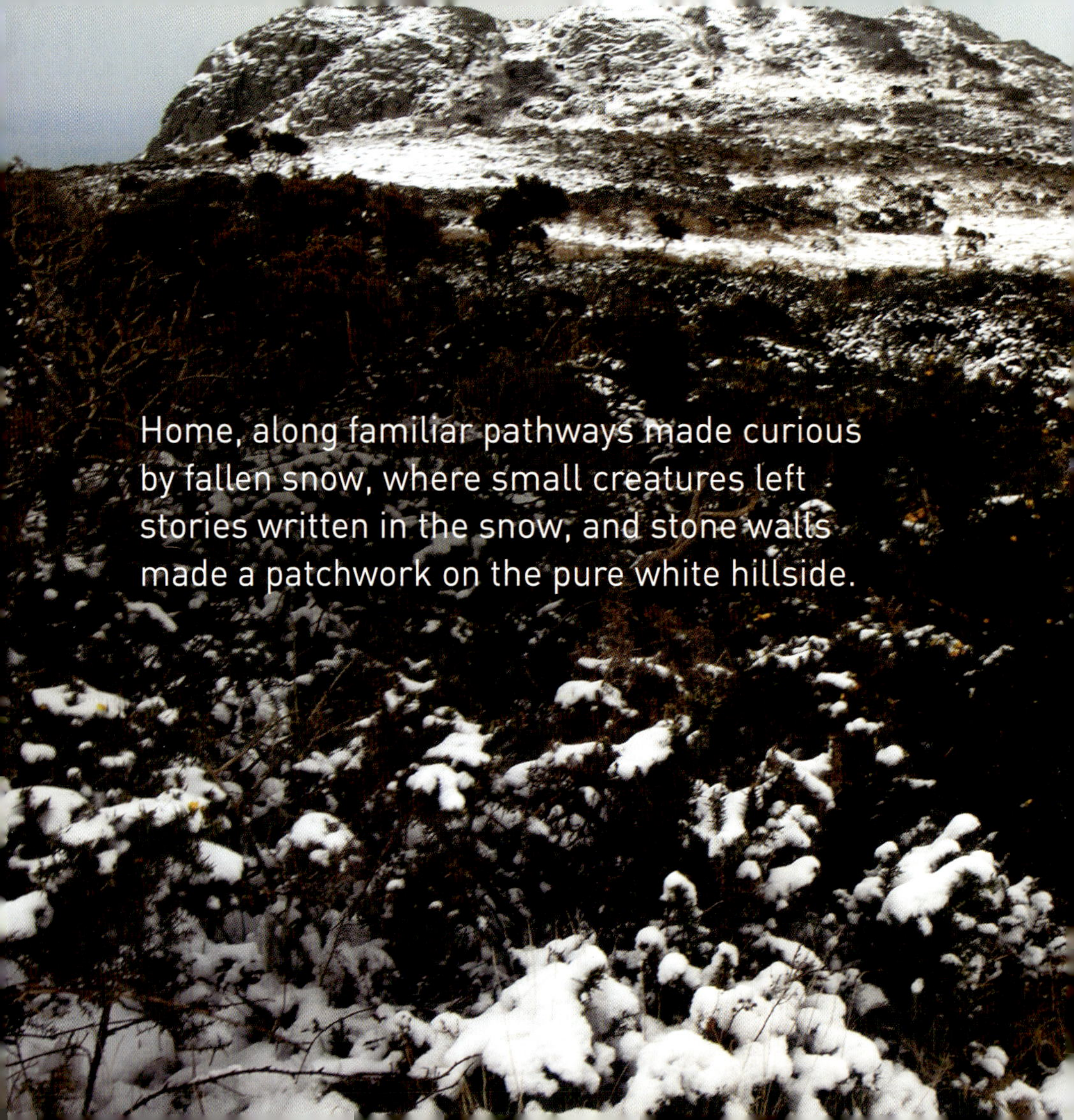


Home, along familiar pathways made curious
by fallen snow, where small creatures left
stories written in the snow, and stone walls
made a patchwork on the pure white hillside.

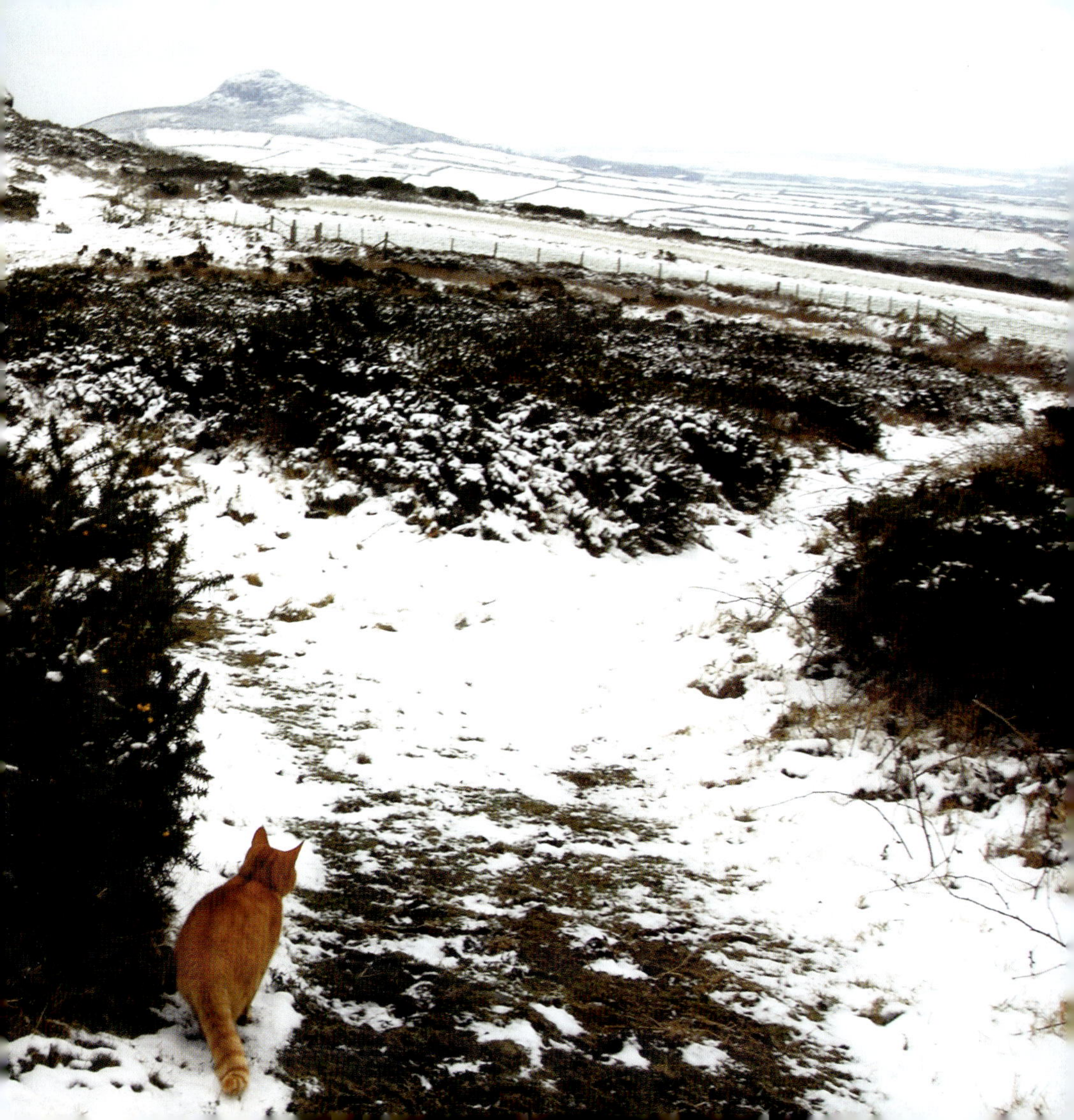

Cat. Logs.

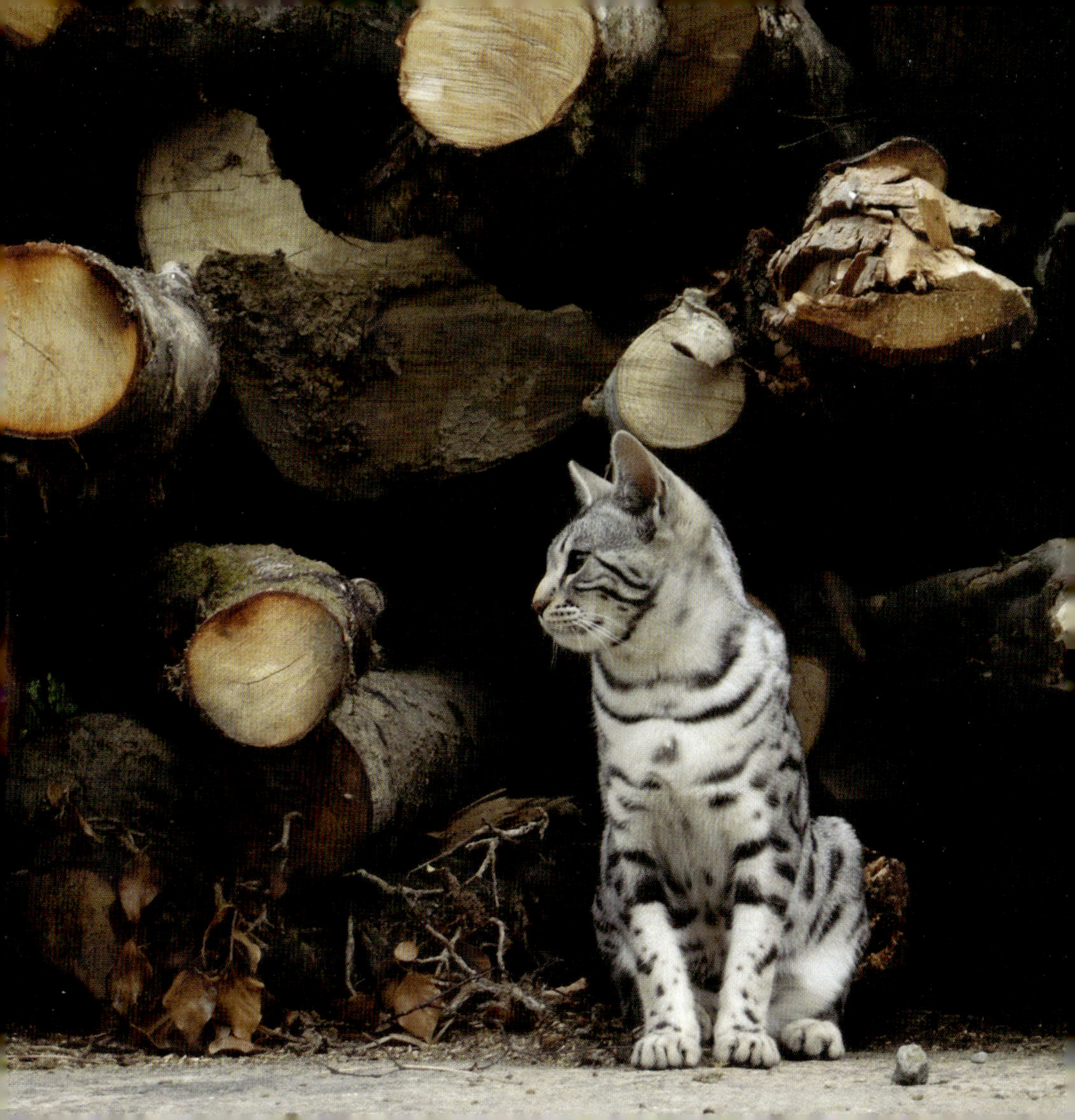

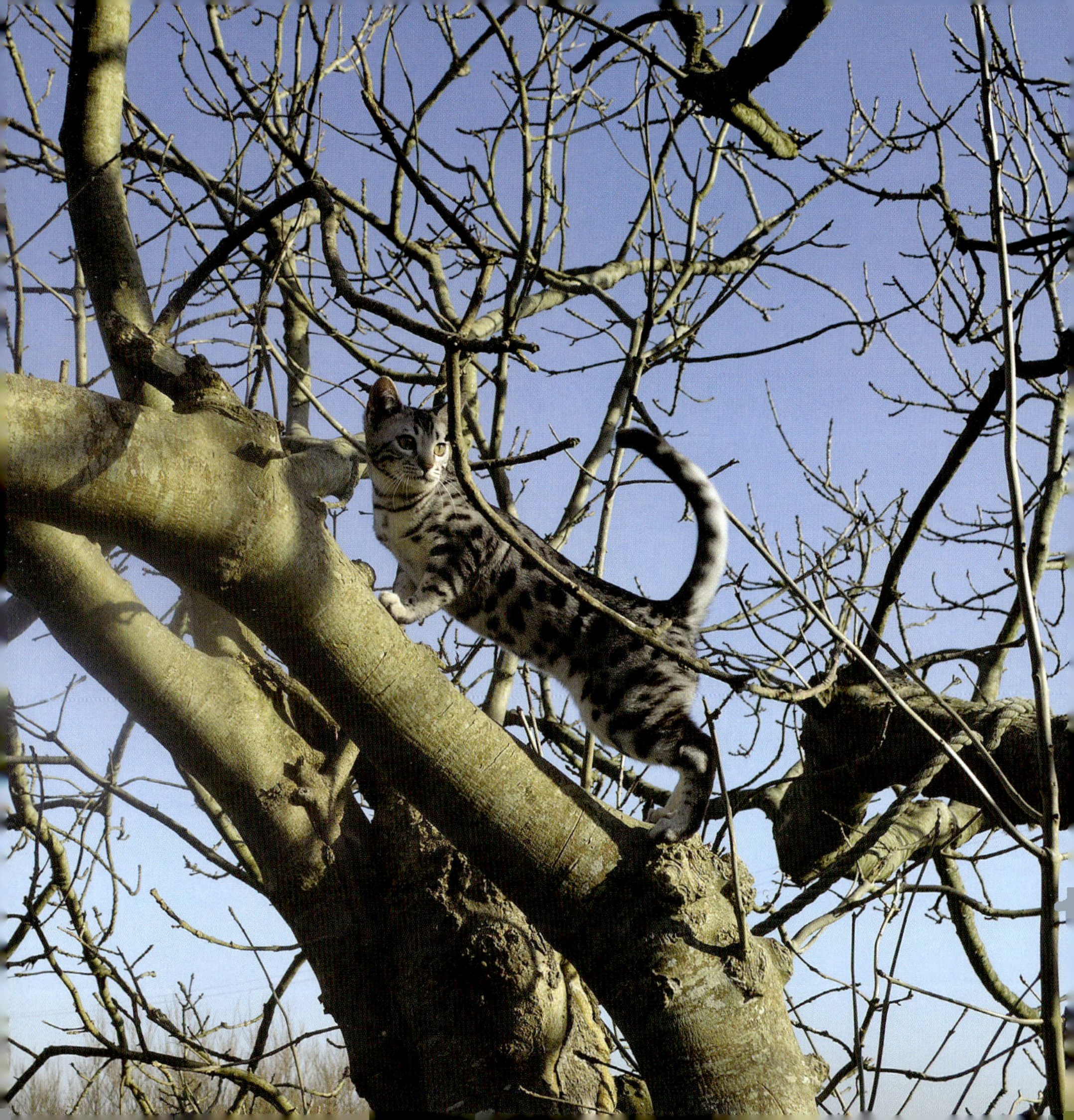

The bare bone branches of the winter tree cut the blue sky into mosaic patterns. Here the small cats can climb high, to watch the birds fly, the world turn.

A climbing frame, a scratching post, a look-out, a safe haven, and the sky an early morning winter blue still carrying a piece of the night in its hue.

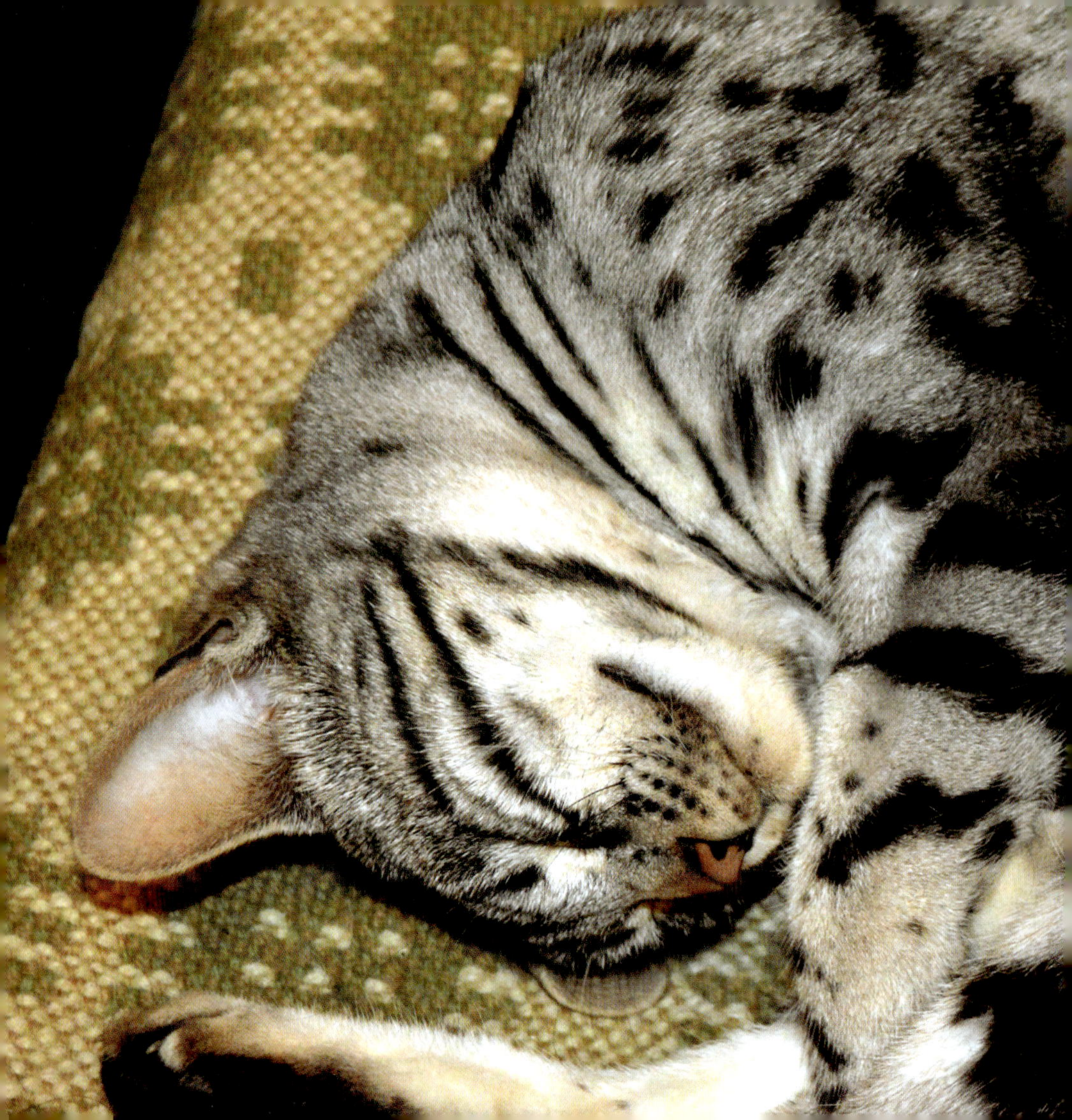

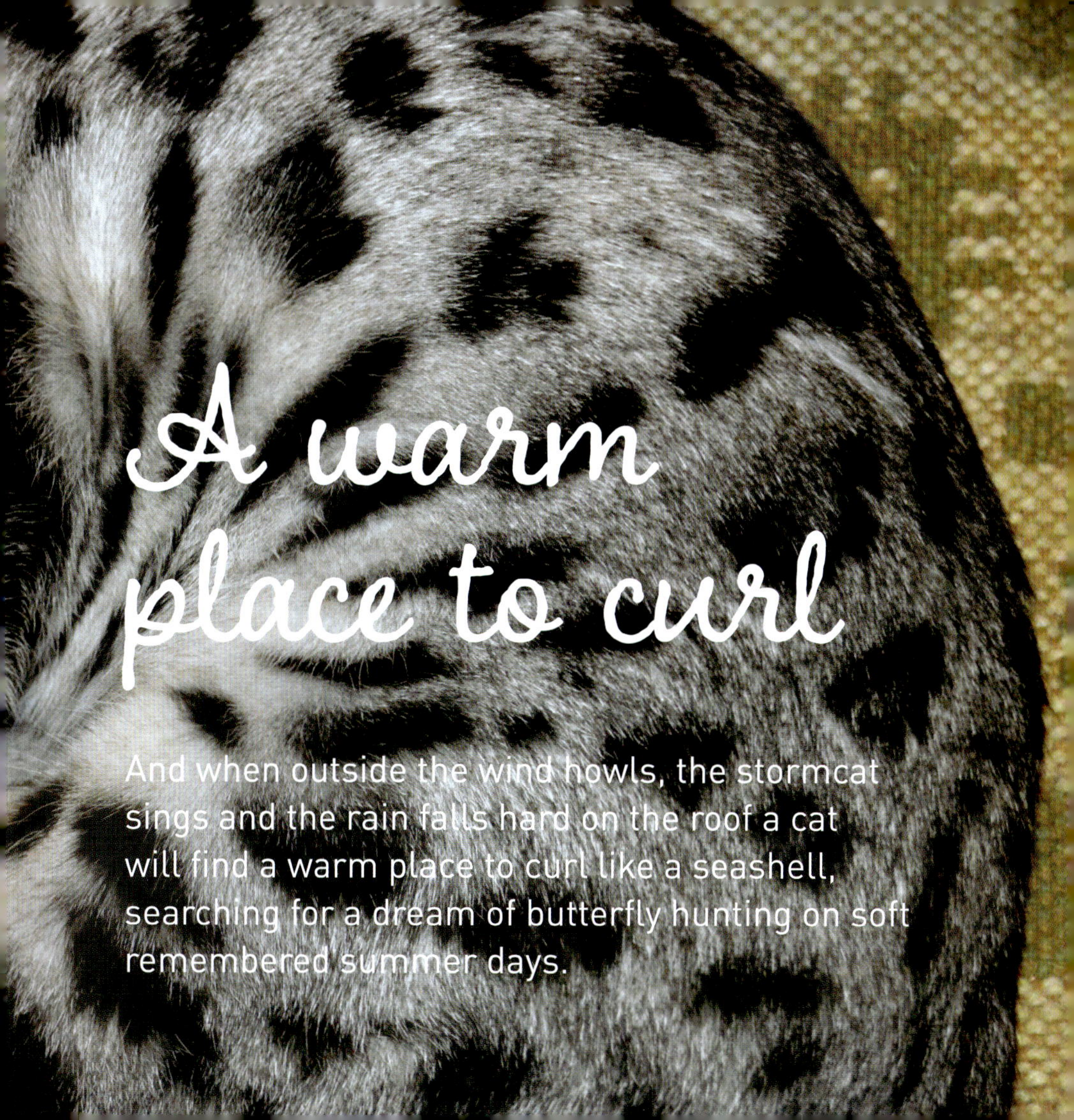

A warm
place to curl

And when outside the wind howls, the stormcat
sings and the rain falls hard on the roof a cat
will find a warm place to curl like a seashell,
searching for a dream of butterfly hunting on soft
remembered summer days.

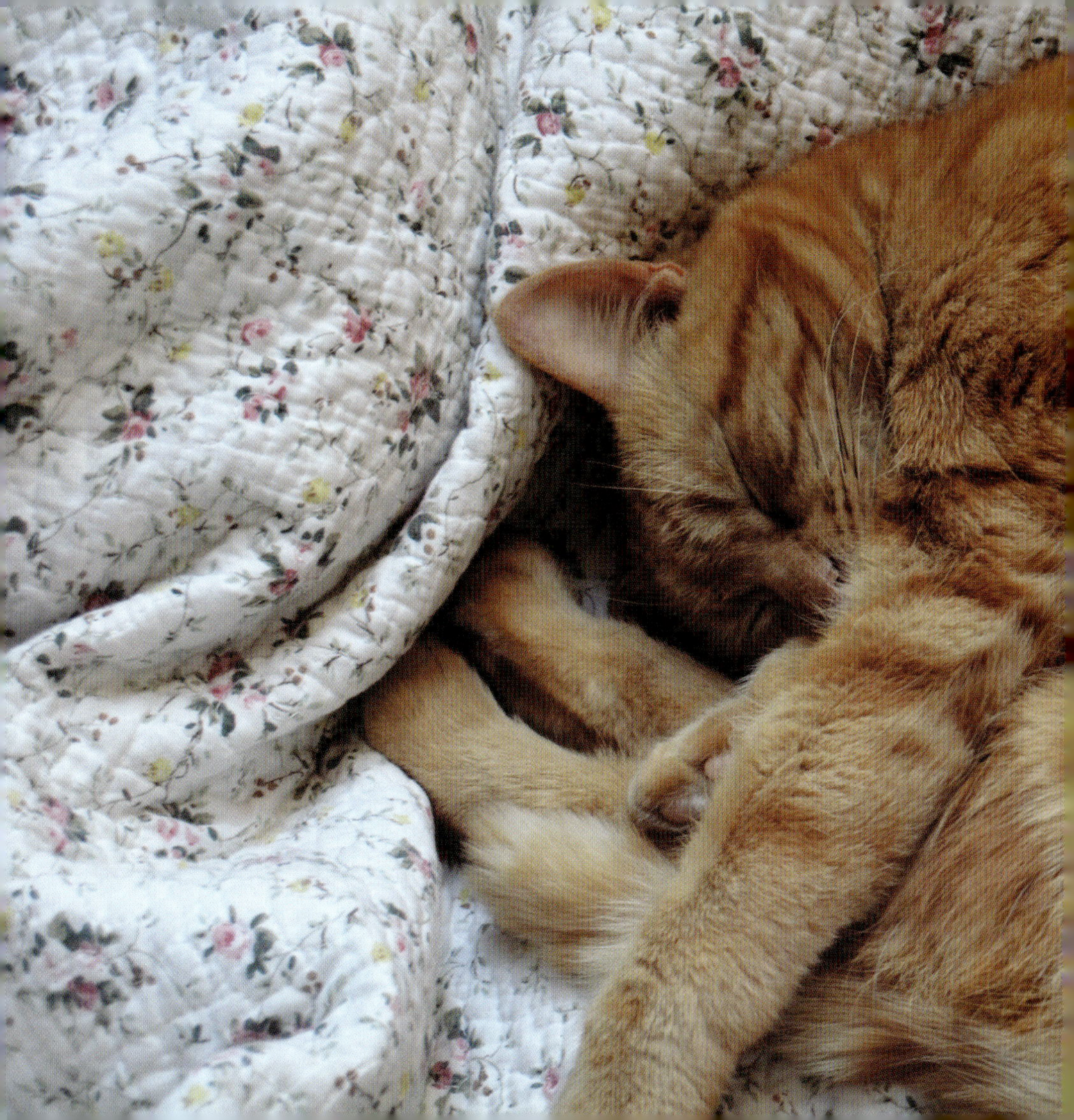

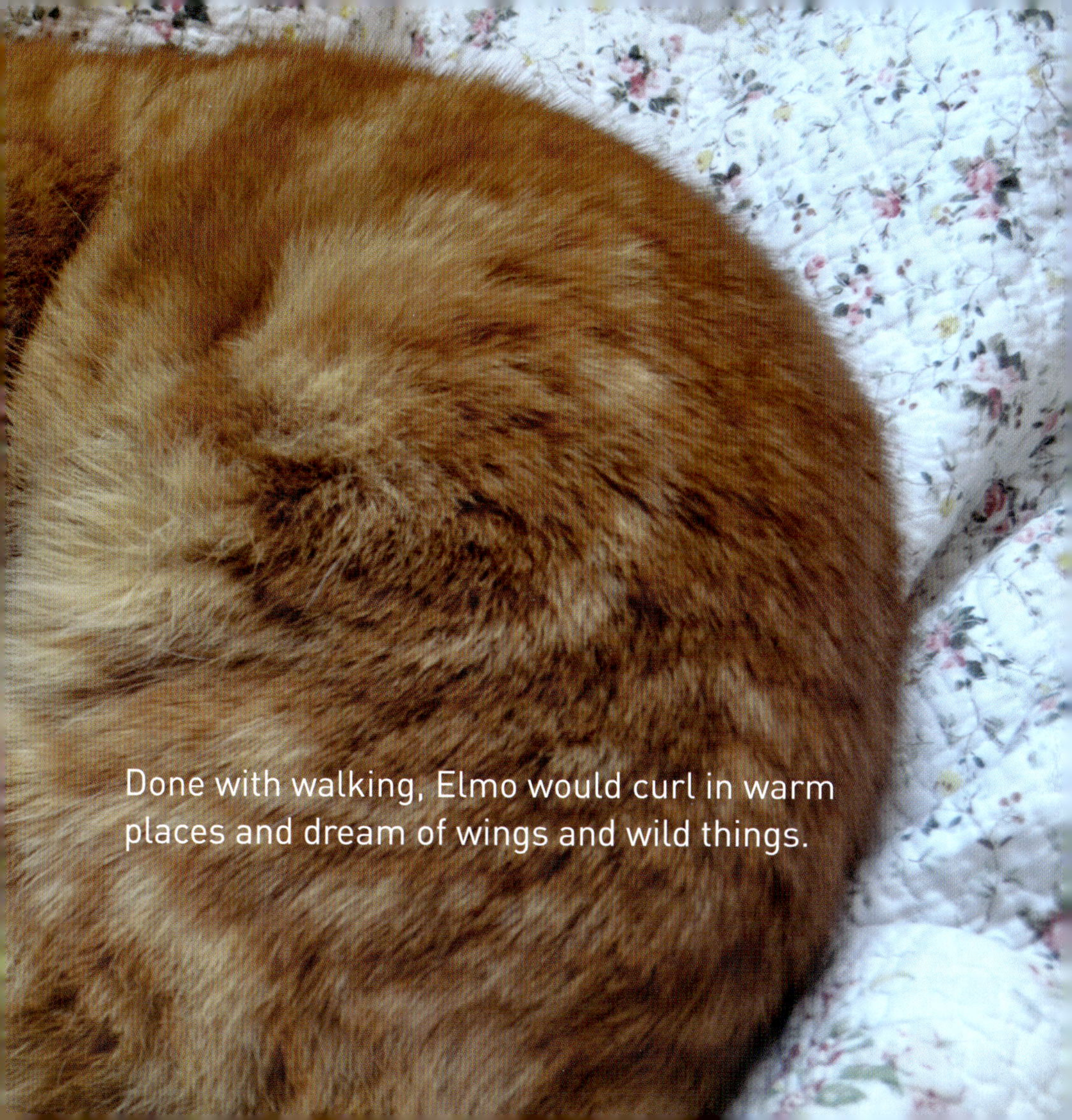
Done with walking, Elmo would curl in warm
places and dream of wings and wild things.

And when the wild wind blows across the land
the cats will curl inside, finding a warm corner
and sometimes the company of others in which
to dream shared dreams of summer sun and
butterflies.

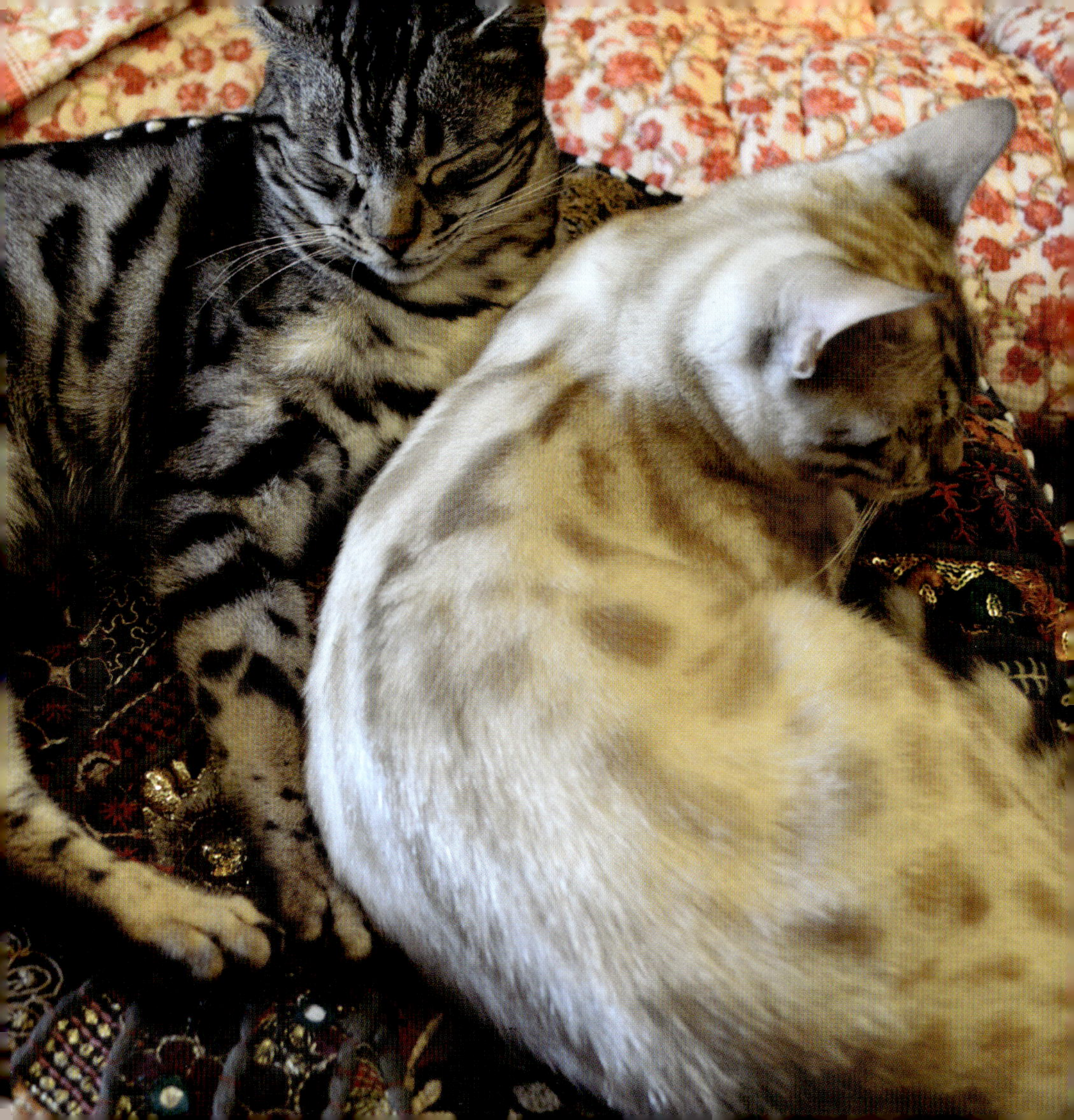

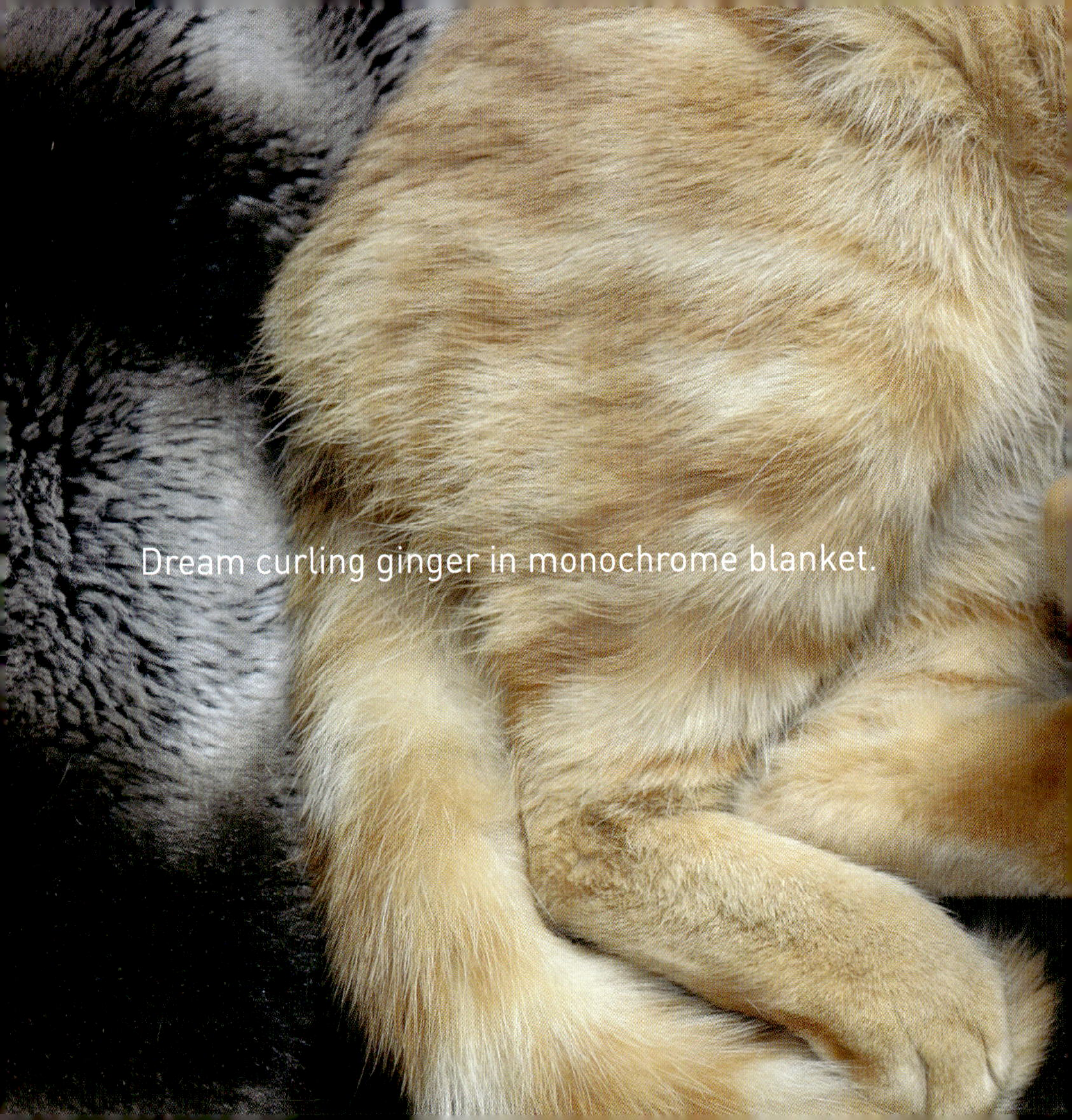
Dream curling ginger in monochrome blanket.

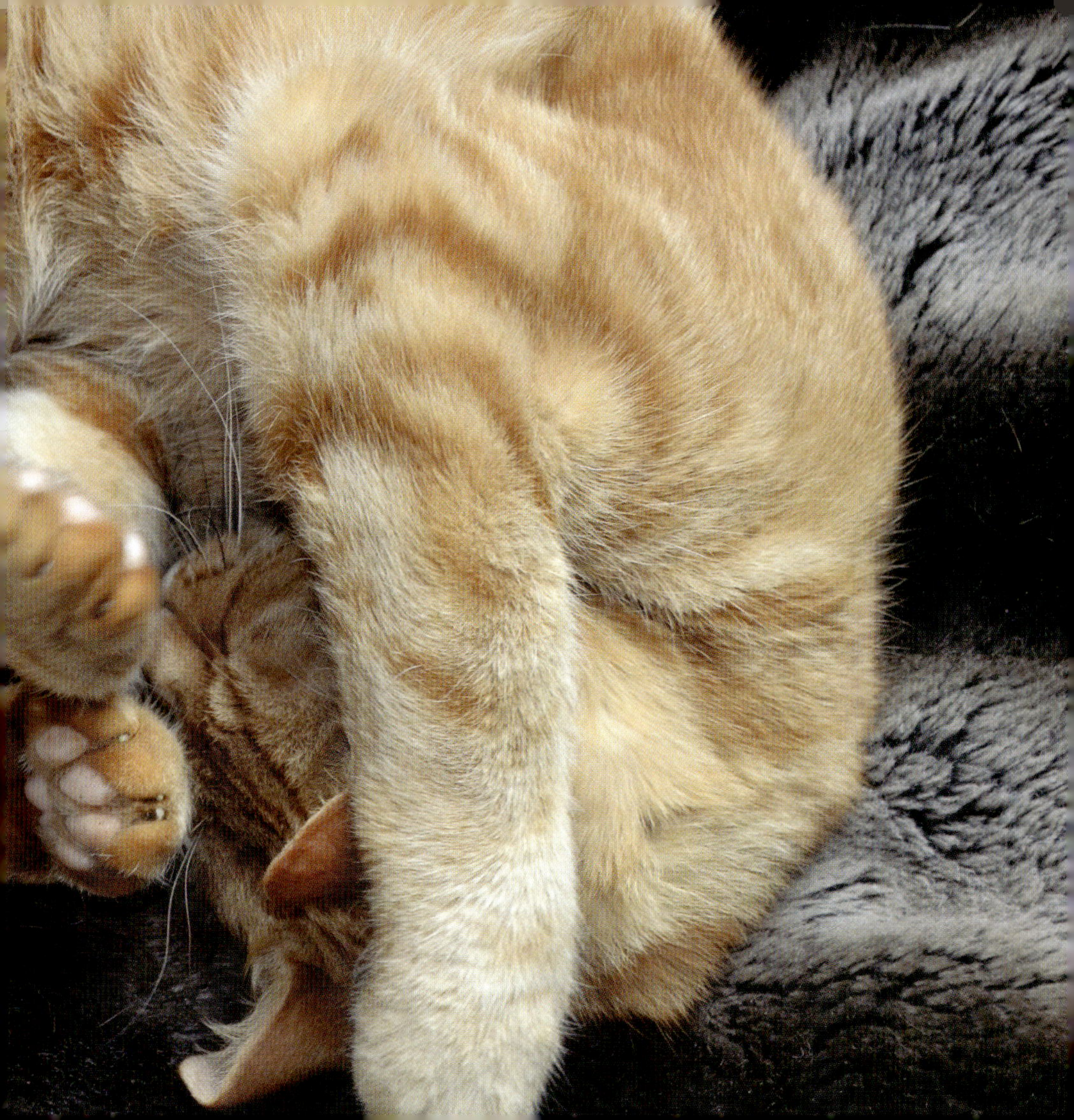

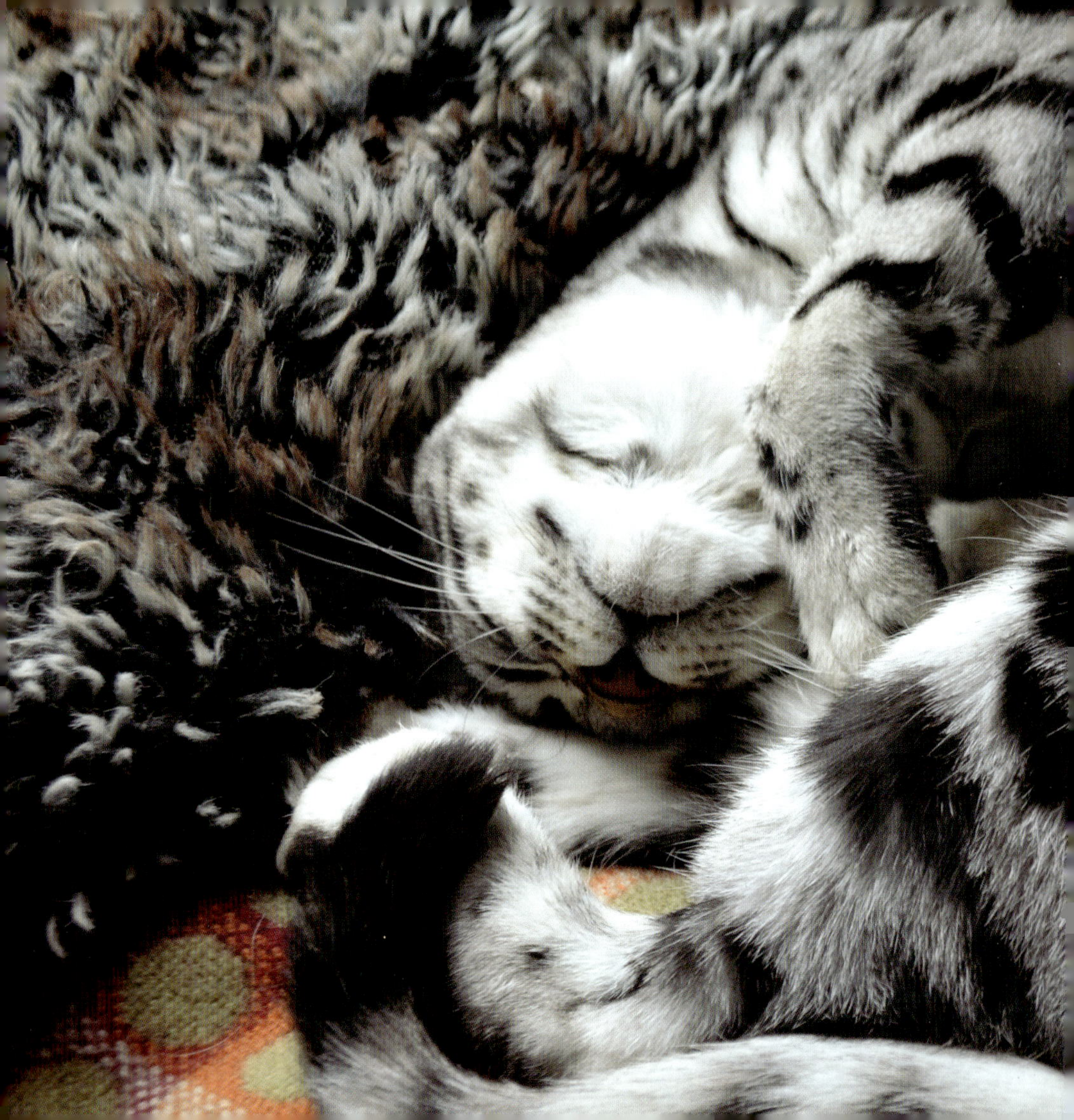

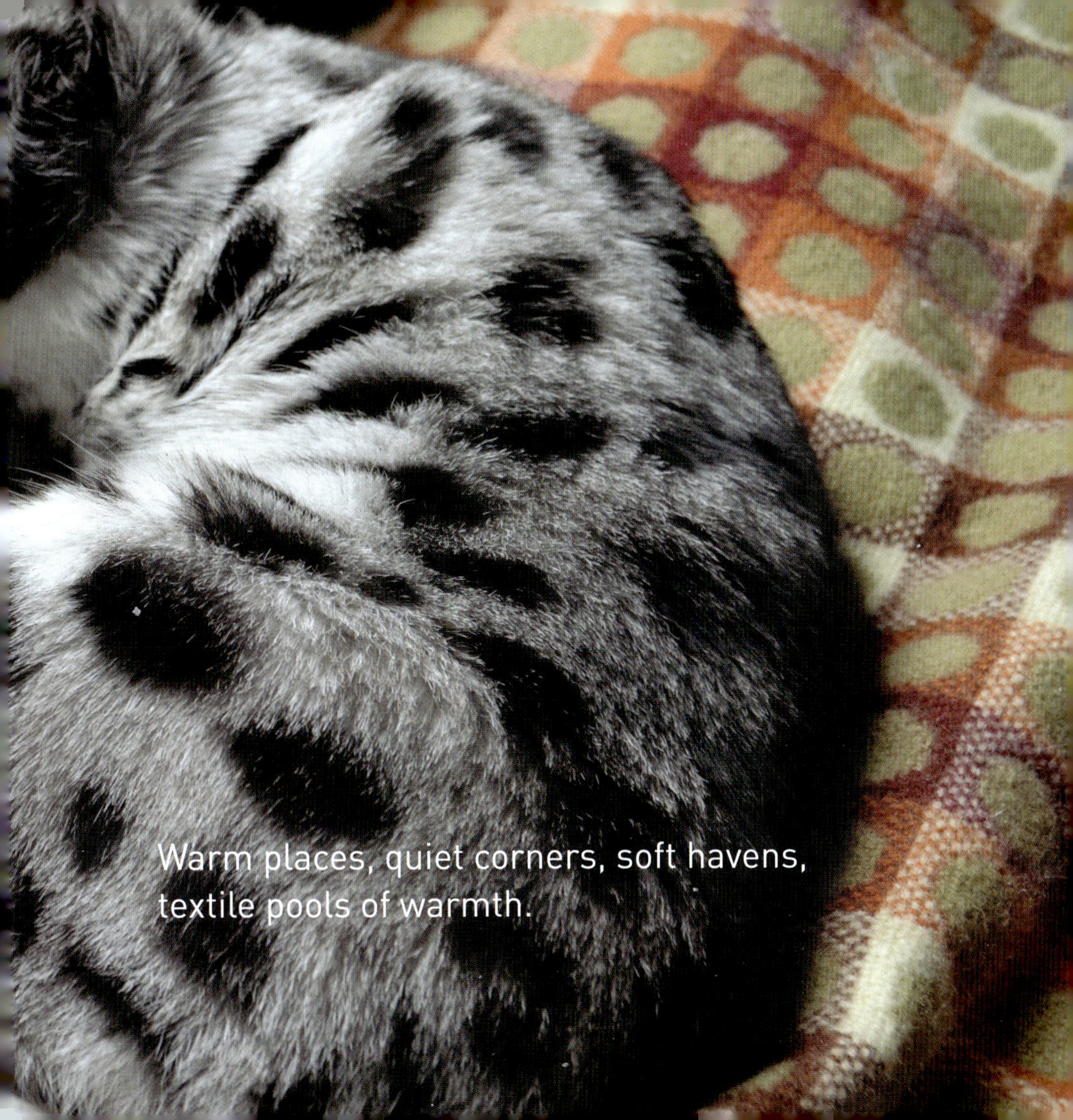

Warm places, quiet corners, soft havens,
textile pools of warmth.

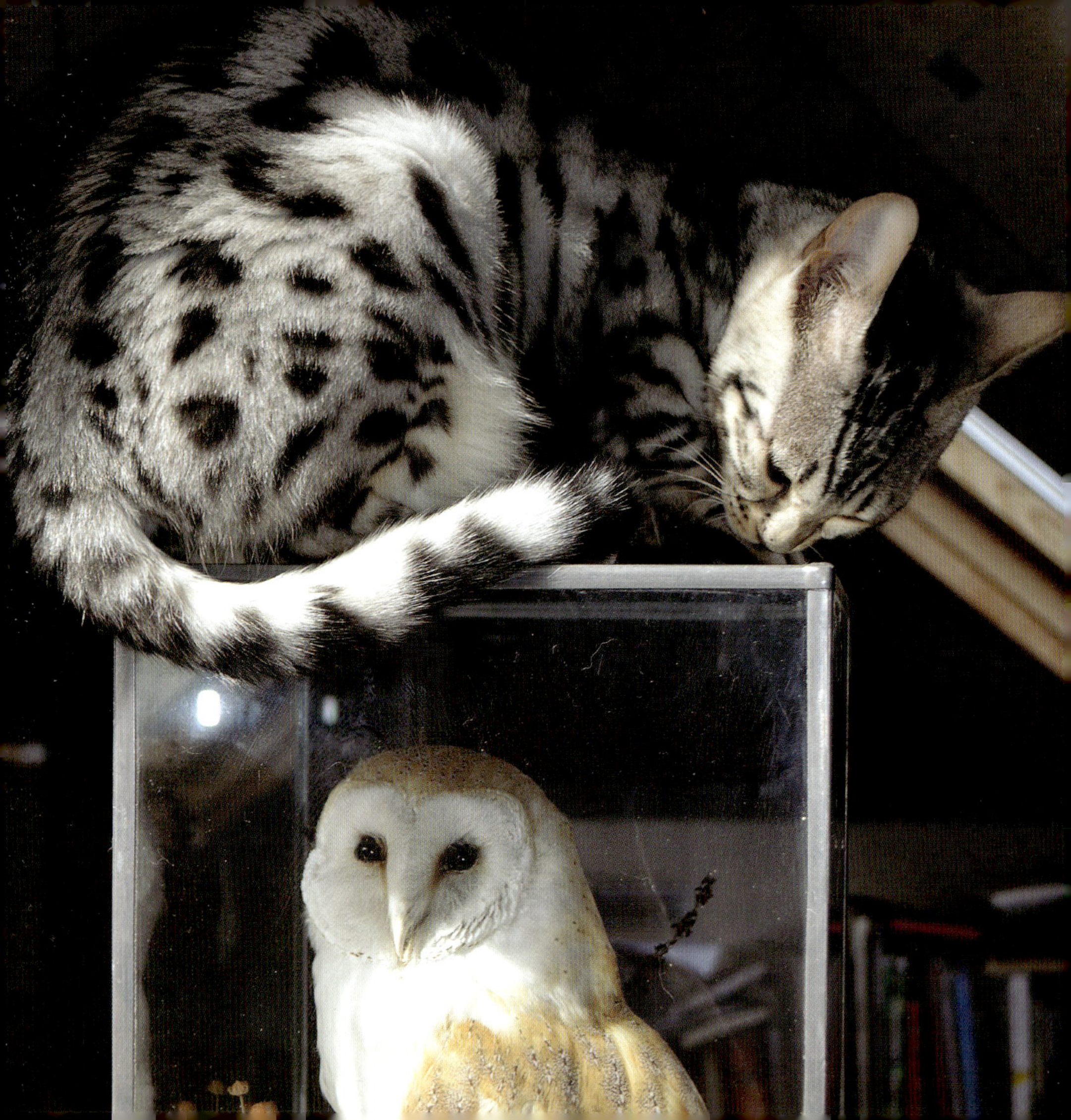

He was beautiful.

He was soft, warm, fierce.

His fur sparkled in sunshine, in moonshine. He was
two halves of the same coin with his small sister. He
loved to sit close, to sleep curled in the curve of your
arm, melt into the shape of your back.

He would follow, up the high hill, walking fast,
coming when called, always ready for adventure.

He would sit in a pool of shade through the heat of
day or wander the small wood, hunting mice as I
hunted words.

He loved company. Wherever you were there he
would be.

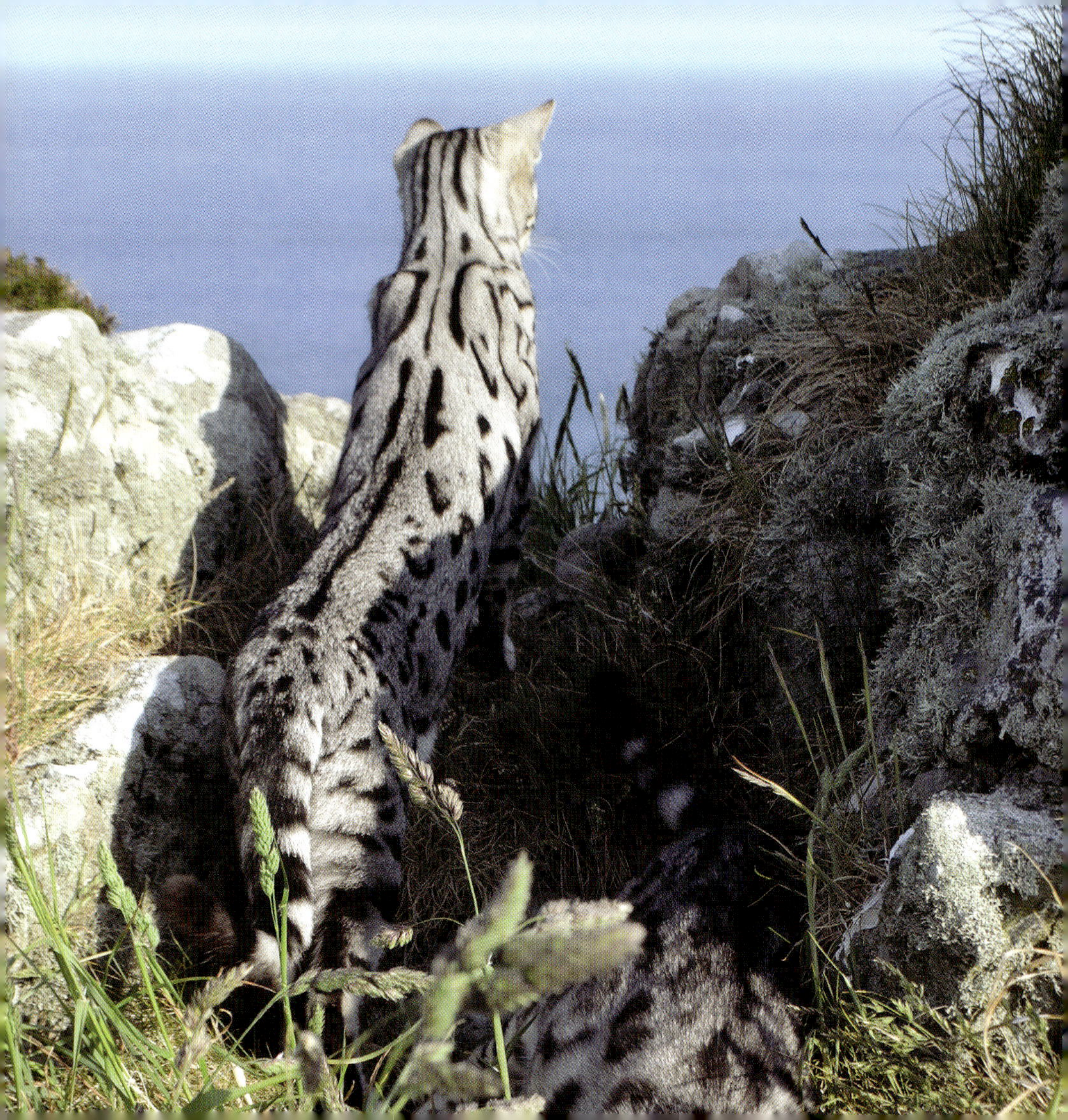

He was named Genji, after the shining one, from an ancient Japanese novel. Too beautiful to live long on this earth for the wild gods did not wish to share his beauty, and called him back to them too soon. Not even a year old. Mischief may have been his middle name. Loki would have suited him.

And though I miss him, and my heart still aches for him, I am glad to have known him during his brief butterfly life, those months when we walked the same pathways, up to the top of the high hill.

The fresh
green of early
spring

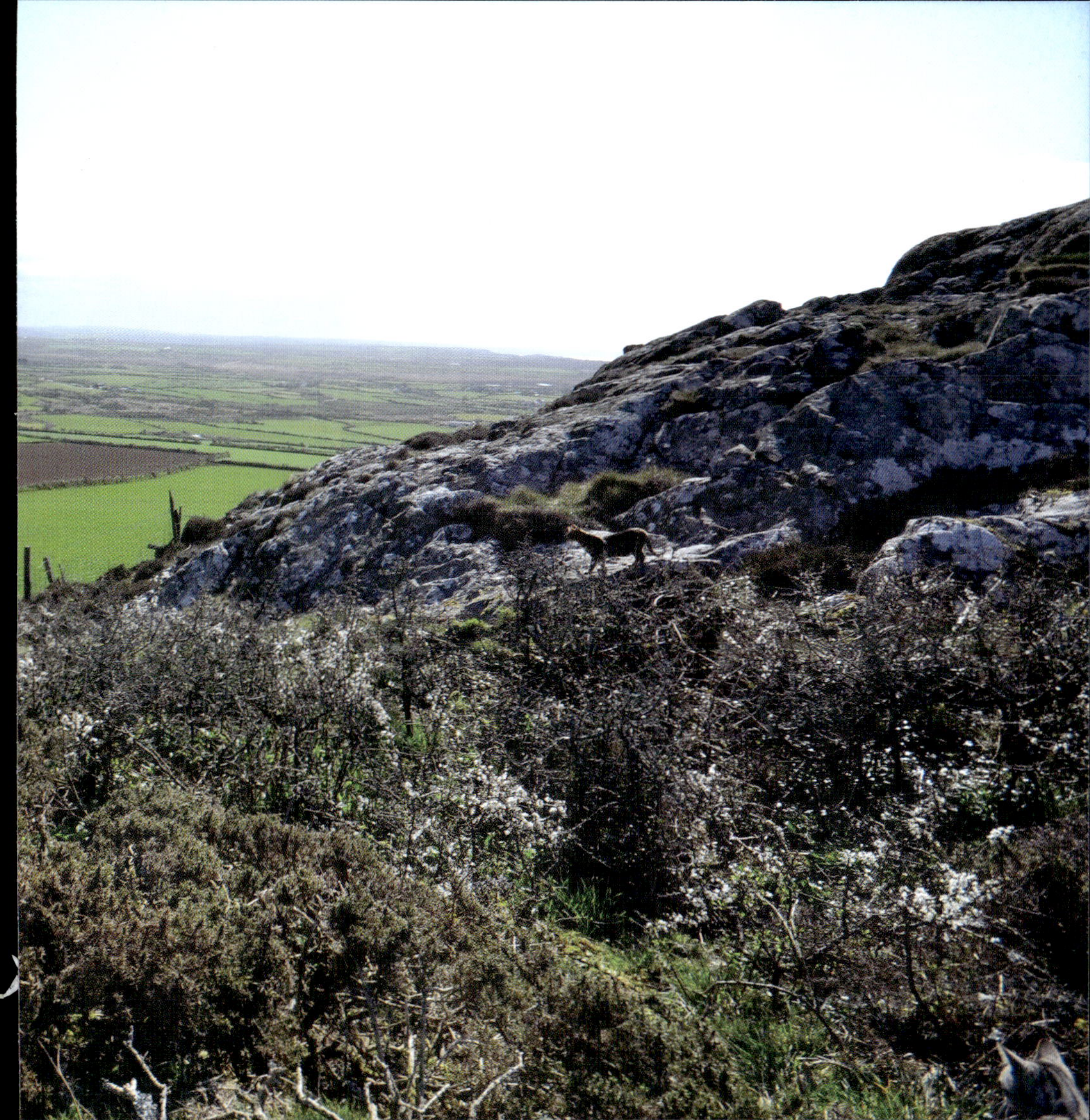

The world was flushed by the fresh green of early spring. In the sunshine the small leopard was almost invisible in the landscape.

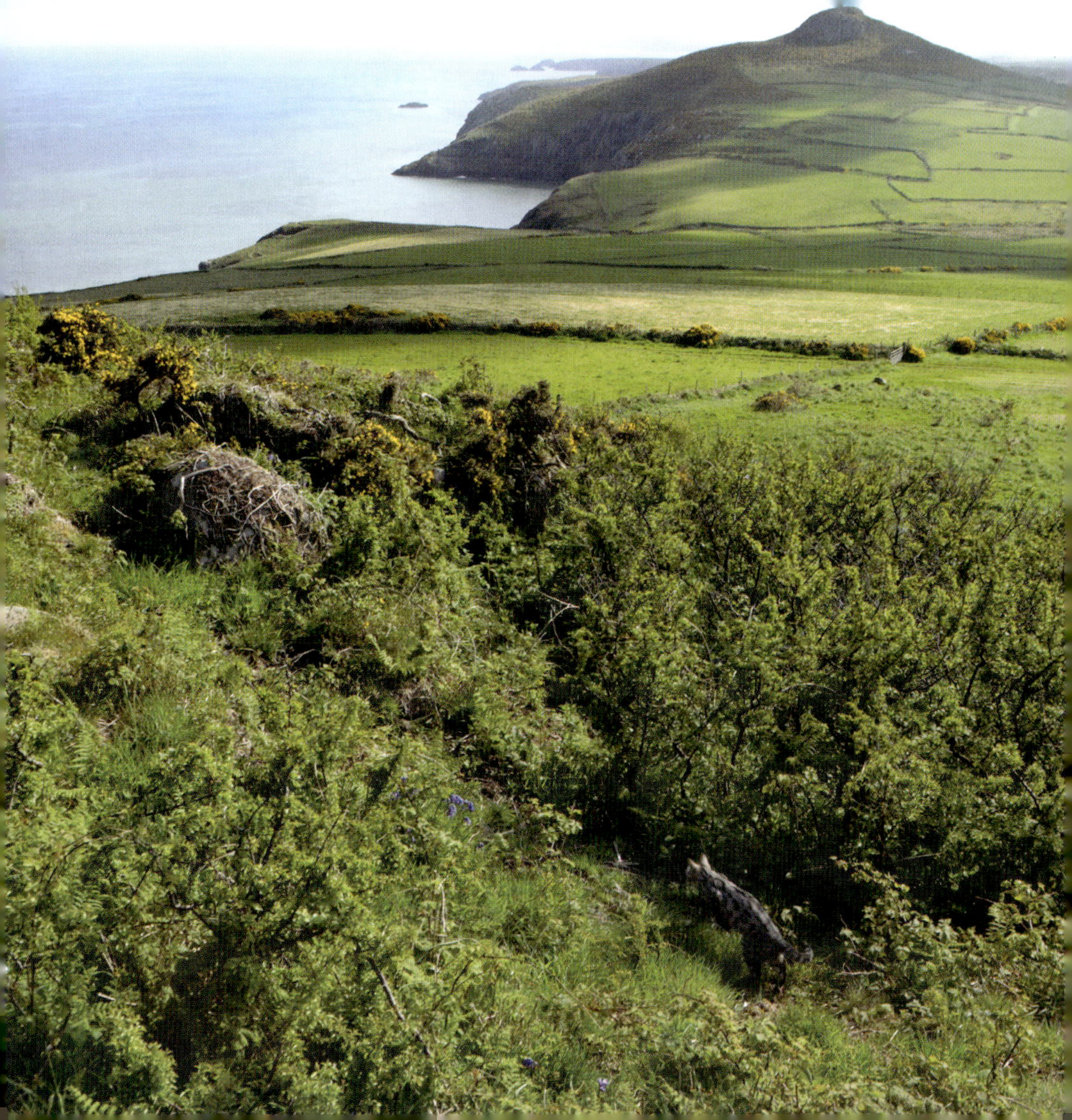

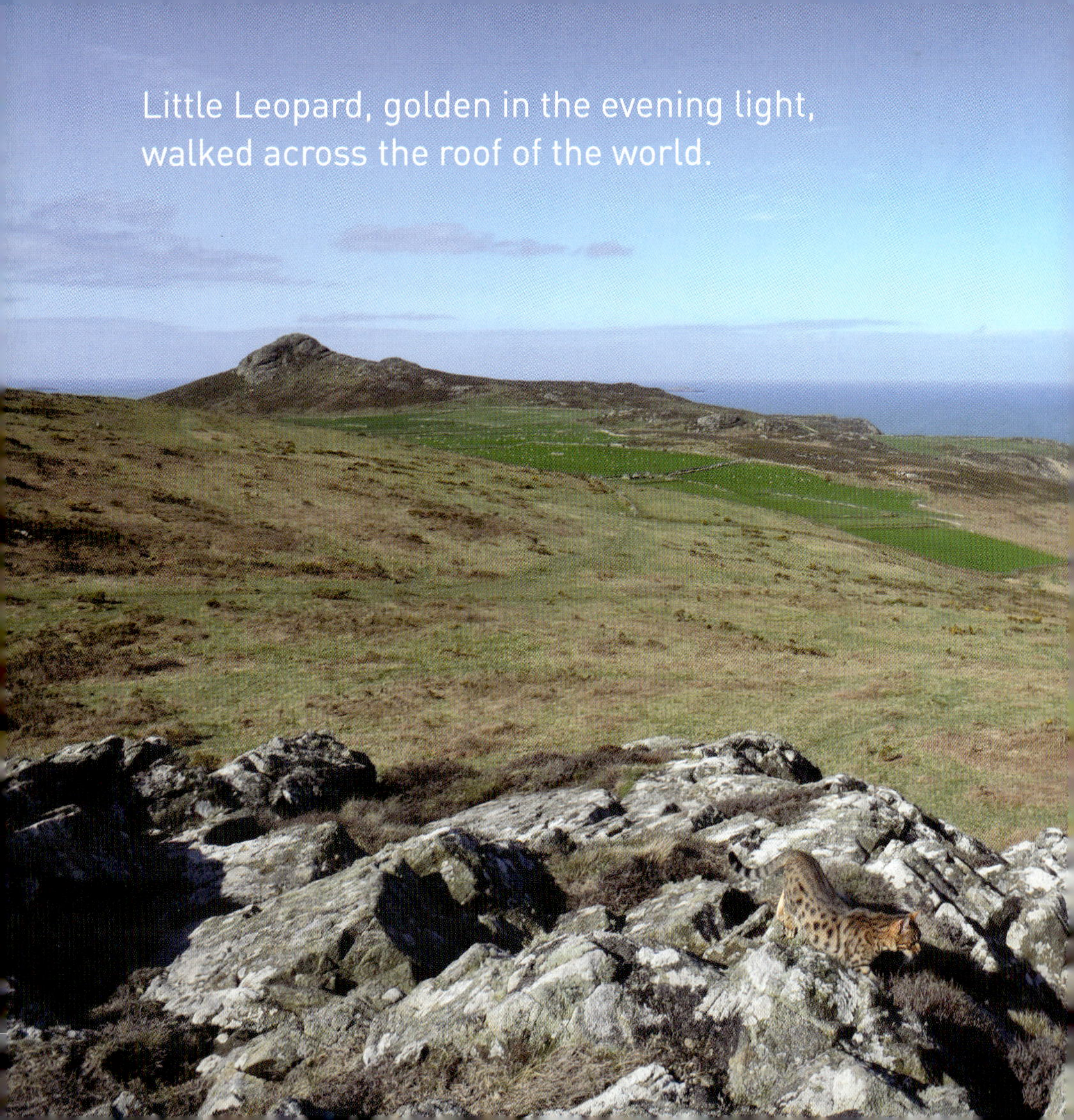

Little Leopard, golden in the evening light,
walked across the roof of the world.

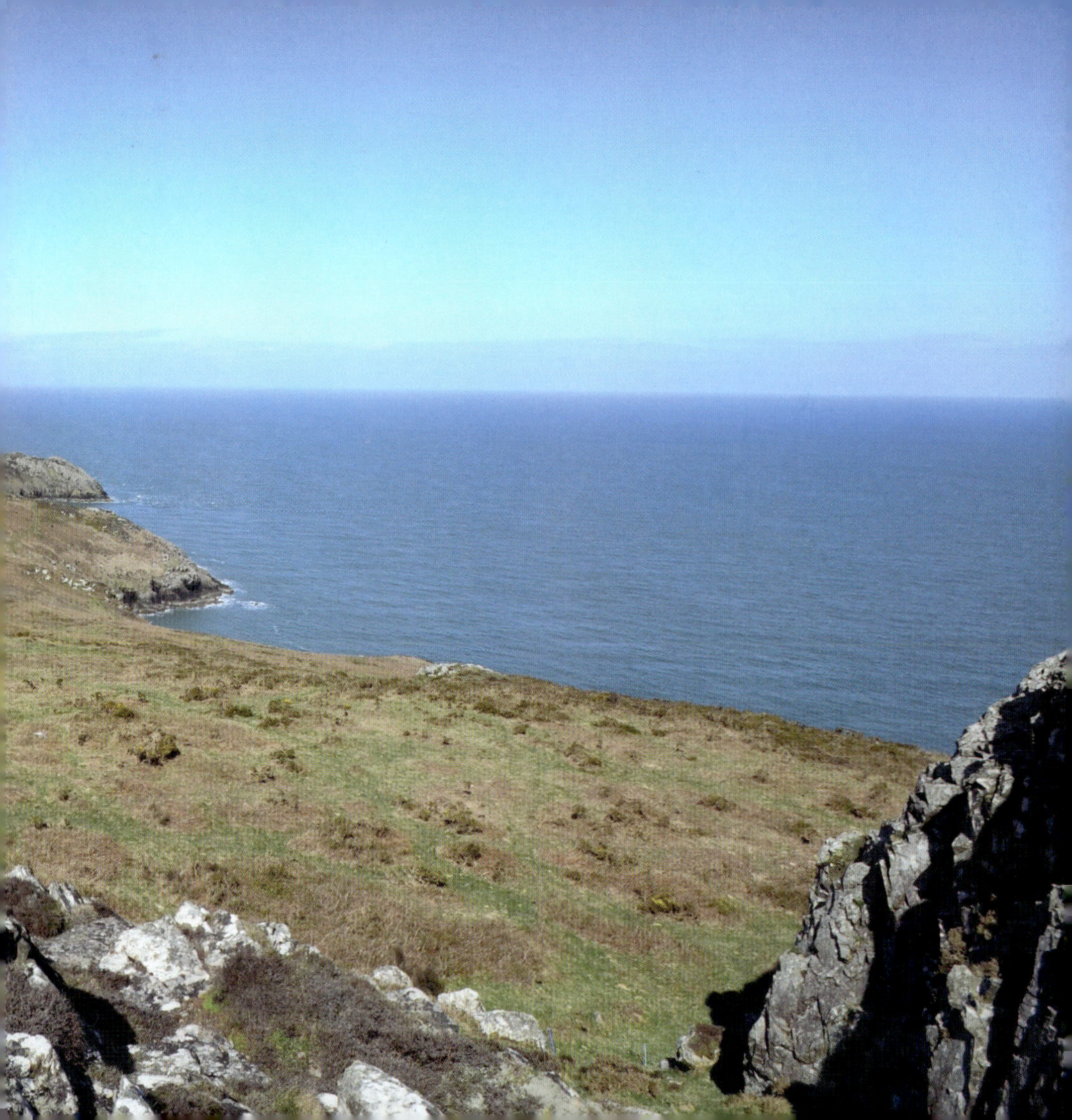

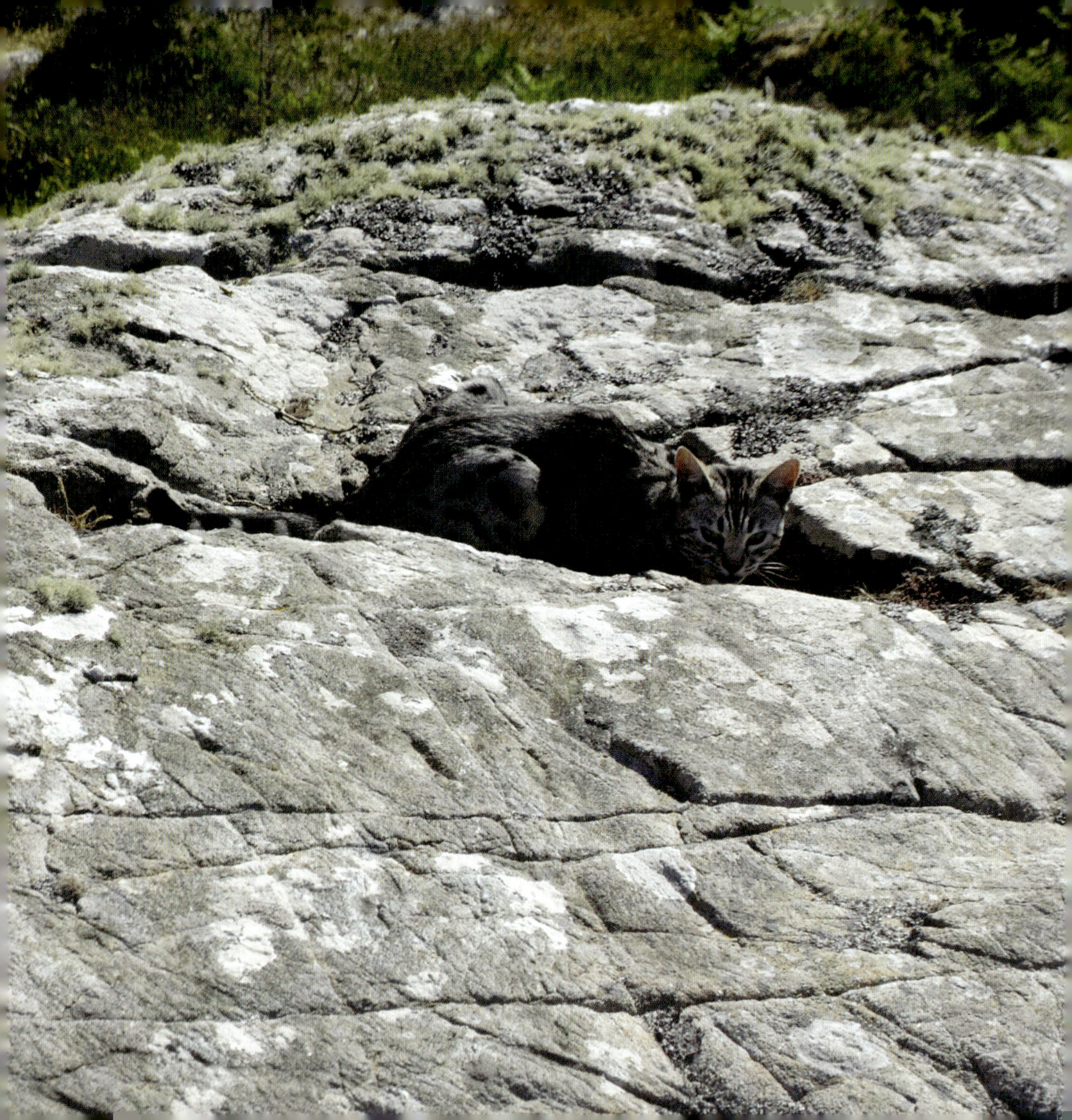

The silver cat crouched, camouflaged by a
curious combination of lichen covered stone,
light and shade.

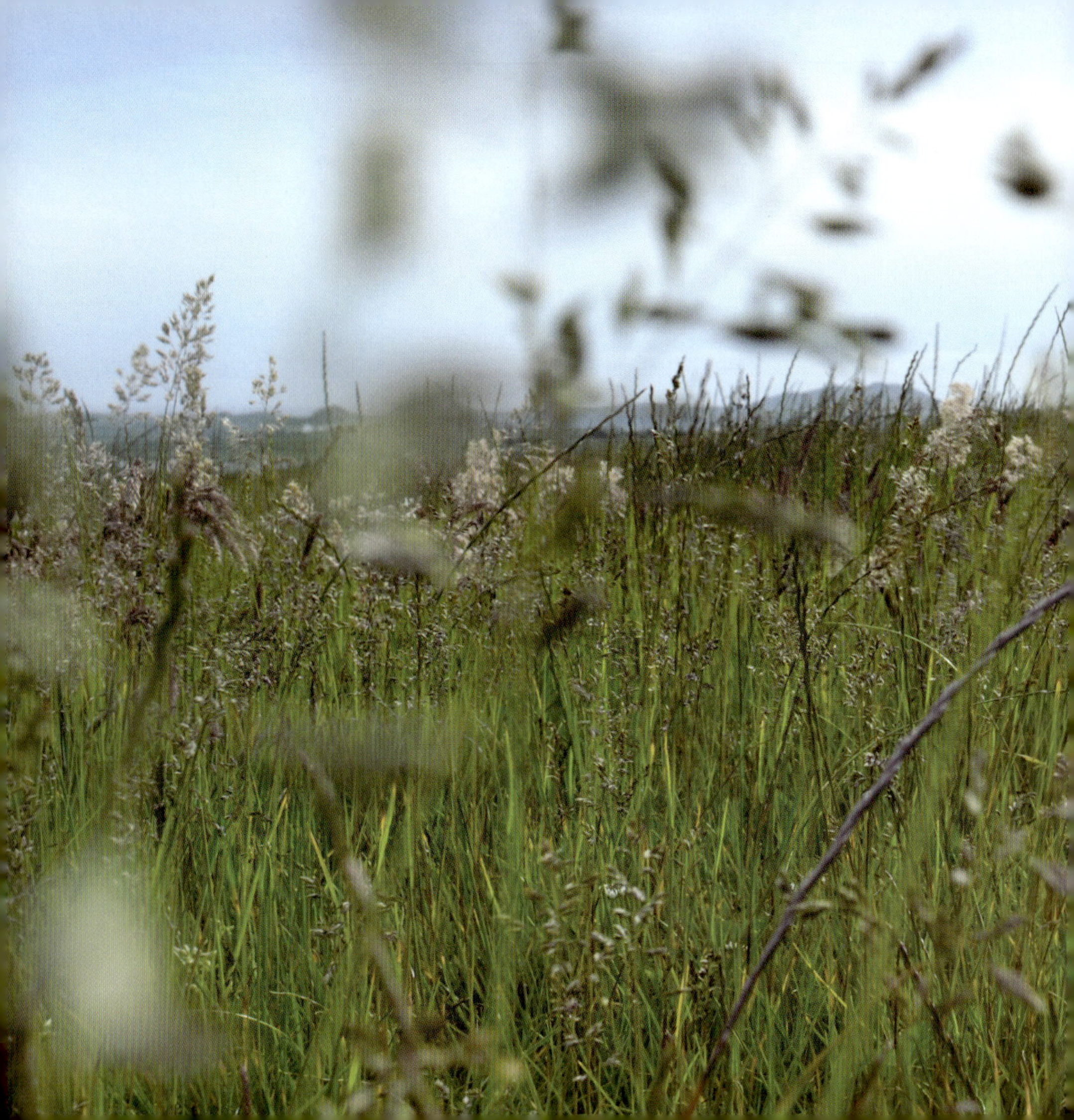

Somewhere in the tangled jungle of grass flowers, a small ginger cat.

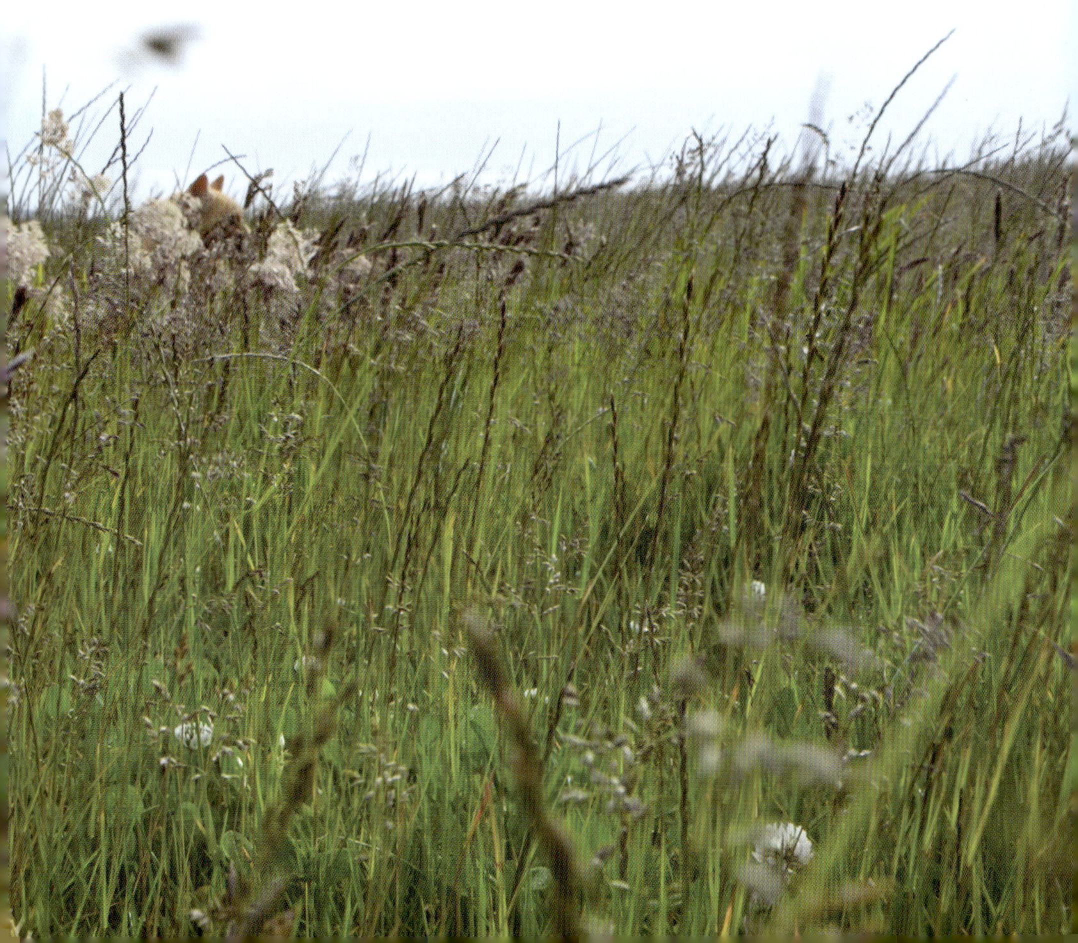

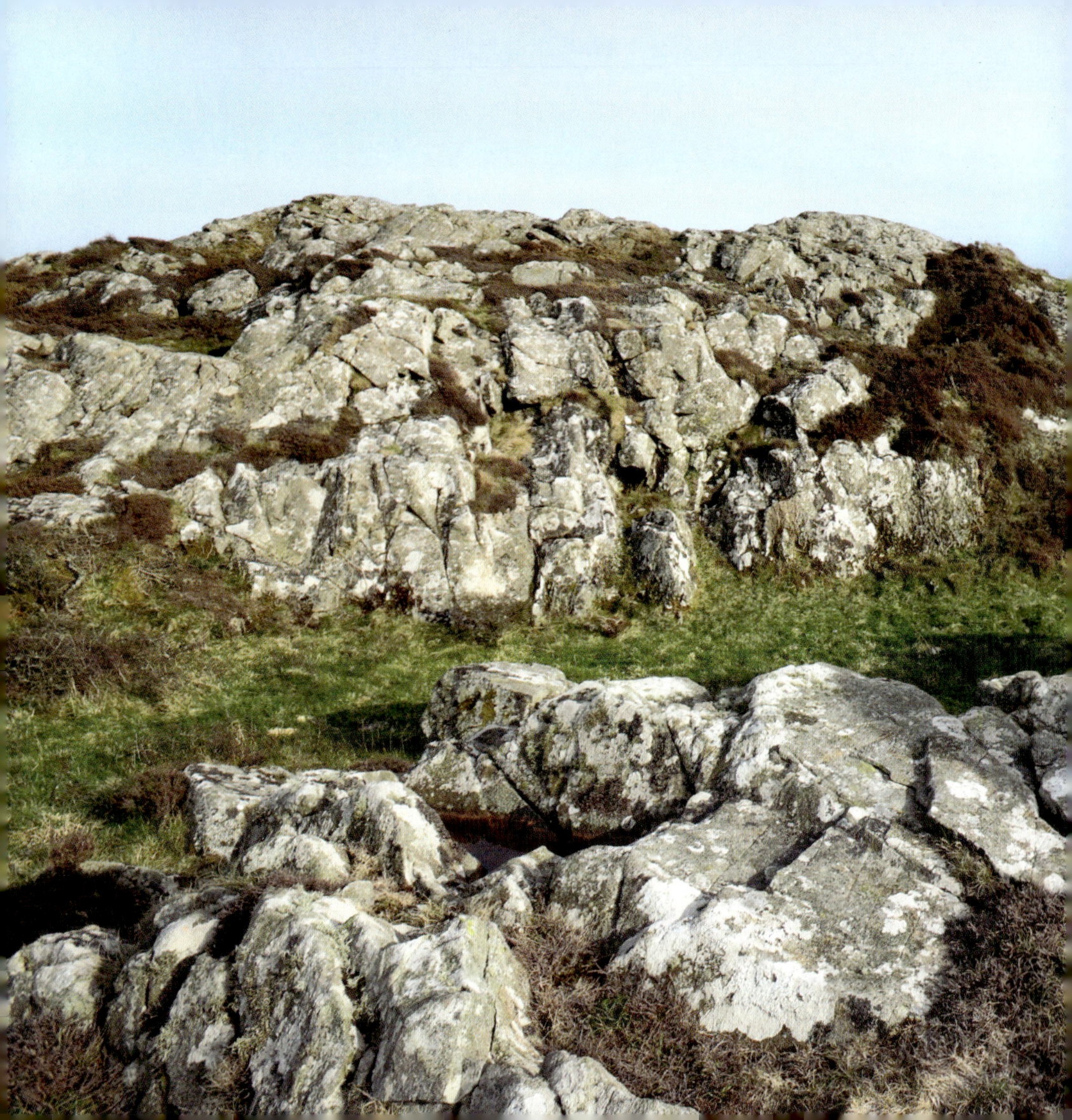

Over stone, under sky, beside the sea.

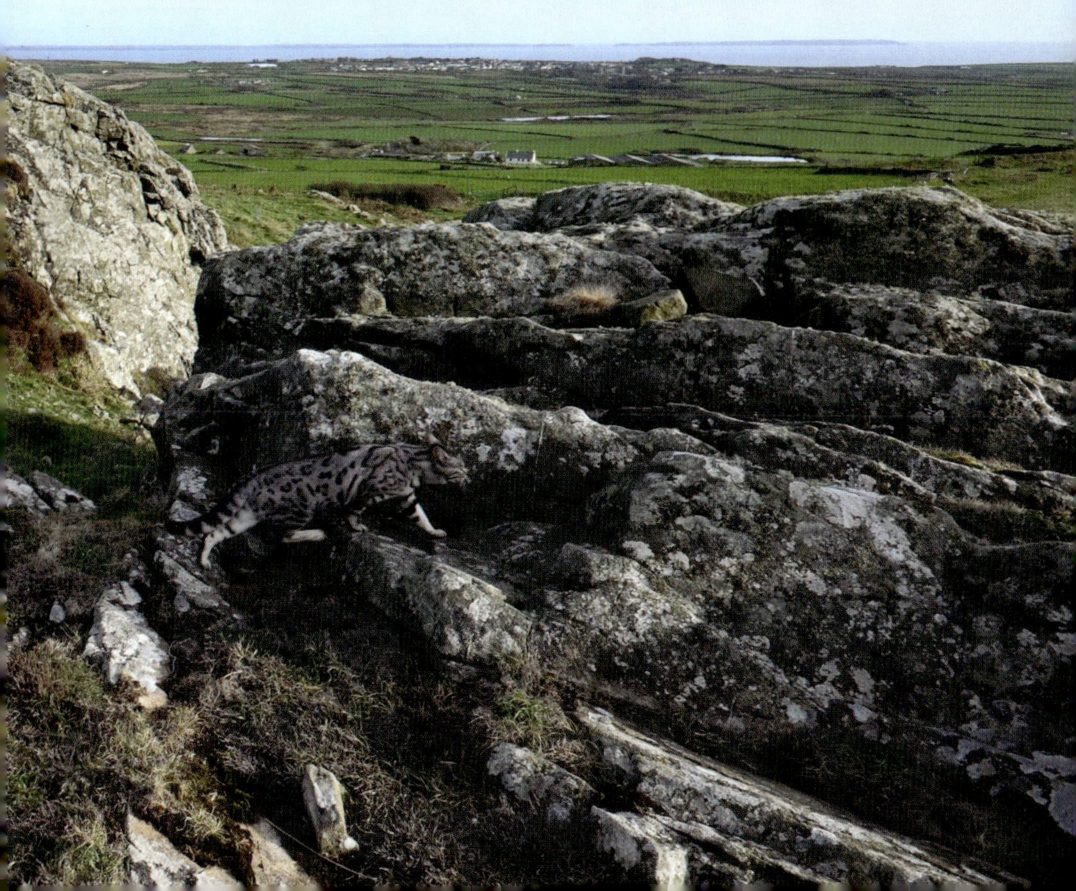

The arm of the land stretched out into the sea
as the small cat hunted over the stones, almost
invisible, mottled like the stones beneath his
small paws.

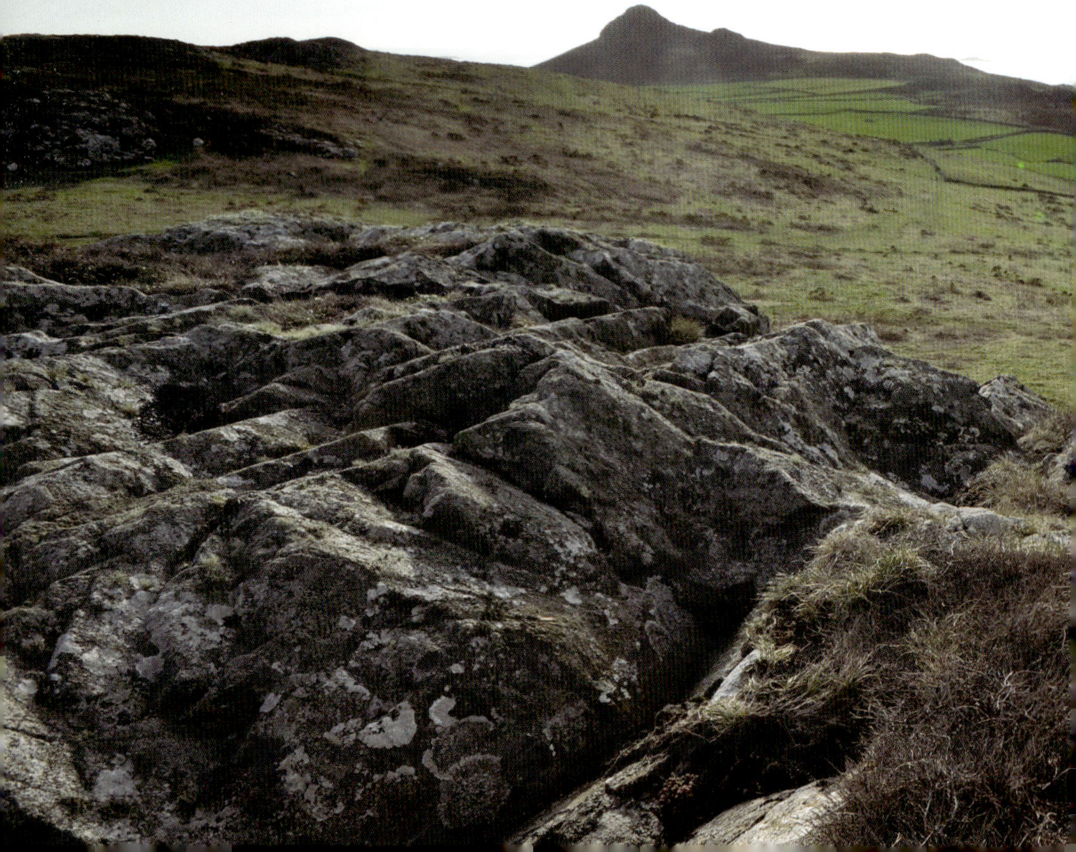

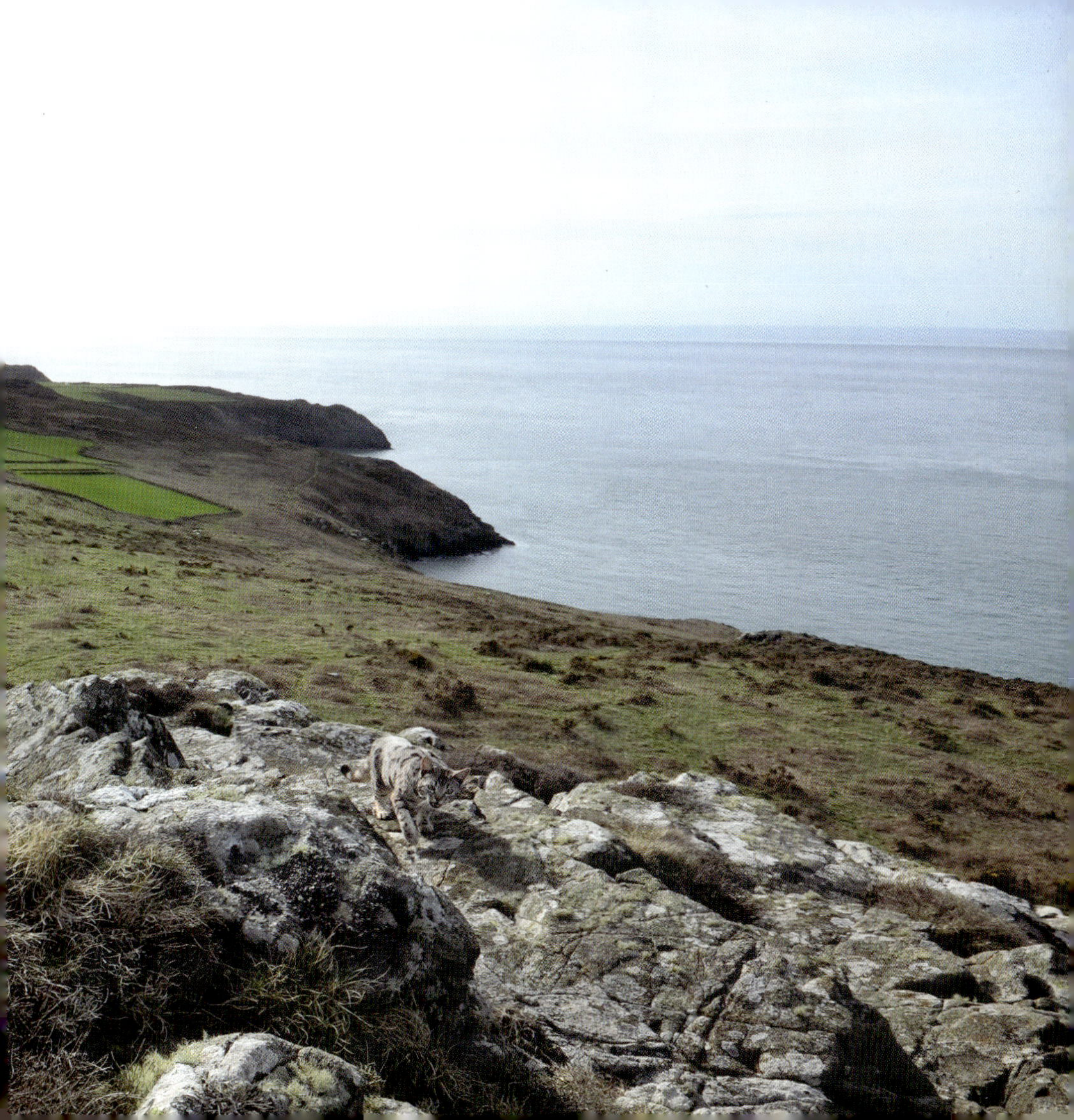

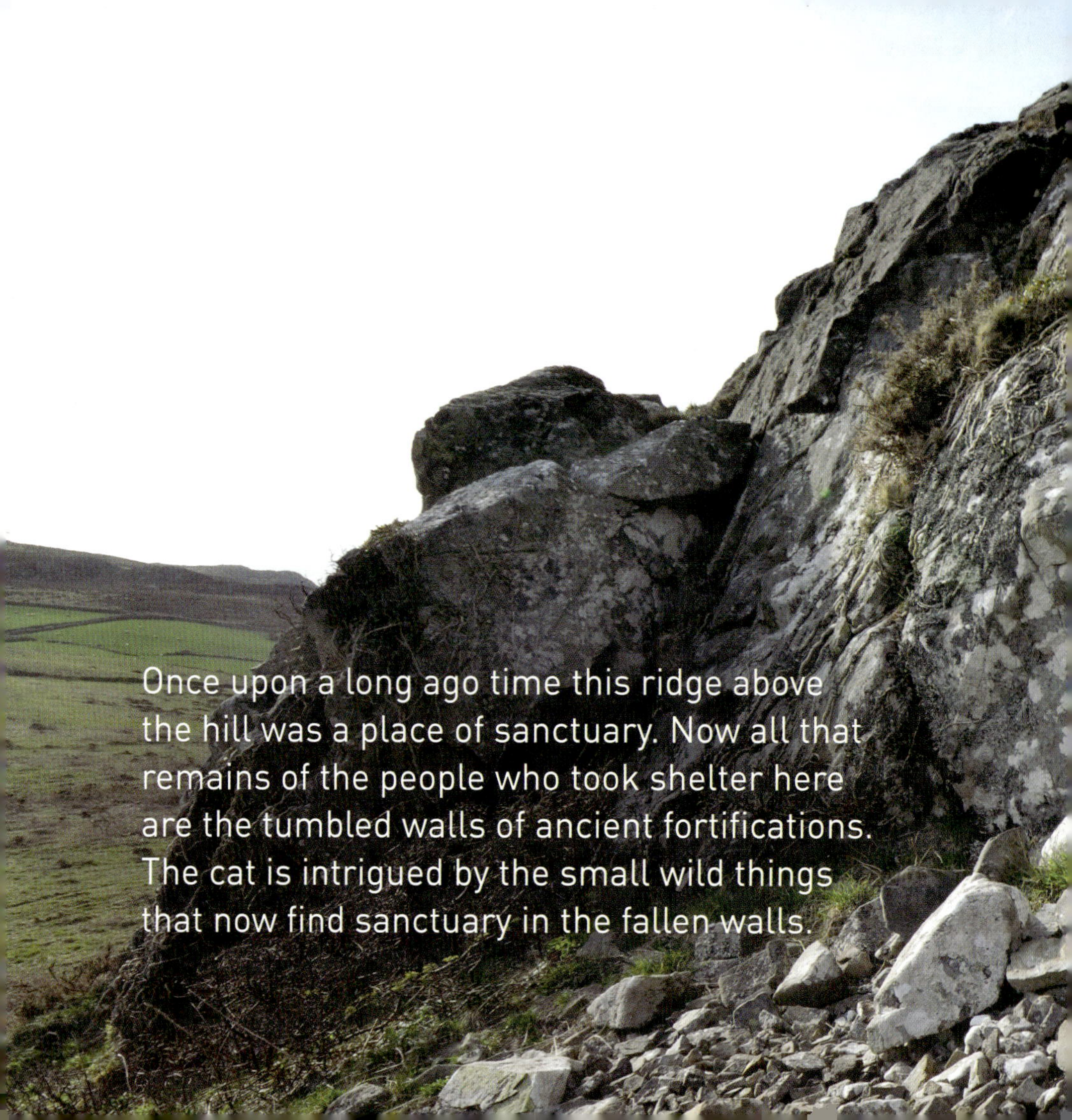

Once upon a long ago time this ridge above
the hill was a place of sanctuary. Now all that
remains of the people who took shelter here
are the tumbled walls of ancient fortifications.
The cat is intrigued by the small wild things
that now find sanctuary in the fallen walls.

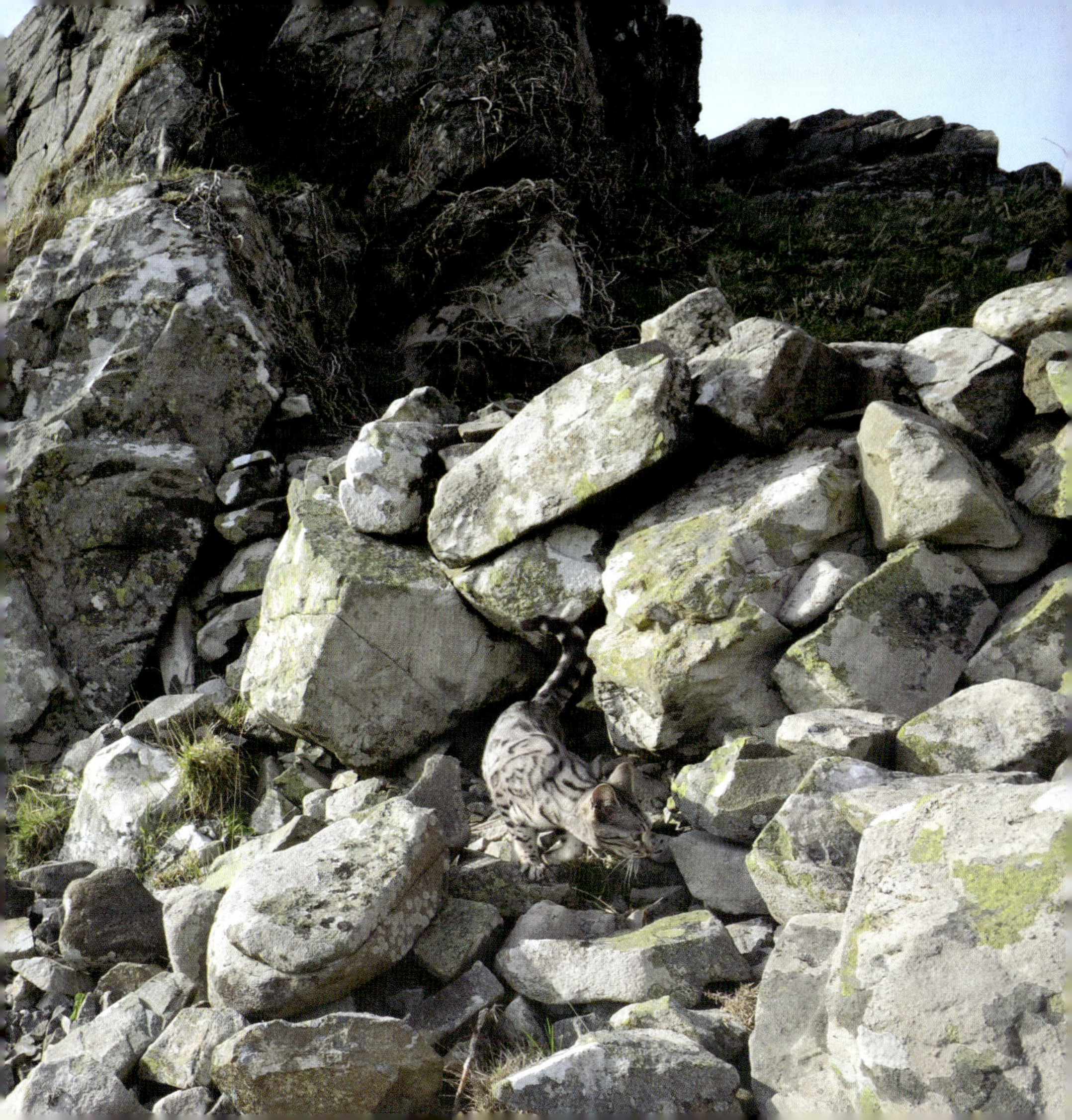

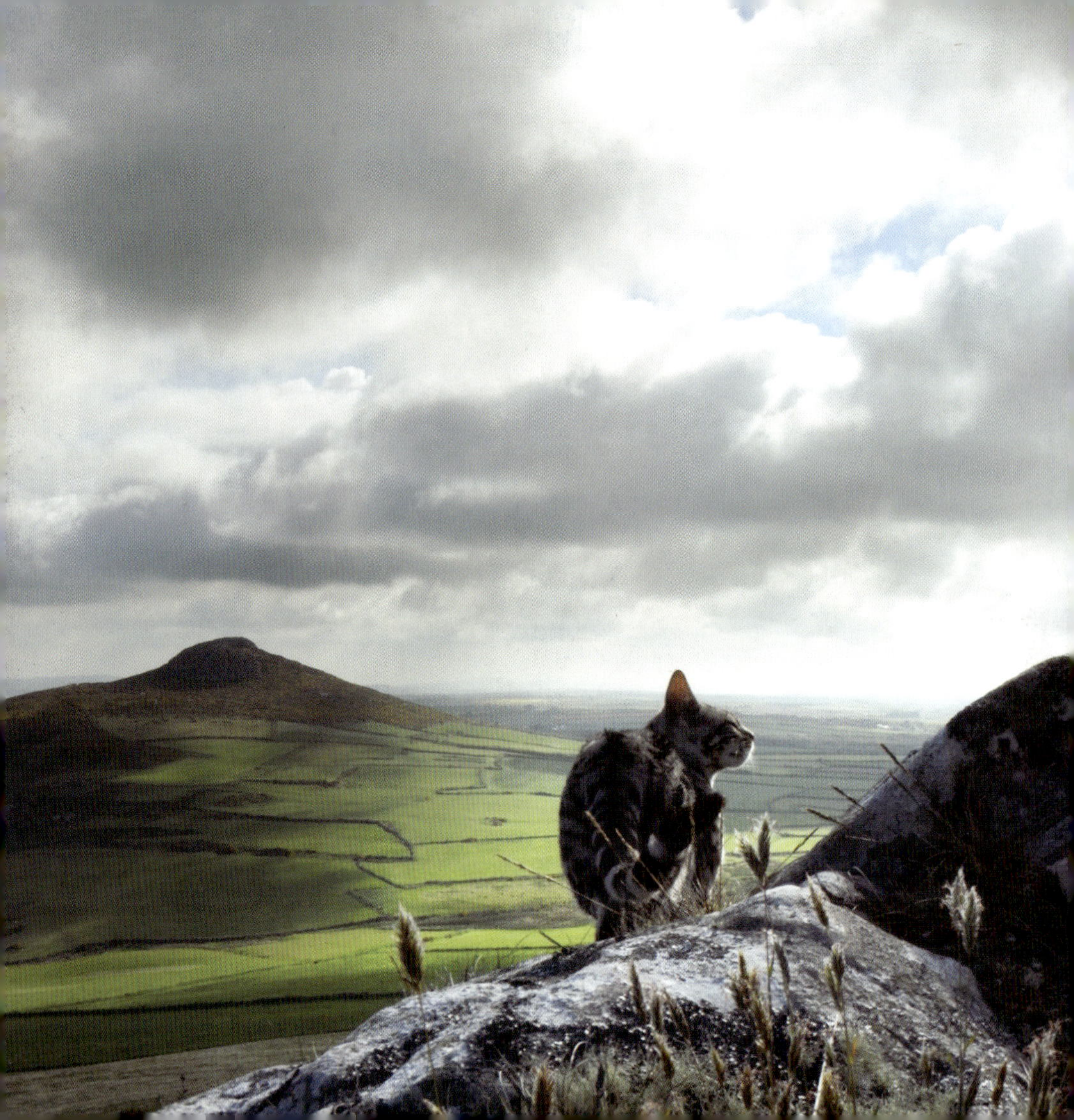

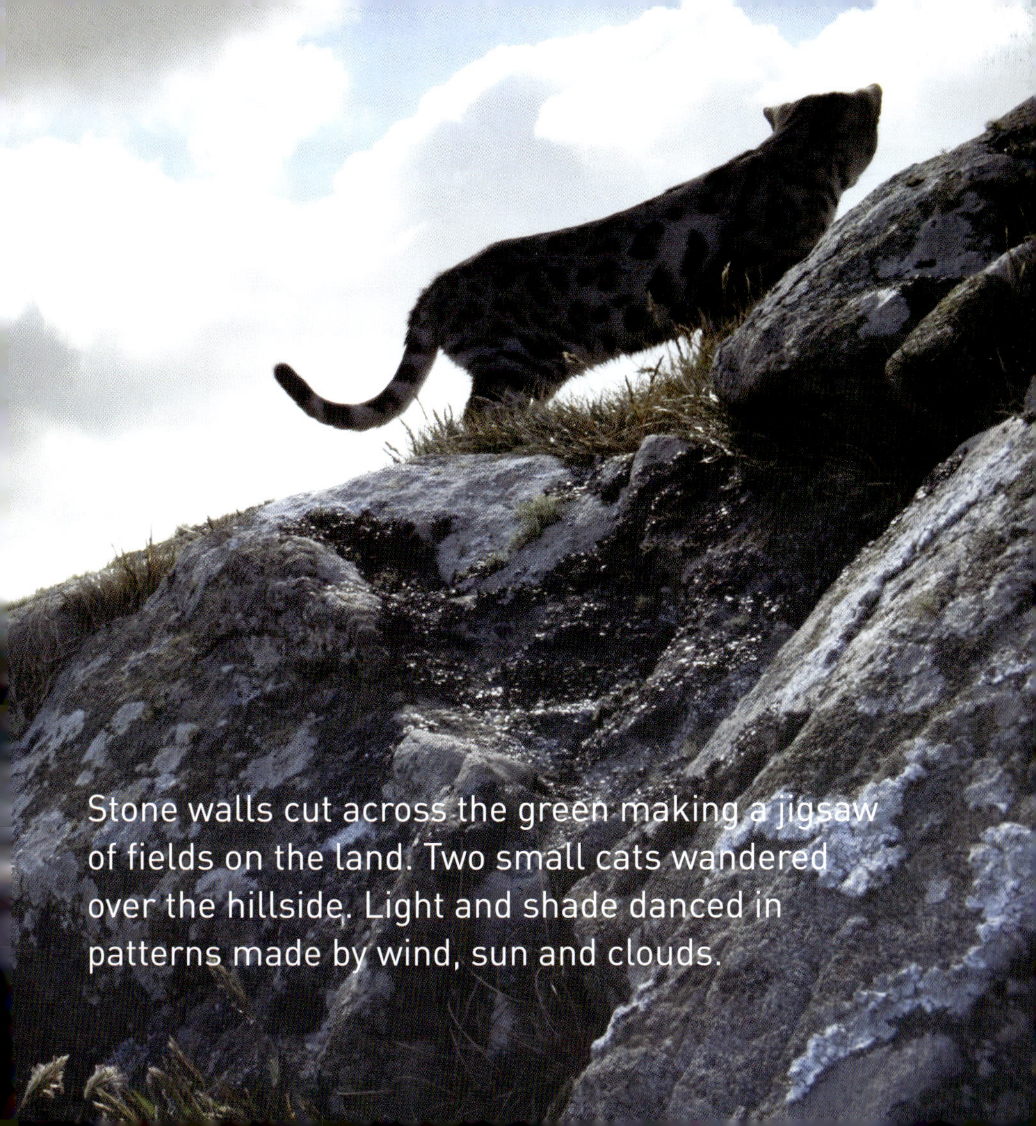

Stone walls cut across the green making a jigsaw of fields on the land. Two small cats wandered over the hillside. Light and shade danced in patterns made by wind, sun and clouds.

# Glossary

**Cat**: a creature that hunts for mice and patches of sunlight.

**Walk**: to move on foot, a step at a time, one foot in front of the other, sometimes with a purpose, sometimes with a cat. To amble, to ramble, to roam, to wonder, meander along pathways.

**Writer**: someone who hunts for words in order to express ideas, tell stories.

With special guest appearances from Floss the Collie and Kiffer the almost ginger cat.

This book is dedicated to Tom, who loves Elmo, and to Audrey and Brian who love Tom.

With thanks to Jane Messore for finding lost cats from long ago.

Cat Walk, author Jackie Morris
Published by Graffeg
Text and photographs © Jackie Morris 2014
Book copyright © Graffeg 2014
ISBN 9781909823273

Designed and produced by Graffeg
Graffeg Limited, 24 Stradey Park Business Centre, Mwrwg Road, Llangennech, Llanelli, Carmarthenshire SA14 8YP
Wales UK Tel 01554 824000
sales@graffeg.com www.graffeg.com

Graffeg are hereby identified as the authors of this work in accordance with section 77 of the Copyrights, Designs and Patents Act 1988.

A CIP Catalogue record for this book is available from the British Library.